D0477331

Tennis
AND THE
Olympic
Games

To Jean
Best wishes
Wimbledon.
12th December.
2013

Tennis
AND THE
Olympic
Games

Alan Little

WIMBLEDON
LAWNTENNIS
MUSEUM

First published 2009

Published by
Wimbledon Lawn Tennis Museum,
All England Lawn Tennis Club,
Church Road, Wimbledon,
London, SW19 5AE

Copyright © Alan Little and Wimbledon Lawn Tennis Museum, 2009

ISBN 978 0 906741 47 4

Designed by Roger Walker
Typeset in Optima and Bembo

Printed and bound in Great Britain by
L&S Printing Company Limited,
Worthing, West Sussex

FRONTISPIECE
A triumphant Elena Dementieva of Russia celebrates winning
the Ladies' singles gold medal in Beijing

Contents

ACKNOWLEDGEMENTS

I wish to thank the following people who have made a contribution to this book: Douglas Dickson of London, Heiner Gillmeister of Bonn, Germany, David Godfree of London, Heinz Grimm of Basle, Switzerland, Bjorn Hellberg of Laholm, Sweden, Richard A. Hillway of Colorado Springs, USA, Jim McManus of Jacksonville, USA, Jean-Pierre Picquot of Paris, France and Barbara Travers and Joanne Burnham of the International Tennis Federation in London for their assistance and kindly providing many of the illustrations.

Thanks also go to the staff of the Wimbledon Lawn Tennis Museum for their assistance: Honor Godfrey (Curator), Ashley Jones (Commercial Manager), Matthew Glaze, Kay Crooks and especially Audrey Snell (Assistant Librarian) for her sterling support throughout.

I am most grateful to Roger Walker for his excellent design of the book.

Picture Credits:
Ron Angle: page 67 (bottom left); Tony Barnard: page 10; Getty Images: pages 50-51; Tommy Hindley: pages 56-57, 58, 59, 61, 62, 63 (top right), 64-65, 66, 69, 71 (bottom right), 78-79; Tom Lovelock: pages 4, 7; Angelo Tonelli: pages ii, 26, 72-73, 74, 75, 77, 80, 81; Stephen Wake: pages 70-71; Paul Zimmer: pages 63 (bottom), 67 (bottom right)

Foreword

The All England Lawn Tennis Club is honoured to have the opportunity to host the Olympic tennis event at Wimbledon, for the second time, in 2012.

On the first occasion, in 1908, the Club grounds were located in Worple Road, Wimbledon, but given the popularity of Lawn Tennis, the club moved to its current Church Road site in 1922.

It is perhaps appropriate that Olympic tennis should return to Wimbledon where the first Grand Slam tournament was held in 1877 – shortly after an Englishman called Major Walter Wingfield 'invented' the game of Lawn Tennis by capitalising on the inventions of both the lawn mower and the vulcanisation of rubber to make bouncy balls. The Championships here at Wimbledon of course continue to be played on the original, and we still think the best, surface of grass – and so will the Olympics in 2012.

And who better to tell the story of Olympic tennis than Alan Little, the Honorary Librarian of the All England Club who established and developed the most comprehensive tennis library in the world at the Wimbledon Lawn Tennis Museum? Alan's services to tennis have been recognised both by the All England Club, who made him an Honorary Member, and by The British Lawn Tennis Writers who presented him with their Annual Award for Services to Tennis in 2008.

I do hope you find this comprehensive story of Olympic tennis to be both entertaining and absorbing as well as being a complete record.

Tim Phillips,
Chairman,
All England Lawn Tennis Club, Wimbledon

INTERNATIONAL OLYMPIC COMMITTEE PRESIDENTS

1894–1896	Dimitrios Vikelas (GRE)
1896–1925	Pierre de Coubertin (FRA)
1925–1942	Henri de Baillet-Latour (BEL)
1942–1946	Johannes Sigfrid Edstrom (SWE) (Acting)
1946–1952	Johannes Sigfrid Edstrom (SWE)
1952–1972	Avery Brundage (USA)
1972–1980	Michael Morris Killanin (IRE)
1980–2001	Juan Antonio Samaranch (ESP)
2001–	Jacques Rogge (BEL)

Introduction

In 2012, London will host the Olympic Games for the third time, following 1908 and 1948. Tennis, one of the 26 sports to be contested, has a long association with the Games, reaching back to 1896, when only nine sports were represented in Athens.

However, the presence of tennis has been far from continuous over the years. At the conclusion of the 1924 meeting the International Tennis Federation could not come to an agreement with the International Olympic Committee over the amateur question and the general management of the tournament, which resulted in tennis being side-lined for 64 years, until 1988.

In August 2012 the tennis tournament will be staged on the lawns of The All England Lawn Tennis Club at Church Road, Wimbledon, a south-west suburb of London.

The organization of the event is in the hands of the London Organising Committee of the Olympic Games, working closely with the International Tennis Federation. Ten match courts and six practice courts are planned to be used, with the Centre, No.1 and No.18 Courts designated as show courts. Competing for the singles Gold Medal will be 64 men and 64 ladies, while 32 teams will enter each doubles event.

The facilities available to all involved at the tournament are of the very highest calibre, being the result of the Club's intensive programme over the past decade or so, in erecting new show courts, completely renovating the buildings and grounds and providing a retractable roof for the Centre Court.

This book describes briefly the history of tennis within the Olympic movement and the pattern of play at each tournament over the years. In addition there is a large section containing the detailed scores of all matches and tables summarizing the events.

Tennis and the Olympic Games

The Olympic Games, which originated in Greece around 776 BC, were revived in modern times by a French nobleman, Baron Pierre de Coubertin. Born on 1st January, 1863 in Paris, he was a brilliant scholar but not an athlete. He always took a great interest in sport and the effect this had on society.

For years he had visualized the inception of sporting championships to include all the world's nations. Healthy competition, where the reward came from the activity, was his aim. Any monetary, material, or business connections would immediately nullify a player's amateur status. He first put forward his ideas at a lecture in Paris during November, 1892, but there appeared little interest. Undeterred, he invited sportsmen from all around the world to participate in a conference at the Sorbonne in Paris in June 1894.

At this meeting there were 79 delegates representing 49 organisations from 13 nations. Pierre de Coubertin was given further encouragement by receiving 21 letters from other nations offering him support.

The meeting was well in accord with de Coubertin's vision and ideals and resolved that "sports competitions should be held every four years on the lines of the Greek Olympic Games and that every nation should be invited to compete."

The new Movement was established as the International Olympic Committee (IOC) with its members being Viktor Balck (Sweden), Aleksei Butorsky (Russia), Pierre de Coubertin (France), Willibald Gebhardt (Germany), Jiri Guth (Bohemia), Ferenc Kemeny (Hungary) and Dimitrios Vikelas (Greece). The last named was elected President and de Coubertin initially acted as Secretary General, but in 1896 he became President, a post he held to 1925.

Left: Baron Pierre de Coubertin (1863–1937). The inspiration behind the modern Olympic Games.

At the conclusion of the Paris Conference in 1894, members of the newly formed International
Olympic Committee commence the task of organizing the first Games.
From left: Willibald Gebhardt (Germany), Pierre de Coubertin (France, Secretary), Jiri Guth
(Bohemia), Dimitrios Vikelas (Greece, President), Ferenc Kemeny (Hungary),
Aleksei Butovsky (Russia) and Viktor Balck (Sweden)

By 1896 new delegates added to the Committee included Lord Arthur
Ampthill and Charles Herbert (British Isles), Ernest Callot (France), Leonard Cuff
(New Zealand), Ferdinado Lucchesi-Palli (Italy), William Stone (USA) and Jose
Zubiaur (Argentina).

Appropriately, the Committee decided that the first Games should be held in
Athens in 1896. The choice was a popular one with the Greek people, but soon the
authorities ran into financial difficulties. Crown Prince Constantine stepped in and
set up an organizing committee, which invited donations, ran lotteries and sold postage stamps to raise the necessary funds. They were spurred on by the thought that
Budapest was hovering in the background ready to take over the Games. On 6th
April, King George of Greece formally opened the first modern Olympic Games.

Surprisingly, lawn tennis was one of the nine sports chosen. There appears to
be no record as to why this was so. The lawn tennis programme consisted of Men's
Singles and Doubles events, played on three courts in the middle of the Velodrome,

at the conclusion of the cycling each day. 13 players from six nations actually hit a ball, with an unknown Irishman, John Boland, winning both titles. A start had been made.

After Athens, the Greek authorities felt that they had the right to stage all future games, but, because of the short Greco-Turkish war and general unrest in the country, their quest faded and the games for 1900 were awarded to Paris. As events unfolded, this was not a good choice as the six month period of the Games coincided with the staging of the World Exhibition, which attracted millions to the capital to see the newly constructed Eiffel Tower and Great Globe. Consequently, this caused confusion among the spectators, who quite often were not sure which event they were witnessing.

Ladies were invited to compete in some of the peripheral events.

In contrast to 1896, the standard of play of the lawn tennis was extremely high and had on show four Wimbledon Singles Champions – Harold Mahony, Laurence Doherty, Reginald Doherty and Miss Charlotte Cooper – all from the British Isles.

The IOC allocated the 1904 Games to St. Louis in the heart of the United States, no doubt with the thought of expanding the frontiers of sport. Originally the Games were awarded to Chicago but, after pressure from the United States Olympic authorities, the venue was changed to St. Louis to coincide with the World's Fair Exposition, being held to commemorate the centenary of the purchase of the Louisiana Territory from France. This led to a situation similar to that which occurred four years earlier, when many of the competitors and visitors to the ground were quite often unable to distinguish between Fair and Games events. The Exposition was a huge success, attracting vast numbers. Consequently attendance at the events of the Games benefitted accordingly.

St. Louis was hardly in a position to attract competitors to the Games from Europe and beyond, who would have to devote much time to the lengthy travel involved in those days. The upshot was that the two lawn tennis events, Men's Singles and Doubles, attracted 32 competitors, but all except one were from the home country. This was hardly expanding world competition.

The poor presentation of the two previous Games had left a stain on the Olympic Movement. Many lessons were learnt for the future, primarily not to stage the Games in tandem with another International event. Keen to present a better image to the sporting world, the IOC decided to hold an additional Games between the set four year period. So in 1906, Athens was awarded the privilege and the venture was most successful.

Because of this, the Greek authorities felt they should repeat the exercise every four years but, well before 1910 arrived, the political unrest in Greece caused the

Badges from 1908. Left – Olympic Games London Committee (blue enamel) and right –
British Olympic Council (red enamel)

abandonment of the idea. The 1906 Games were recognized as official and called
'Intercalated', but they were never accorded the title of 4th Olympics. The tennis
tournament ran smoothly. The entry consisted mainly of Greek players, but three of
the events were won by French competitors.

Originally scheduled for Rome, the 1908 Games were reallocated to London,
when the Italian authorities were forced to withdraw due to financial problems.
King Edward VII and Queen Alexandra opened the Games and gave great support
throughout. The participation of ladies was, by now, well recognized. Both indoor
and outdoor lawn tennis tournaments were held in well established venues.

The 1912 Games held in Stockholm were regarded as the best organized so far.
Led by King Gustav V, the people of the city took much interest in all the events,
which were attended to full capacity. For the first time electrical timing equipment
was used and an official poster issued. As four years earlier indoor and outdoor lawn
tennis tournaments were staged but the former, played in early May, attracted so few
competitors that the idea was abandoned in the future.

Preparations for the 1916 Games in Berlin were well advanced when the outbreak of World War I in August 1914 caused them to be abandoned. However, the
Games were still designated the 6th Olympics. Lawn Tennis was one of the sports
scheduled.

After hostilities had ceased, Antwerp was chosen for 1920. Although aspects of
the organization of these Games were criticized, the general overall feeling was that
the city had risen to the enormous task of overcoming, in less than two years, the

Generally over the years, winners of medals also received an accompanying certificate.
The one above was awarded to Kathleen McKane, the winner of the Ladies' Doubles at
Antwerp in 1920. The certificate, illustrated by Jean Malraux, shows an image of
Athena crowning the winner with a laurel wreath. (29 × 22 inches)

ravages of the War, which had severely affected the country. On show for the first
time was the Olympic Flag, consisting of five interlaced rings coloured blue, yellow,
black, green and red, symbolizing all nations who had at least one of these colours
in their national flag. Also, the Olympic Oath was introduced. The number of lawn
tennis competitors attending was satisfactory, but some parts of the management of
the event were poor.

Four years later, the Games, which originally had been scheduled for Amsterdam, were held in Paris to honour the retirement of de Coubertin. The French
authorities were pleased to be given the opportunity to eradicate the poor image
of their organization 24 years earlier and, generally, this they did. However, after
these Games, feelings in the lawn tennis world ran high against the IOC. Although
recognition was given for having attracted double the number of countries and competitors to take part in the tournament, the organization had been in many respects

very poor. The hospitality towards the players had been practically non-existent. When they first arrived at the ground the stands were unfinished as were most of the courts. The dressing room accommodation was primitive with the ladies assigned to a large wooden shed with a tin roof and provided with only one shower. The men suffered more as they had to walk nearly half a mile for their facility. Reports stated that at times the players' tempers became frayed and in turn the umpiring suffered. The Olympic spirit was very much under strain.

No lawn tennis authority could be blamed for the situation as the officials appointed by the IOC had very little experience in running a tournament. The International Lawn Tennis Federation (ILTF) was not allowed to take part.

Soon after the Games, a meeting took place between delegates of the ILTF and the IOC. Here preliminary discussions were held on matters to come before the Olympic Congress in Prague in May 1925. The IOC suggested that the ILTF's definition of an amateur should be revised according to their own views. This was an attempt to get a worldwide definition of an amateur – something which at that time appeared an impossibility. The ILTF had their own definition considered satisfactory for lawn tennis. The IOC also suggested that during the year of the Olympics no official championships should be held by members of the ILTF. This put the big four Championships at risk. Also, possibly the Davis Cup would have to miss a year.

Following this meeting the ILTF circulated all members to ascertain their views. A Council meeting of The Lawn Tennis Association (LTA) held in London on 23rd September 1924, came out very strongly against the suggestions of the IOC and conveyed their views in a letter to the governing body.

Six months later at the Annual Meeting of the ILTF in Paris on 20th March 1925, Mr R.J. McNair put forward the strong feelings of the LTA, but the meeting took no definite action and decided to send two representatives, Messrs. Paul de Borman (Belgium) and Karl Robertin (Czechoslovakia), to the meeting in Prague.

During the next year matters were fairly quiet but when on 19th March 1926 the ILTF met again and the report of the Prague delegates was read, the IOC's attitude had not altered. In the course of discussion, a suggestion was made that any decision by the Federation to leave the IOC should not take effect until after the 1928 Olympics. This did not satisfy the majority of the meeting who felt that immediate action should be taken. Finally, the following resolution, proposed on behalf of Great Britain, was put to the meeting and carried unanimously. "The ILTF, having considered the report of Messrs. de Borman and Robertin as to the proceedings at the Olympic Congress in Prague, resolve:

MEDALS

1908
Gold

1912
Bronze

1920
Gold

1924
Silver

The following medals are in the Wimbledon Lawn Tennis Museum collection:
1908 – Covered Courts: Gold (singles and doubles), A.W. Gore. Bronze (singles) M.J.G. Ritchie.
Grass Courts: Gold (singles), Silver (doubles), M.J.G. Ritchie. **1912 – Covered Courts:** Bronze (singles), Mrs M.B. Parton. **1920:** Gold (doubles), Silver (mixed), Bronze (singles), Miss K. McKane.
1924: Silver (doubles), Bronze (singles), Miss K. McKane.

(a) That the participation by the affiliated associations in the Olympic Games is rendered practically impossible unless the following requirements are agreed to:

(1) The ILTF be granted one representative at least on the IOC.

(2) The ILTF be allowed to co-operate in the technical and material organization of lawn tennis at the Olympic Games.

(3) The definition of an amateur, as adopted by the ILTF, be accepted so far as lawn tennis is concerned.

(4) The holding of the Olympic Games in any one year shall not cancel or supersede the holding during that year of any officially recognized Lawn Tennis Championships or Competitions, nor shall the Olympic Games be regarded as a 'championship of the world' in lawn tennis.

(b) A copy of this resolution be sent to the IOC and to all International Sporting Associations."

A year later the final step to break away was taken at the Annual Meeting of the ILTF, held in Paris on 18th March 1927. The representatives of Holland, supported by Belgium, initially opposed this (not surprisingly as Holland was to stage the next Games in 1928) but after discussion the following resolution was carried unanimously: "The ILTF, not having obtained the satisfaction of all the requirements placed before the IOC by the previous meeting (1926), resolves not to take part in the Olympic Games until such time as full satisfaction shall have been obtained." Obviously the ILTF was in no mood to compromise and there the matter rested. No one could possibly envisage that lawn tennis would not fully appear in the Olympic Games for more than 60 years.

Amsterdam was the venue in 1928, followed by Los Angeles and Berlin. The 1940 Games, originally allocated to Tokyo, were transferred to Helsinki, because of the Sino-Japanese War, but the outbreak of the Second World War in September 1939 brought further cancellation, likewise the 1944 Games, which had been chosen for London. With all hostilities over, London became the hosts in 1948 and so began the unbroken sequence of the Games, every four years – Helsinki (1952), Melbourne (1956), Rome (1960) and Tokyo (1964). In the meantime, the Olympic Movement went from strength to strength, with over 90 countries and 5,000 competitors, including nearly 700 ladies, at the Games.

Around 1963, voices were heard making a case for the return of lawn tennis to the Olympic Games. The ILTF put the matter on the Agenda and when the Annual Meeting was held in Vienna on 8th July 1964, the matter was fully discussed. Many of the delegates were in favour, particularly when they heard Georges de Stefani of Italy, an IOC member, state that the present policy of the IOC was to allow all sports to assist in the organization of the Games.

There was overwhelming support for the motion to go forward, with 35 nations in favour, five against, with six abstentions. Great Britain voted against, which was not surprising knowing the background.

The announcement that the IOC had agreed to add the ILTF to their list of Sports Federations was made at the Annual Meeting of the ILTF, held in Munich on 7th July 1965. This, of course, did not mean that lawn tennis would automatically be included in future Olympic Games. Generally, at that time, the IOC accepted the word of their Sports Federations as to whether the amateur status of the competitor was good. This had been a difficult issue in the past as two or three times the ILTF had nearly agreed to stage Open tournaments, while certain lawn tennis associations, including Great Britain, had pressed for all to be called "players". Most of the nations well realized that the top players under their jurisdiction were far from amateur, but were quite powerless to do anything. There was also the possibility that a problem could arise trying to fit the Olympic Games into the crowded ILTF International Calendar.

The rules of the IOC allowed two "additional sports" to be added by an organizing committee of a Games and so, consequently, an approach was made to Mexico City for tennis to be one of the extra sports in 1968.

After two years had elapsed, the ILTF announced at the Annual Meeting held in Luxembourg on 12th July 1967 that lawn tennis would be included at Mexico City as a demonstration sport. Because of the high altitude of the city the tournament was staged at Guadalajara at the Country Club, where Manuel Santana of Spain and Helga Nielsen of West Germany won the singles. There was also an Exhibition event held in Mexico City.

Unfortunately, having got so far, the process to advance came swiftly to a halt. Earlier in the year, the most significant change ever in tennis came about with the introduction of

Over the years, numerous postage stamps depicting the Olympic Games have been issued by many countries. Although Greece issued the first set of stamps in 1896 to commemorate the inaugural Games, Monaco was the first in 1948 to produce a stamp showing a tennis player (unnamed), with an Olympic background. This referred to the 10th Olympic Games in Wembley (London) event though tennis was not one of the sports held that year.

The new Los Angeles Tennis Centre, which hosted the 1984 Olympic 'demonstration' tennis. Four years later, tennis was back in the Olympics as a full medal sport

'Open' tennis. As far back as 1959 The All England Lawn Tennis Club, with Chairman Herman David at the helm, put forward to the LTA a proposal that The Championships at Wimbledon be made 'open' to all players.

At the Annual Meeting of the ILTF on 6th July 1960, this was rejected and several years followed in which argument persisted at all levels. In 1964 the Club tried to persuade the LTA to declare unilaterally The Championships 'open', but support was not forthcoming. However, on 14th December 1967, at their Annual Meeting, the LTA voted overwhelmingly to admit all categories of players to Wimbledon and other tournaments in Great Britain. There was much activity in the world of tennis but, at a Special Meeting held in Paris on 30th March 1968, the ILTF faced with a *fait accompli*, yielded and allowed each nation to determine their own legislation regarding amateur and professional players. Bournemouth was the first 'open' tournament in the world and in June, The Championships at Wimbledon followed suit. All this, of course, automatically debarred lawn tennis from the Olympic Games, where the IOC's ideal of strict amateur status lived on.

During the next few years the IOC had other matters on their mind with the staging of the Games. At Munich (1972), a terrorist attack by Palestinian guerrillas on the Israeli team, left 17 people dead. Also, South Africa was banned and Rhodesia expelled. Montreal (1976) was boycotted by 22 African countries objecting to New Zealand's rugby team touring South Africa. Another large scale boycott took place at Moscow (1980), when the United States were absent, protesting at the Soviet Union's invasion of Afghanistan. West Germany and Japan were also missing.

In 1984, at Los Angeles, the Soviet Union and some of her allies boycotted the Games, alleging that the security arrangements were not satisfactory, but this appeared to be a cover for the real reason as retaliation for four years earlier.

However, gradually the IOC recognized that times were changing in the world of sport and that many authorities were edging towards professionalism. David Gray, the General Secretary of the ITF (the word 'Lawn' was dropped from the title

International Tennis Federation President, Philippe Chatrier, left, and General Secretary, David Gray, worked continually to persuade the International Olympic Committee to reinstate tennis as part of the Games

in 1977), felt passionately that tennis should be reinstated and had for some years devoted much time trying to convince the IOC to alter their approach. He was given tremendous backing by his President, Philippe Chatrier, and in the end persuasion carried the day, with the IOC agreeing to include tennis as a demonstration sport at the 1984 Games, to be held in Los Angeles. Credit must also be given to the Americans, Jack Kramer, Joseph Bixler and Patricia Yeomans who applied continual pressure to the IOC. A stipulation was laid down by the IOC that all the players must be 21 or under, but this was not a sticking point with the ITF who were only too willing to agree.

The tournament, held during August, was a great success, with over 6,000 spectators attending daily at the Los Angeles Tennis Center. There were two singles events each of 32 competitors, from 34 nations, won by Stefan Edberg of Sweden and 15 year-old Steffi Graf of West Germany. The way was clearly open for tennis to be a full Olympic sport again and so, four years later in 1988, players from all over the world descended upon Seoul in South Korea to contest the first tournament for 64 years.

A major problem prior to the Games was the insistence of North Korea on staging half the events. They were offered a few sports but declined and in the end refused to attend. A number of small Communist countries gave them support. Overshadowing the Games was the failure of ten competitors to pass a drugs test, the most notable being the Canadian runner, Ben Johnson.

None of this had an effect on the tennis tournament which, by being present, consolidated the acceptance of a fully professional sport by the IOC. There were a number of changes to the format which brought the meeting up to modern day practices, such as restricted draws, seeding, wildcards and tie-break sets. There were no third place play-offs.

The Games which followed at Barcelona in 1992 were notable in that no nations boycotted the event, the television income reached new records and the organization was at a very high level and included a spectacular opening ceremony. The tennis tournament was well supported by the players. The ladies' draw was increased to 64 and the doubles to 32 pairs.

Surprisingly, the Centenary meeting of the Olympic Games was not held in Athens but at Atlanta, Georgia, USA. A terrorist bomb that exploded in the Olympic Park three days before the opening of the Games did not spoil the celebrations and the performance of most participants reached record-breaking levels. The tennis tournament ran smoothly, but there was disappointment that so many of the leading men were absent. In some players' minds the Olympic Games still did not rate against the attraction of the normal tournament schedule, in particular the Grand Slams.

After 44 years the Olympic Games returned to the Southern Hemisphere in 2000, with their staging in Sydney. As an incentive to attract players, ATP computer ranking points were awarded to the men but, despite this, a number of top players failed to appear. The new Centre Court, built on the lines of the No.1 Court at Wimbledon, and other accommodation were outstanding, likewise the facilities.

Athens was the venue for 2004. There would be little comparison between this and the original Games staged in the capital, 108 years earlier. In stark figures, over 10,000 athletes from 200 nations appeared as opposed to only 14 nations and just over 200 entries in 1896. Also, nearly 300 events were held in contrast to the 43 originally held. Coverage of the modern Games, with TV, radio and the Press, bore no resemblance with the past. However, the tennis tournament did not attract good coverage and attendance fell short, which also applied to many of the other sports.

The cost of staging the Beijing Games was an estimated 23 billion pounds. The Chinese authorities went to extraordinary lengths to ensure the event was a complete success and this they well achieved. There were no boycotts, no drug scandals and no air pollution, which had been a source of contention for years beforehand. The players' support for the tennis tournament was almost total, which resulted in good crowds, particularly as the week progressed.

So to 2012, when the Games will be held in London for the third time. In 1908 the tennis tournament was held at The All England Lawn Tennis Club at their old ground, situated off Worple Road at Wimbledon. The same Club will stage the event 104 years later, still on grass, but at their Church Road ground, which over recent years has been completely transformed and modernized to present the best facilities available, second to none.

Olympic Medallists

1896 – Athens

	Silver Medal
Men's Singles	J.M.P. Boland (IRE)
Men's Doubles	J.M.P. Boland (IRE)
	F.A. Traun (GER)

1900 – Paris

	First
Men's Singles	H.L. Doherty (BRI)
	(value FF 1,500)
Ladies' Singles	Miss C.R. Cooper (BRI)
	(value FF 350)
Men's Doubles	H.L. Doherty (BRI)
	R.F. Doherty (BRI)
	(value FF 800 each)
Mixed Doubles	R.F. Doherty (BRI)
	Miss C.R. Cooper (BRI)
	(value FF 300 each)

Copper Medal	**Third**	
D. Kasdaglis (GRE)	K. Paspatis (GRE)	In Singles, Boland was also awarded a certificate and olive branch and Kasdaglis a laurel sprig. No medals were awarded for third place.
	M. Tapavica (HUN)	
D. Kasdaglis (GRE)	E.H. Flack (AUS)	
D. Petrokokkinas (GRE)	G.S. Robertson (BRI)	

Second	**Third**	
H.S. Mahony (BRI)	R.F. Doherty (BRI)	No medals were awarded but a prize money voucher was given to all winners, runners-up and the men's singles third place. H.L. Doherty's singles prize was a coffee and liqueur service table. Defeated semi-finalists did not play-off for third place.
(value FF 500)	A.B.J. Norris (BRI)	
	(value FF 350) each	
Miss H. Prevost (FRA)	Miss M. Jones (USA)	
(value FF 150)	Miss H. Rosenbaum (BOH)	
M.O. Decugis (FRA)	G. de la Chapelle (FRA)	
B.S. de Garmendia (USA)	A. Prevost (FRA)	
(value FF 400 each)	H.S. Mahony (BRI)	
	A.B.J. Norris (BRI)	
H.S. Mahony (BRI)	H.L. Doherty (BRI)	
Miss H. Prevost (FRA)	Miss M. Jones (USA)	
(value FF 100 each)	A.A. Warden (BRI)	
	Miss H. Rosenbaum (BOH)	

1904 – St. Louis

	Gold Medal
Men's Singles	B.C. Wright (USA)
Men's Doubles	B.C. Wright (USA)
	E.W. Leonard (USA)

1906 – Athens

	Silver Medal
Men's Singles	M.O. Decugis (FRA)
Ladies' Singles	Miss E. Simiriotou (GRE)
Men's Doubles	M.O. Decugis (FRA)
	M. Germot (FRA)
Mixed Doubles	M.O. Decugis (FRA)
	Mrs M. Decugis (FRA)

1908 – London

	Gold Medal
(Covered courts)	
Men's Singles	A.W. Gore (BRI)
Ladies' Singles	Miss G.S. Eastlake-Smith (BRI)
Men's Doubles	H.R. Barrett (BRI)
	A.W. Gore (BRI)
(Grass courts)	
Men's Singles	M.J.G. Ritchie (BRI)
Ladies'Singles	Mrs D.K. Chambers (BRI)
Men's Doubles	R.F. Doherty (BRI)
	G.W. Hillyard (BRI)

Silver Medal	**Bronze Medal**	
R. LeRoy (USA)	A.E. Bell (USA)	A bronze medal was awarded to both defeated semi-finalists who did not play-off for third place.
	E.W. Leonard (USA)	
A.E. Bell (USA)	C.O. Gamble (USA)	
R. LeRoy (USA)	A.Y. Wear (USA)	
	J.W. Wear (USA)	
	A.T. West (USA)	

Second	**Third**	
M. Germot (FRA)	Z. Zemla (BOH)	The Jury decided that in the Mixed Doubles, G. Simiriotis and Miss S. Marinou had achieved a better result than X. Kasdaglis and Miss A. Matsa against the eventual champions and awarded them second place. In the Men's Singles Z. Zemla was awarded third place.
Miss S. Marinou (GRE)	Miss E. Paspati (GRE)	
I. Ballis (GRE)	L. Zemla (BOH)	
X. Kasdaglis (GRE)	Z. Zemla (BOH)	
G. Simiriotis (GRE)	X. Kasdaglis (GRE)	
Miss S. Marinou (GRE)	Miss A. Matsa (GRE)	

The silver medal awarded to the singles winners differed to the doubles winners.

Silver Medal	**Bronze Medal**
G.A. Caridia (BRI)	M.J.G. Ritchie (BRI)
Miss A.N.G. Greene (BRI)	Mrs M. Adlerstrahle (SWE)
G.A. Caridia (BRI)	W. Bostrom (SWE)
G.M. Simond (BRI)	G. Setterwall (SWE)
O. Froitzheim (GER)	W.V. Eaves (BRI)
Miss P.D.H. Boothby (BRI)	Mrs R.J. Winch (BRI)
J.C. Parke (BRI)	C.H.L. Cazalet (BRI)
M.J.G. Ritchie (BRI)	C.P. Dixon (BRI)

1912 – Stockholm

	Gold Medal
(Covered courts)	
Men's Singles	A.H. Gobert (FRA)
Ladies' Singles	Miss E.M. Hannam (BRI)
Men's Doubles	A.H. Gobert (FRA)
	M. Germot (FRA)
Mixed Doubles	C.P. Dixon (BRI)
	Miss E.M. Hannam (BRI)
(Hard courts)	
Men's Singles	C.L. Winslow (RSA)
Ladies' Singles	Miss M.M. Broquedis (FRA)
Men's Doubles	H.A. Kitson (RSA)
	C.L. Winslow (RSA)
Mixed Doubles	H. Schomburgk (GER)
	Miss D. Koring (GER)

1920 – Antwerp

	Gold Medal
Men's Singles	L.B. Raymond (RSA)
Ladies' Singles	Miss S.R.F. Lenglen (FRA)
Men's Doubles	O.G.N. Turnbull (BRI)
	M. Woosnam (BRI)
Ladies' Doubles	Miss K. McKane (BRI)
	Mrs W.M. McNair (BRI)
Mixed Doubles	M.O. Decugis (FRA)
	Miss S.R.F. Lenglen (FRA)

Silver Medal

C.P. Dixon (BRI)
Miss T.G.S. Castenschiold (DEN)
C. Kempe (SWE)
G. Setterwall (SWE)
H.R. Barrett (BRI)
Miss F.H. Aitchison (BRI)

Bronze Medal

A.F. Wilding (AUL)
Mrs M.B. Parton (BRI)
A.E. Beamish (BRI)
C.P. Dixon (BRI)
G. Setterwall (SWE)
Mrs S. Fick (SWE)

After the 1912 Olympics, solid gold medals were replaced with a gold (silver gilt, with six grams of fine gold) medal.

H.A. Kitson (RSA)
Miss D. Koring (GER)
F. Piepes (AUT)
A. Zborzil (AUT)
G. Setterwall (SWE)
Mrs S. Fick (SWE)

O. Kreuzer (GER)
Miss A.M. Bjurstedt (NOR)
A.H. Canet (FRA)
E.M.M. Meny (FRA)
A.H. Canet (FRA)
Miss M.M. Broquedis (FRA)

Silver Medal

I. Kumagae (JPN)
Miss E.D. Holman (BRI)
S. Kashio (JPN)
I. Kumagae (JPN)
Mrs W.A. Beamish (BRI)
Miss E.D. Holman (BRI)
M. Woosnam (BRI)
Miss K. McKane (BRI)

Bronze Medal

C.L. Winslow (RSA)
Miss K. McKane (BRI)
P.H.M. Albarran (FRA)
M.O. Decugis (FRA)
Miss E.P.S.M. d'Ayen (FRA)
Miss S.R.F. Lenglen (FRA)
L. Zemla (TCH)
Miss M. Skrbkova (TCH)

1924 – Paris

	Gold Medal
Men's Singles	V. Richards (USA)
Ladies' Singles	Miss H.N. Wills (USA)
Men's Doubles	F.T. Hunter (USA)
	V. Richards (USA)
Ladies' Doubles	Mrs H.V. Wightman (USA)
	Miss H.N. Wills (USA)
Mixed Doubles	R.N. Williams (USA)
	Mrs H.V. Wightman (USA)

1988 – Seoul

	Gold Medal
Men's Singles	M. Mecir (TCH)
Ladies' Singles	Miss S.M. Graf (FRG)
Men's Doubles	K.E. Flack (USA)
	R.A. Seguso (USA)
Ladies' Doubles	Miss Z.L. Garrison (USA)
	Miss P.H. Shriver (USA)

Silver Medal	**Bronze Medal**
H.J. Cochet (FRA)	U.L. de Morpurgo (ITA)
Miss J.P. Vlasto (FRA)	Miss K. McKane (GBR)
J. Brugnon (FRA)	J.R. Borotra (FRA)
H.J. Cochet (FRA)	J.R. Lacoste (FRA)
Mrs P.L. Covell (GBR)	Mrs D.C. Shepherd-Barron (GBR)
Miss K. McKane (GBR)	Miss E.L. Colyer (GBR)
V. Richards (USA)	H. Timmer (NED)
Mrs M.H. Jessup (USA)	Miss K. Bouman (NED)

Silver Medal	**Bronze Medal**	
T.S. Mayotte (USA)	S.B. Edberg (SWE)	A bronze medal was
	B.N. Gilbert (USA)	awarded to both
Miss G.B. Sabatini (ARG)	Miss Z.L. Garrison (USA)	defeated semi-finalists
	Miss M.G. Maleeva (BUL)	who did not play-off
S. Casal (ESP)	M. Mecir (TCH)	for third place.
E. Sanchez (ESP)	M. Srejber (TCH)	
	S.B. Edberg (SWE)	
	A.P. Jarryd (SWE)	
Miss J. Novotna (TCH)	Mrs E.M. Smylie (AUS)	
Miss H. Sukova (TCH)	Miss W.M. Turnbull (AUS)	
	Miss S.M. Graf (FRG)	
	Miss C.G. Kohde-Kilsch (FRG)	

1992 – Barcelona

	Gold Medal
Men's Singles	M. Rosset (SUI)
Ladies' Singles	Miss J.M. Capriati (USA)
Men's Doubles	B.F. Becker (GER)
	M.D. Stich (GER)
Ladies' Doubles	Miss B.C. Fernandez (USA)
	Miss M.J. Fernandez (USA)

1996 – Atlanta

	Gold Medal
Men's Singles	A.K. Agassi (USA)
Ladies' Singles	Miss L.A. Davenport (USA)
Men's Doubles	T.A. Woodbridge (AUS)
	M.R. Woodforde (AUS)
Ladies' Doubles	Miss B.C. Fernandez (USA)
	Miss M. J. Fernandez (USA)

Silver Medal	Bronze Medal	
J. Arrese (ESP)	G. S. Ivanisevic (CRO)	
	A. Cherkasev (CIS)	
Miss S.M. Graf (GER)	Miss A.I.M. Sanchez-Vicario (ESP)	
	Miss M.J. Fernandez (USA)	
W. Ferreiro (RSA)	J.A. Frana (ARG)	
P. Norval (RSA)	C. Miniussi (ARG)	
	G.S. Ivanisevic (CRO)	
	G. Prpic (CRO)	A bronze medal
Miss I.C. Martinez (ESP)	Miss L.Meskhi (CIS)	was awarded to
Miss A.I.M. Sanchez-Vicario (ESP)	Miss N.M. Zvereva (CIS)	both defeated
	Miss R. McQuillian (AUS)	semi-finalists who did not play-off
	Miss N.A-L. Provis (AUS)	for third place.

Silver Medal	Bronze Medal
S. Bruguera (ESP)	L.A. Paes (IND)
Miss A.I.M. Sanchez-Vicario (ESP)	Miss J. Novotna (CZE)
N. Broad (GBR)	M.K. Goellner (GER)
T.H. Henman (GBR)	D. Prinosil (GER)
Miss J. Novotna (CZE)	Miss I.C. Martinez (ESP)
Miss H. Sukova (CZE)	Miss A.I.M. Sanchez-Vicario (ESP)

2000 – Sydney

	Gold Medal
Men's Singles	Y. Kafelnikov (RUS)
Ladies' Singles	Miss V.E.S. Williams (USA)
Men's Doubles	S. Lareau (CAN)
	D.M. Nestor (CAN)
Ladies' Doubles	Miss S.J. Williams (USA)
	Miss V.E.S. Williams (USA)

2004 – Athens

	Gold Medal
Men's Singles	N.A. Massu (CHI)
Ladies' Singles	Mrs J. Henin-Hardenne (BEL)
Men's Doubles	F.F. Gonzales (CHI)
	N.A. Massu (CHI)
Ladies' Doubles	Miss T. Li (CHN)
	Miss T.T. Sun (CHN)

2008 – Beijing

	Gold Medal
Men's Singles	R. Nadal (ESP)
Ladies' Singles	Miss E. Dementieva (RUS)
Men's Doubles	R. Federer (SUI)
	S. Wawrinka (SUI)
Ladies' Doubles	Miss S.J. Williams (USA)
	Miss V.E.S. Williams (USA)

Silver Medal	Bronze Medal
T.M. Haas (GER)	A. DiPasquale (FRA)
Miss E. Dementieva (RUS)	Miss M. Seles (USA)
T.A. Woodbridge (AUS)	A. Corretja (ESP)
M.R. Woodforde (AUS)	A. Costa (ESP)
Miss K. Boogert (NED)	Miss E. Callens (BEL)
Miss M.J.M.M. Oremans(NED)	Miss D. Van Roost (BEL)

Silver Medal	Bronze Medal
M. Fish (USA)	F.F. Gonzales (CHI)
Miss A. Mauresmo (FRA)	Miss A.H. Molik (AUS)
N. Kiefer (GER)	M. Ancic (CRO)
R. Schuettler (GER)	I. Ljubicic (CRO)
Miss I.C. Martinez (ESP)	Miss P. Suarez (ARG)
Miss V. Ruano Pascual (ESP)	Miss P. Tarabin (ARG)

Silver Medal	Bronze Medal
F.F. Gonzales (CHI)	N. Djokovic (SRB)
Miss D. Safina (RUS)	Miss V. Zvonareva (RUS)
S.O.K. Aspelin (SWE)	M.C. Bryan (USA)
T.K. Johansson (SWE)	R.C. Bryan (USA)
Miss A. Medina Garrigues (ESP)	Miss Z. Yan (CHN)
Miss V. Ruano-Pascual (ESP)	Miss J. Zheng (CHN)

With the return of tennis to the Olympic Games after 64 years, Miloslav Mecir of Czechoslovakia won the men's singles gold medal at Seoul.

The Tennis Tournaments

1896

1st Olympic Games – Athens, Greece

8,9,11 April

Irishman, John Boland wins first medal

The lawn tennis tournament was staged over three days in the middle area of the Velodrome Stadium at Phaliron. There were three clay courts in use, two singles and one doubles, but play did not take place until around 5pm each day, on the completion of the cycling.

There were two events, a Men's Singles and Doubles, which were contested by 13 players and six pairs, respectively. Of the six nations who were represented, Greece had seven players, British Isles two and Australia, France, Germany and Hungary, one each. Unfortunately, due to the passage of time, early round detailed results do not exist, but the two final scores are available.

The honour of being Britain's first Olympic champion fell to John Boland, an Irishman born in Dublin in 1870, when he won the lawn tennis events. While at Oxford University in 1895 he learnt that the first modern Games would be held the following year. Very interested, he accepted an invitation to visit Athens from a Greek undergraduate at the University, Constantine Mano, who was involved in the organization of the Games. Soon after arriving in Athens, Boland met another Greek, Dionysios Kasdaglis, who suggested that he contest the Olympic tennis tournament. So, with a racket and shoes, purchased locally, he entered the Men's

Top: Cover of official Olympic Report
Left: The first Olympic Tennis Champion – John Boland from Dublin

One of the three courts situated in the middle of the Velodrome Stadium

Singles and Doubles and emerged as champion in both. To win the singles he beat four players, Friedrich Traun from Hamburg, Evangelos Rallis and Konstantinos Paspatis – both from Greece – and in the final, Kasdaglis, 6–2 6–2. His partner in the doubles was Traun and they defeated Kasdaglis and Dimitrious Petrokokkinos in the final, 5–7 6–3 6–3. Strangely, the doubles final was played before the singles final.

A number of spectators watched the final stages of the matches, but Boland felt they took away a poor impression of tennis as a game. His play was superior to the other competitors but his overall standard was difficult to judge as there was no record of him competing in tournaments, either before or after.

He received a Silver Medal, a certificate and an olive branch as his prize in both events, while the runners-up were presented with a Copper Medal and a laurel sprig. The prizes were presented by King George I on the last day of the Games.

Boland had a distinguished life. After being educated at Edgbaston, Bonn University, London University and Christ Church, Oxford he was called to the Bar in 1897, but never practised. He was a Member of Parliament for South Kerry from 1900–1918, during which time he served on many national committees and was often a leading light in bringing about change to the Irish situation. He then settled in London and became Secretary of the Catholic Truth Society for 21 years. He married Eileen Moloney in 1902 and they had one son and five daughters. He died in London on 17th March 1958, aged 87.

1900

2nd Olympic Games – Paris, France

6–11 April

Britain dominates meeting

The lawn tennis tournament was scheduled to be played on the newly-constructed courts of the Cercle du Bois de Boulogne, but they were considered not ready for continuous play and the venue was changed at short notice to the exclusive Puteaux Club on L'Ile de Puteaux. Here the players found first class facilities, with outstanding dressing rooms, restaurant etc., all located in beautiful surroundings. Another bonus was the delightful weather throughout the week, which attracted a large attendance each day.

Very few people realized that the tournament was part of the Olympics. 'Lawn Tennis and Croquet', the official organ of the British Lawn Tennis Association, devoted more than four large pages to a very detailed report, including full scores, under the heading of "Paris Exhibition" but there was no reference to the Olympics or medals.

The tournament did not attract a large entry, but those who competed were generally of high standard. No doubt if earlier notice had been possible in announcing the Puteaux Club as the venue, many more competitors, particularly from the Continent, would have entered. As it was, the four events were completely dominated by British Isles players, three of whom were present or past Wimbledon champions, who captured the titles. In the Men's Singles, listing 15 names, the legendary Doherty brothers, Laurie and Reginald, unfortunately were drawn together at the semi-final stage and, as quite often, one of them retired. On this occasion Laurie went through to easily win the final from Irishman, Harold Mahony, 6–4 6–2 6–3. The five French players did not excel.

The Doherty brothers had matters their own way in the doubles, crushing all resistance from Max Decugis and Basil de Garmendia, a French/American combination, in the final, 6–1 6–1 6–0.

Above left: Three times Wimbledon champion, Charlotte Cooper became the first lady to win an Olympic title when she captured the Ladies' singles event. She also won the mixed doubles

Above right: Englishman, Laurie Doherty won the Men's singles title and combined with his brother, Reginald, to take the doubles event

Facing page: One of several Olympic posters

The Ladies' Singles presented an easy passage for Britain's Charlotte Cooper, who was only called upon to play three matches. In the semi-final her victim was Marion Jones, the United States champion in 1899 (and 1902), 6–2 7–5, the second set being well contested. In the final, Charlotte Cooper was always in control, defeating Parisian, Helen Prevost, 6–1 6–4. This gave her the honour of being the first British lady to win an Olympic event. As expected, Reginald Doherty and Charlotte Cooper won the Mixed Doubles.

The winners and runners-up, plus the two defeated semi-finalists in the Men's Singles, received a prize money voucher. In the case of Laurie Doherty the value was 1,500 francs, which was sufficient for him to be given a coffee table.

Besides the four Olympic events, five handicap competitions and a top-class Professional Singles Championship were staged to augment the programme.

1904

3rd Olympic Games – St. Louis, USA

29 August – 3 September

Only one foreign player competes

The lawn tennis competition took place on three dirt courts situated in The Francis Field, near the main Stadium where the athletic events were being held at the same time. The programme consisted of two events, a Men's Singles and Doubles. Both were contested by matches decided over the best of three sets, except the Men's Doubles final, which was best of five sets.

All competitors were from the home country, except a Dr Hugo Hardy of Germany. In the singles, 34 players entered their names, but only 24 competed. The very experienced, left-handed, Beals Wright won the singles without losing a set, defeating Robert LeRoy in the final, 6–4 6–4. In the round before, Wright beat Alphonso Bell, 6–3 6–4, while LeRoy defeated Edgar Leonard, 6–3 6–3. One of Wright's victims was Hardy in the second round. A close look at the draw reveals the name of Dwight Davis, donor of the famous Davis Cup, the worldwide International Team Championship.

In the doubles 15 pairs competed. The last four of the singles contested the final, with Leonard and Wright outplaying Bell and LeRoy, 6–4 6–4 6–2. Apparently both finals attracted a good attendance.

There were four other tennis events held simultaneously, but these were of a much lesser standard and not recognized as being of Olympic status.

Left-handed American, Beals Wright won the Men's singles gold medal without losing a set in five matches

Below: The entrance gates to The Francis Field, scene of the World's Fair Exposition and the Olympic Games of 1904. The commemorative gates were installed in 1914

1906

Intercalated Games – Athens, Greece

23–26 April

France wins three events

Unlike the Games of 10 years earlier, the lawn tennis tournament was held on the clay courts of the Athens Lawn Tennis Club. Only six nations sent representatives and from an entry of 29 in the Men's Singles, only 18 actually took the court.

Head and shoulders above the field were the two Frenchmen, Max Decugis and Maurice Germot, who comfortably steered their way through the event to the final, where Decugis won in four sets, 6–1 7–9 6–4 6–1. The semi-finalists were Guus Kessler and Gerrard Scheurleer, both from Holland.

The two Frenchmen paired to win the Men's Doubles, but were given much to think about in the final, before overcoming Ioannis Ballis and Xenophon Kasdaglis from Greece, 6–3 9–7 3–6 0–6 6–0.

All the entrants for the Ladies' Singles were from Greece, apart from Marie Decugis from France, who withdrew without striking a ball. In the final, Esmee Simiriotou beat Sophia Marinou, 2–6 6–3 6–3. Decugis won his third event when, partnered by his wife, he took the Mixed Doubles. A Silver Medal was presented to the winners of the four competitions, but the medal differed for singles and doubles.

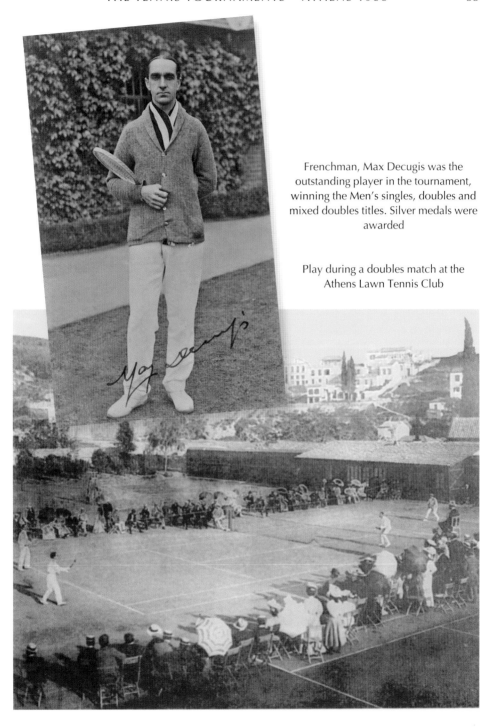

Frenchman, Max Decugis was the outstanding player in the tournament, winning the Men's singles, doubles and mixed doubles titles. Silver medals were awarded

Play during a doubles match at the Athens Lawn Tennis Club

1908

4th Olympic Games – London, England

6–11 May

Sweden is the only nation from abroad

The organizing Committee decided to hold two competitions for lawn tennis - a covered court and a grass court meeting. Unfortunately, the tournament held on wood at the Queen's Club, West Kensington, failed to attract players from abroad, apart from two men and two ladies from Sweden who, by their fine sportsmanship and manner, were well received.

The draw for the Men's Singles had only nine entries, two of them Australasians, who withdrew. There was argument as to whether they had even entered.

Queen's Club covered wood courts, West Kensington

Left: Twice Wimbledon champion, Arthur Gore (British Isles) played only two matches to win the Men's singles gold medal. He also captured the doubles title with Roper Barrett

Right: Representing the British Isles, Gladys Eastlake-Smith won the third set 6–0 in the final against Alice Greene, to capture the Ladies' singles gold medal

The British Isles players were all top-class performers. Arthur Gore, twice Wimbledon champion, beat Major Ritchie at the semi-final stage in a contest of very high standard, 4–6 6–3 5–7 6–1 6–4, while in the other half of the draw, Wilberforce Eaves was forced to default to George Caridia after the first set, suffering from the intense heat.

Gore had little difficulty in overcoming Caridia in the final, 6–3 7–5 6–4, to take the Gold Medal. The two Swedes gave opposite accounts of themselves, with Gunnar Setterwall losing easily to an in-form Caridia, 6–2 6–1 6–1, and Wollmar Bostrom who, with his excellent service and backhand strokes, pushed Eaves to win 7–5 6–2 9–7.

The draw for the Ladies' Singles listed nine players, but only seven struck a ball. In the second round Elsa Wallenberg, one of the visitors, fought bravely against Mildred Coles who, when leading 9–11 6–4 5–4 40–15 had the misfortune to sustain a severe injury to her arm, which forced her to retire. The other Swedish lady, Marthe Adlerstahle, had a bye and walkover to reach the semi-final, where she was comfortably beaten by Alice Greene's good serving, 6–1 6–3. At the same stage, Gladys Eastlake Smith was too strong for Elsa Wallenberg who, at one time, lost nine games in a row, 6–4 6–4.

In the title round the first two sets were shared before Gladys Eastlake Smith reeled off six games in succession for victory over Alice Greene, at 6–2 4–6 6–0. Two days later, Gladys Eastlake Smith became Mrs. Lamplough. Marthe Adlerstahle beat her colleague in the Bronze Medal play-off.

Five pairs played in the Men's Doubles, which was won by the old firm of Roper Barrett and Gore, who beat Caridia and George Simond, 6–2 2–6 6–3 6–3, in the last match. Setterwall and Bostrom returned home with a Bronze Medal each, by defeating Lionel Escombe and Ritchie in the play-off, 4–6 6–3 1–6 6–0 6–3.

The absence of players was equalled by the lack of interest in the competition by the public, which showed by the very meagre attendance and on the final day amounted to only a mere handful of spectators.

6–11 July

Britain wins all medals bar one

The second competition was held on the lawns of The All England Lawn Tennis Club, then situated off Worple Road, Wimbledon, in the week immediately after The Championships.

There was great disappointment from the public that Arthur Gore and Charlotte Sterry, the two champions from the previous week, withdrew from the singles after being listed. Also, favourites Hugh Doherty and Anthony Wilding did not appear. However, the admission of some of the younger first class British players representing their country for the first time, compensated, likewise the presence of the Germans, South Africans and Dutch, together with the new contingent from Austria and Bohemia which gave the field a new atmosphere.

Undoubtedly, the feature of the Men's Singles was the success of the boyish looking German champion, Otto Froitzheim, appearing practically for the first time on grass. He seemed to win matches in his stride by advancing with victories over Kenneth Powell, 6–1 6–3 6–4, Oscar Kreuzer, 6–2 6–3 6–3, James Parke, 6–4 11–9 6–4, George Caridia, 6–4 6–1 5–7 6–1 and John Richardson, 2–6 6–1 6–4 6–4, until he reached the final against Major Ritchie. Here he tried for much of the time to play the Englishman at his own game from the back of the court, but he could not sustain the momentum and fell, 7–5 6–3 6–4. There were some other fine matches in this event, which attracted 31 players, but the impression left by Froitzheim was the most memorable.

The Ladies' Singles developed into a farce. From the original entry of thirteen, only five players, all British, actually appeared on court, with Dora Boothby reaching the final without hitting a ball! Dorothea Chambers, three times Wimbledon champion, was in invincible form when she defeated Agnes Morton, 6–2 6–3, Ruth Winch, 6–1 6–1 and Dora Boothby, 6–1 7–5, to take the Gold

Above: In the Ladies' singles, only four matches were played. Dorothea Chambers, three times Wimbledon champion, won three of them to become champion

Left: 37 year-old Englishman, Major Ritchie won the Men's singles gold medal, on grass, at the All England Lawn Tennis Club

The All England Lawn Tennis Club Centre Court at Worple Road, Wimbledon.
Above: Dorothea Chambers smashes to Dora Boothby in the Ladies' singles final.
Below: The Men's doubles final – Reginald Doherty and George Hillyard (far side)
versus Major Ritchie and James Parke

MEN'S SINGLES.

First Prize—Olympic Gold Medal.   Second Prize—Olympic Silver Medal.
Third Prize—Olympic Bronze Medal.
Those who are beaten in the Semi-Final Round will compete for the Bronze Medal.

LADIES' SINGLES.

First Prize—Olympic Gold Medal.   Second Prize—Olympic Silver Medal.
Third Prize—Olympic Bronze Medal.
Those who are beaten in the Semi-Final Round will compete for the Bronze Medal.

MEN'S DOUBLES.

First Prizes—Two Olympic Gold Medals.   Second Prizes—Two Olympic Silver Medals.
Third Prizes—Two Olympic Bronze Medals.
The Pairs who are beaten in the Semi-Final Round will compete for the Bronze Medals.

OLYMPIC GAMES, 1908.

Grass-Court Lawn Tennis Section

SATURDAY, JULY 11th,

UPON THE LAWNS OF THE

ALL ENGLAND

Lawn Tennis & Croquet Club,

WIMBLEDON.

Committee of Management:

E. R. CLARKE.   S. A. E. HICKSON.   R. J. McNAIR.
W. H. COLLINS.   G. W. HILLYARD.   G. R. MEWBURN.
                  R. B. HOUGH.

Honorary Referee - - W. H. COLLINS.
Honorary Manager - - G. W. HILLYARD.

The Gentlemen's Singles Olympic Championship.

The Gentlemen's Doubles Olympic Championship.

The Ladies' Singles Olympic Championship.

PRICE 3d.

PRINTED BY E. TRIM AND CO. HOMEFIELD ROAD, AND HILL ROAD.

The Official Programme for the Grass Court tournament, played at the All England Lawn Tennis Club, showing the draws of the three events

Medal. In the only other match, Agnes Morton beat Alice Greene in the opening round, 8–6 6–2. Ruth Winch took the Bronze Medal by default. None of the six foreign players even appeared.

The Men's Doubles produced some excellent matches, with Reginald Doherty and George Hillyard overcoming many narrow escapes before eventually beating Clement Cazalet and Charles Dixon in the semi-final, 5–7 2–6 6–4 17–15 6–4, and Parke and Ritchie in the final, 9–7 7–5 9–7.

At the conclusion, Queen Alexandra presented the medals, all of which were won by the British Isles, except the Silver taken home by Froitzheim.

Attendance was low at the start of the week, perhaps due to poor weather, but towards the end the numbers increased considerably.

1912

5th Olympic Games – Stockholm, Sweden

5–12 May

Gold medals shared by Britain and France

For the lawn tennis event, Sweden decided to follow the pattern set by London four years earlier, by holding covered court and outdoor competitions. The first, held at the Royal Lawn Tennis Club, Idrottsparken, where there was a newly constructed pavilion, attracted a high standard of entry from six nations. Both the British Isles and Sweden fielded full teams, which were well supported by leading players from Australia, Bohemia, Denmark and France.

When the covered court building was erected 12 years earlier, there were difficulties with the lighting. A glass roof could not support the weight of winter snow and the Club was forced to place the two courts end to end to allow high level windows to access the light on both sides. The accommodation for the spectators was in a gallery between the two courts and in boxes along the sides. The surface of the courts was wood, painted black. Spacious dressing rooms had hot and cold showers, while an attractive lounge was provided for relaxation. The building does not exist today.

Never before in Sweden had tennis matches attracted so much public interest with spectators filling the courts to capacity each day. Unfortunately, only 400 people could be accommodated around the two courts. King Gustav V and the Crown Prince and Princess and other members of the Royal Family were avid followers of the play throughout the week. Those who failed to attend found the Stockholm newspaper columns brimming with information.

The favourite for the Men's Singles title was Anthony Wilding of New Zealand, champion at Wimbledon for the past two years. Without being pressed he reached the semi-final, where he met British stalwart Charles Dixon, who on the day was more resourceful and accurate in winning, 6–0 4–6 6–4 6–4. In the final Dixon met Andre Gobert of France, who had eliminated another Englishman, Gordon Lowe,

Left: Andre Gobert of France, winner of two gold medals, singles and doubles

Below: Englishwoman, Edith Hannam, won the gold medal in the Ladies' singles without losing a set. She also triumphed in the mixed event

Bottom: One of the two covered courts at the Royal Lawn Tennis Club at Idrottsparken

at the semi-final stage, in five long sets. So much interest was taken in the final that spectators queued for three hours before the doors were opened. Dixon played very well but Gobert's ability to raise his game at crucial moments when really needed, gave him the control to win, 8–6 6–4 6–4. Gobert won a second Gold Medal by combining with fellow countryman, Maurice Germot, to beat the top Swedish pair, Gunnar Setterwall and Carl Kempe in the final, after a marathon battle, 4–6 14–12 6–2 6–4. This was considered the finest match of the tournament.

Edith Hannam of the British Isles was clearly outstanding when capturing the Ladies' Singles title without the loss of a set. In the final her superior speed and strength overcame the defence of Thora Castenschiold of Denmark who, leading 3–0 in both sets, fell at 6–4 6–3. Another Englishwoman, Mabel Parton, won the singles Bronze Medal, while Dixon and Edith Hannam took home the gold medal in the Mixed Doubles event. At the conclusion, the King presented the medals and that evening a dinner at the Hasselbacken successfully wound up the proceedings.

28 June –5 July

South Africa and France take top honours

Although twice the number of nations and competitors took part in the outdoor event, the gathering was of relatively poor standard. The matches were played on a surface called "Adekvat", a kind of clay, at Ostermalms Idrottsplats, not far from the capital. There were four courts available with the main court accommodating approximately 1,500 spectactors. The event was very well organized by the Swedish Lawn Tennis Association.

Charles Winslow defeated fellow South African, Harold Kitson in the final of the Men's singles. They combined to win the doubles

The British Isles did not send any representatives, while France was without their leading players. Earlier in the year both these nations had agreed that as the dates of the outdoor meeting clashed with those of The Championships at Wimbledon they would concentrate their top entry at the earlier tournament. The Swedish authorities would not change their arrangements and consequently the standard of play suffered. The United States decided not to send an official team, but one player entered individually.

Left: Gold medallist in Ladies' singles, Marguerite Broquedis of France

Below: Marguerite Broquedis receives her Ladies' singles gold medal at the courtside from King Gustav V

South Africa's two representatives, Harold Kitson and Charles Winslow completely dominated the Men's Singles to reach the final where the latter, in a fiercely contested and spirited encounter, won after 54 games, 7–5 4–6 10–8 8–6. During the lead up, both were pressed only once – Kitson to overcome Ladislav Zemla of Bohemia 2–6 6–3 6–2 4–6 6–3 and Winslow to edge out against the German, Lois-Maria Heyden, 6–1 6–4 8–10 4–6 6–3. The Bronze Medal was taken by another German, Oscar Kreuzer, who beat Zemla in the play-off.

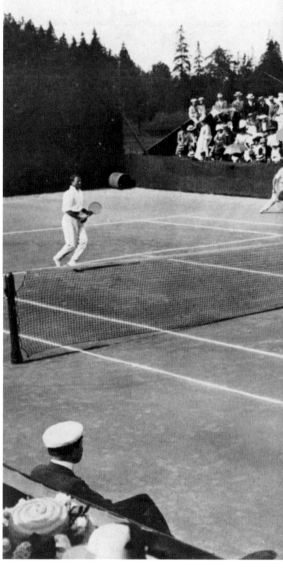

Marguerite Broquedis of France won the Ladies' Singles Gold Medal. In the last two rounds she was taken to the limit, just succeeding in both in the 10th game of the third set. She beat Margrethe Bjurstedt from Norway, 6–3 2–6 6–4 and then Dora Koring of Germany in the final, 4–6 6–3 6–4. Much more was to be heard in the future of Margrethe Bjurstedt as she later became Mrs Mallory and won the United States Singles Championships eight times.

Although Kitson and Winslow conceded three sets along the way, they proved to be the best team in the Men's Doubles, beating the Austrians, Felix Piepes and Arthur Zborzil in the final, 4–6 6–1 6–2 6–2. In the round before, the runners-up eliminated Albert Canet and Eduard Meny, but not before the Frenchmen had saved 12 match points.

The Gold Medal for the Mixed Doubles was won by Heinrich Schomburgk and Dora Koring who defeated Gunnar Setterwall and Sigrid Fick of Sweden, 6–4

The Men's doubles final being played out on the main court

6–0. Unfortunately, the contest was spoilt when Setterwall received a blow to his mouth from his partner's racket and was virtually out of action afterwards. Following this match, the medals for all four events were presented from the courtside by King Gustav.

1920

7th Olympic Games – Antwerp, Belgium

15–24 August

South Africa and France retain both singles titles

Unlike the previous two Olympics, the authorities wisely decided to stage just one lawn tennis competition – an outdoor hard court event at the Beerschot Lawn Tennis Club.

The organization of the tournament left much to be desired. The main complaint was that the courts being very close to the main Athletic Stadium, the continual loud cheering from the crowd upset the players' concentration. Also, the dressing room accommodation was poor, offering no hot water, soap or facilities for drying clothes. This was particularly inconvenient for those who had to travel each evening to Antwerp for their hotel accommodation.

Although the newly constructed courts were quite satisfactory, the surface was inclined to cut up and when the rain came in the middle of the week, they did not drain quickly and became very slow. However, most players entered into the spirit of the occasion and, generally, there was accord.

Players from Austria, Bulgaria, Germany, Hungary and Turkey were not invited because of their involvement in World War I. The United States did not send a team. They had requested that the Belgian authorities change the dates of the tennis tournament, as this clashed with the US Championships, but they would not agree.

Although a few of the top players of the day, such as France's Andre Gobert and Gerald Patterson from Australia were missing, the overall standard of play from the record 13 nations who competed was good and included Japan for the first time.

Two South Africans reached the semi-final of the Men's Singles. Charles Winslow fell easily to Japan's Ichiya Kumagae, 6–2 6–2 6–2, while Louis Raymond, after losing the opening two sets, overcame a tired Noel Turnbull of the British

In a battle of two left-handers, Louis Raymond of South
Africa won the Men's singles gold medal, beating Japan's
Ichiya Kumagae, comfortably, in the final

Isles, 2–6 1–6 6–2 6–2 6–1. The final brought two left-handers face to face, with
Raymond having the edge in a baseline duel, 5–7 6–4 7–5 6–4.

A record marathon match was played in the second round, when Gordon
Lowe outlasted the Greek player, Augustos Zerlendi, after five and three-quarter
hours on court, 14–12 8–10 5–7 6–4. Adjourned overnight and then the following
day for lunch, the tactics from both were almost the same – keep the ball in motion
until the other made a mistake. Lowe suffered cramp at 3–1 in the final set and was
treated by a doctor for seven minutes before managing to struggle on. Many of the
other matches were also long-drawn out affairs.

The winner of the Ladies' singles gold medal was never in doubt as confirmed by Frenchwoman, Suzanne Lenglen, who dropped just four games in five matches. She also won the mixed doubles in partnership with Max Decugis

Right: A view of the main court at the Beerschot Lawn Tennis Club in Antwerp

The winning of the Ladies' Singles by Suzanne Lenglen of France was never in doubt. She won three matches without losing a game to reach the semi-final, before sailing past Sweden's Sigrid Fick, 6–0 6–1, and Dorothy Holman of the British Isles, 6–3 6–0, to capture the Gold Medal. Kathleen McKane withdrew from the semi-final to reserve herself for the Ladies' Doubles with Winifred McNair. In consequence a crowded gallery was able to watch the English pair inflict a very rare defeat on Suzanne Lenglen. The Frenchwoman, playing magnificently, did her best to protect her partner, the very inexperienced Elizabeth d'Ayen, but in a very close and exciting finish the French team went down, 2–6 6–3 8–6, after holding two match points in the last set. The victors went on to win the final against

fellow countrywomen, Winifred Beamish and Dorothy Holman, 8–6 6–4, to take
the Gold Medal.

The Men's Doubles, which produced some very exciting encounters, was won
by Turnbull and Max Woosnam, who eventually proved too strong for Seichiro
Kashio and Kumagae in the final, 6–3 5–7 7–5 7–5.

Suzanne Lenglen and Max Decugis dropped a set but were never in trouble
in capturing the Mixed Doubles. In the final they beat Woosnam and Kathleen
McKane, 6–4 6–2. This gave Suzanne Lenglen and Kathleen McKane three medals
each. Including three at the 1906 Intercalated Games, Decugis won his sixth medal
at this meeting – a record.

1924

8th Olympic Games – Paris, France

13–20 July

America wins all five events

The lawn tennis facility at Colombes, an industrial area on the edge of Paris, was situated a hundred yards or so from the main Athletic Stadium and consisted of seating accommodation on four sides, enclosing an area, with three tennis courts. Just outside were a further six courts. Players complained that their concentration was upset by the continuous shouting coming from the Stadium and from spectators applauding, at various times, the players on the adjoining courts in the central area. Only laid the week before, the red clay courts were said to be in good condition, made hard and fast by the hot weather. The dressing room facilities were very poor, with just one shower available.

The entry for the five events was very large compared to earlier years, with 28 nations providing 82 men and 31 ladies. All the war-time enemies were invited, except Germany, who was still not on good terms with France. Ireland and Great Britain competed separately for the first time. The standard was very high. The United States Association, keen to impress, sent an outstanding top class team of four men and five ladies and this paid dividends as, between them, they captured every event. Bill Tilden was not in the team as he was in dispute with the US authorities. Nor was the world's other top player available, Suzanne Lenglen of France, who withdrew before play started, being not fit following her withdrawal from Wimbledon, two weeks earlier. However, the home country was well represented by their four Musketeers, Jean Borotra, Jacques Brugnon, Henri Cochet and Rene Lacoste.

With such a high-powered entry, there were many fiercely fought matches in the earlier rounds of the Men's Singles, which culminated with Cochet beating Borotra, 6–2 5–7 6–2 6–3, and Vincent Richards of the USA defeating the

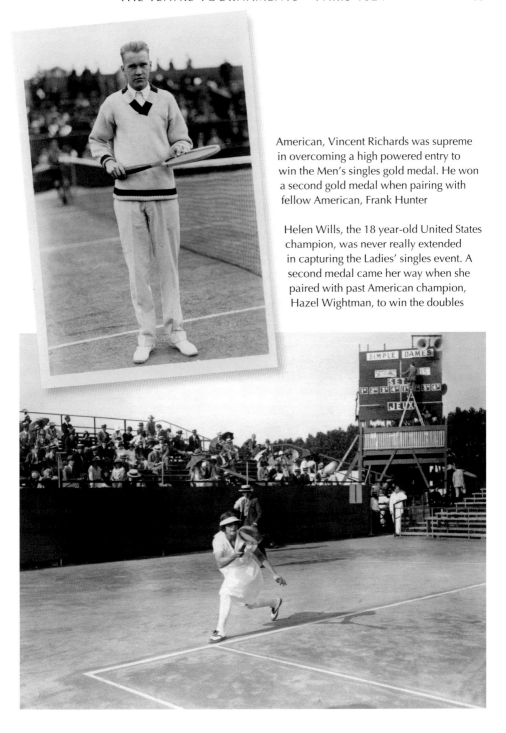

American, Vincent Richards was supreme in overcoming a high powered entry to win the Men's singles gold medal. He won a second gold medal when pairing with fellow American, Frank Hunter

Helen Wills, the 18 year-old United States champion, was never really extended in capturing the Ladies' singles event. A second medal came her way when she paired with past American champion, Hazel Wightman, to win the doubles

A view of the courts at Colombes, where three courts were enclosed in the main area

Italian, Uberto de Morpurgo, 6–3 3–6 6–1 6–4, in the semi-finals. Richards, who had overcome Lacoste in four sets at the quarter final stage, went on to beat Cochet in a thrilling final, after being pulled back to two sets all, 6–4 6–4 5–7 4–6 6–2.

In the Ladies' Singles there was a tremendous upset in the last four when Diddie Vlasto, the newly crowned French Champion, defeated Britain's Kathleen McKane, after losing the first nine games, 0–6 7–5 6–1. In the other half of the draw, Helen Wills, the 18 year old US champion, beat Germaine Golding of France in the semi-final and went on to win the Gold Medal from Diddie Vlasto, 6–2 6–2. Diddie took some time to settle down in the match. At the same time as she was due on court, the gateman at the entrance to the ground was refusing her entry because she had forgotten her ticket. However, she eventually played well but could not match the control of the American.

Richards won a second Gold Medal in partnership with Frank Hunter in the Men's Doubles, beating Brugnon and Cochet in the final over five sets, while Helen

Britain's Kathleen McKane won two medals at the meeting, bringing
her total up to five – a record

Wills did likewise in the Ladies' Doubles, pairing with Hazel Wightman. In this event, Kathleen McKane reached the final and won her fifth Olympic tennis medal – a record for ladies. Norris Williams and Hazel Wightman won the Mixed Doubles event. When the singles finals were contested on the last day, over 6,000 spectators were present, including the newly elected President of France, Gaston Doumergue, and Queen Victoria Eugenia of Spain. Alas, this was the last occasion that lawn tennis was played competitively in the Olympic Games for another 64 years.

1988

24th Olympic Games – Seoul, Korea

19 September – 2 October

Steffi Graf adds gold to her Grand Slam

Legends Jean Borotra of France and Kathleen Godfree from Great Britain, 90 and 92 respectively, were very special guests invited to the reinstated lawn tennis event. Sixty four years earlier both had won medals at the last contested tournament in Paris. What memories must have come flooding back to them, doubtless comparing

the first class organization and facilities before them, with the poor conditions existing when they were the stars of the day.

Now a new Olympic Tennis Centre was created, which housed an excellent floodlit Centre Court, having a capacity of 10,000 spectators, also a secondary court holding 4,000 people. Two other match courts were available plus 14 practice courts, all providing a hard court surface (Neodex). The organization of the tournament was well managed by the Korean Tennis Association, who oversaw the smooth progress of the matches, all made easier by the presence of a fortnight's sun.

As expected, after many years, there were many changes to the format of the competitions. The number of competitors in the draws was restricted to 64 in the Men's Singles and

The Centre Court, holding 10,000 spectators, at the new Olympic Tennis Centre

48 in the Ladies', with 32 and 14 pairs, respectively, in the Doubles. The Mixed Doubles event was discontinued. Leading players were seeded and tie-break sets were employed throughout, except in the deciding set. There were no third place play-offs in any event and defeated semi-finalists received a Bronze Medal.

Disappointing was the absence of several of the world's top players from the 64 draw Men's Singles, with Mats Wilander (Sweden), Ivan Lendl (Czechoslovakia), Boris Becker (Germany) and Pat Cash (Australia) missing.

Stefan Edberg of Sweden, seeded at No.1, played four matches without dropping a set to reach the semi-final where, in a see-saw encounter going the full distance, he fell to the Czech, Miloslav Mecir. At the bottom of the draw, Tim Mayotte of the United States conceded just one set en route to the final, defeating fellow-countryman Brad Gilbert on the way. The match for the Gold Medal turned after the first set when Mecir never looked back to win 3–6 6–2 6–4 6–2.

There was little doubt that Steffi Graf of Germany would win the Ladies' Singles. Two weeks earlier she had captured the US Open crown to complete the Grand Slam, and the winning of the Olympic event gave her a unique Golden

Left: The Men's singles medal winners:
Silver – Tim Mayotte (USA), Gold – Miloslav
Mecir (Czechoslovakia), Bronze – Brad
Gilbert (USA) and Stefan Edberg (Sweden)

Bottom left: Steffi Graf of West Germany
captured the Ladies' singles gold medal, to
add to her four Grand Slam tournaments,
won during the year. A unique
achievement.

Right: Argentina's Gabriela Sabatini
could make little headway against her
old rival, Steffi Graf, in the Ladies singles
final

Grand Slam – possibly never to be repeated. Not all her matches were easy, with two
Russians putting her under some pressure. First Leila Meshki, in the first set of the
second round and then Larissa Savchenko, who took the middle set in the quarter-
final. After swamping Zina Garrison of the USA, Steffi Graf defeated her old rival,
Gabriela Sabatina from Argentina, in the final, 6–3 6–3, after 41 minutes. The upset
of the event was the elimination of the No.2 seed, America's Chris Evert, by the
Italian, Raffaella Reggi in the third round, 2–6 6–4 6–1. Martina Navratilova of the
USA did not compete.

In the Men's Doubles, America's Ken Flach and Robert Seguso won the Gold
Medal, overcoming the Spanish pair, Sergio Casal and Emilio Sanchez, in five sets
lasting 3 hours 40 minutes. The Ladies' Doubles was also won by Americans when
Zina Garrison and Pam Shriver beat the Czechs, Jana Novotna and Helena Sukova,
in a tight struggle, 4–6 6–2 8–6. In the first round, Canadians Carling Bassett Seguso
and Jill Hetherington defeated Mercedes Paz and Gabriela Sabatini in a memorable
match after 63 games, lasting 4 hours 13 minutes, 7–6(10–8) 5–7 20–18. (This is the
second largest number of games ever played in a Ladies' Doubles match).

1992

25th Olympic Games – Barcelona, Spain

28 July-8 August

Medals well-distributed

The tennis matches were played on the red clay surface in the new Barcelona Municipal Tennis Centre at Vall d'Hebron. This facility provided a 10,000 seat Stadium Court, two other show courts, holding 3,500 and 1,500 people, and five outer courts. King Juan Carlos and Queen Sofia were regular visitors to the tournament.

The ITF ruled that to qualify, players had to pledge their availability to the previous year's Davis Cup or Fed Cup competitions. This resulted in three out of the top five ladies missing, Monica Seles and Martina Navratilova (USA) and Gabriela Sabatini from Argentina. The men were well represented with most top players on show, including three past Wimbledon champions. Absent were Andre Agassi, who declined, and John McEnroe, whose ranking at the time was too low.

There were many upsets in the Men's Singles, where the majority of the big names failed to pass the third round. After two comfortable wins, Jim Courier (USA), the top seed, was dispatched by Switzerland's Marc Rosset's powerful serving, in just over two hours, 6–4 6–2 6–2. Stefan Edberg, the No.2 seed, performed poorly and lost in the opening round to the unseeded, Andrei Chesnokov, 6–0 6–4 6–4, while another Russian, Andrei Cherkasov, seeded No.13, put paid to Pete Sampras (USA) in the third round, after being two sets and 1–4 down. He proceeded to take the next nine games and eventually won, 6–7 1–6 7–5 6–0 6–3. In the same round, Boris Becker of Germany, seeded at No.5, fell to France's Fabrice Santoro, 6–1 3–6 6–1 6–3, no doubt feeling the effects of his marathon encounter, played the first day on the Stadium Court. Little known Christian Ruud of Norway kept the triple Wimbledon champion at bay for 4 hours 50 minutes before the German edged out, 3–6 7–6(7–2) 5–7 7–6(7–2) 6–3. At times, the court temperature was 114 degrees. The other top German, Michael Stich, was unhappy with the surface and lost to his compatriot, Carl-Uwe Steeb in four sets. While all this drama unfolded, Rosset proceeded to the quarter-final, where he dismissed the Spaniard, Emilio Sanchez, in a see-saw match, 6–4 7–6(7–2) 3–6 7–6(11–9). His next opponent was the No.4 seed, Goran Ivanisevic of Croatia, who had reached this stage by winning all his four matches over five sets. Rosset served his way to victory against a weary opponent, 6–3 7–5 6–2.

In the other half of the draw, the Spaniard Jordi Arrese, seeded No.16, weaved his way past three unseeded opponents to reach the semi-final, where he beat Cherkasov, 6–4 7–6(7–4) 3–6 6–3. The final, which lasted four hours, was played for much of the time under a very hot sun. Rosset led Arrese by two sets to love, but was pulled back, before eventually edging out to take the Gold Medal, 7–6(7–2) 6–3 3–6 4–6 8–6. Rosset, 6 feet 5 inches tall, served 33 aces during the match. This was Switzerland's only medal at the Games.

The two British entrants were eliminated in the first round. Andrew Castle lost to Sergi Bruguera (Spain) and Chris Wilkinson to Younes El Aynaoui of Morocco, both in straight sets.

The Ladies' Singles followed very close to form, with the top seven seeds reaching their appointed places in the last eight and the highest four contenders going through. The outstanding favourite was Steffi Graf of Germany, who had won the Gold Medal four years earlier. In devastating form she won her first four matches with the loss of just 10 games to reach the semi-final, where Mary Joe Fernandez (USA) was duly dispatched, 6–4 6–2.

Jennifer Capriati from America and seeded at No.3, also moved smoothly through the field to

Marc Rosset (Switzerland) eventually edged out against the Spaniard Jordi Arrese in the Men's singles final to take the gold medal – his country's only medal at the Games

reach the semi-final without dropping a set, although she was taken to a tie-break set by Anke Huber of Germany. Her opponent was Spain's Arantxa Sanchez Vicario, the No.2 seed who, in the round before, had disposed of her Fed Cup colleague, Conchita Martinez, 6–4 6–4. The match for a place in the final was played out at a furious pace. The Spaniard managed to pull back a set to even matters but thereon Jennifer Capriati's controlled driving gave her a 6–3 3–6 6–1 victory.

Jennifer Capriati had never beaten Steffi Graf and the loss of the opening set appeared to suggest the same result. But never discouraged, the American fought back to serve out for the second set at 5–3. The deciding set proceeded game for game with the tension mounting, until the American broke for 5–4. Without faltering she served out for the match, which had taken 2 hours 8 minutes, 3–6 6–3 6–4. A very hard-earned Gold Medal.

Three British ladies took part. Unfortunately, Sara Gomer and Samantha Smith were drawn together in the first round. The latter won 2–6 6–3 6–1 but then went down to Natalia Zvereva (CIS), 6–1 6–2. Monique Javer fell to the Austrian, Barbara Paulus, 6–7(9–11) 6–4 6–3.

As consolation for their disappointment in the singles, Becker and Stich combined to win the Men's Doubles. In the final they defeated the South African pair, Wayne Ferreira and Pieter Norval, 7–6(7–5) 4–6 7–6(7–5) 6–3. Gigi

Fernandez and Mary Joe Fernandez defeated the top seeds, Arantxa Sanchez Vicario and Conchita Martinez in the Ladies' Doubles final, 7–5 2–6 6–2.

Left: The Stadium Court at the new Barcelona Municipal Tennis Centre at Vall d'Hebron

Right: In a match lasting over two hours, Jennifer Capriati (USA) defeated the holder Steffi Graf, in the Ladies' singles final to win a very hard-earned gold medal

Below: After disappointing displays in the singles, Michael Stich and Boris Becker combined to win the Men's doubles gold medal

1996

26th Olympic Games – Atlanta, USA

23 July–3 August

America captures both singles gold medals

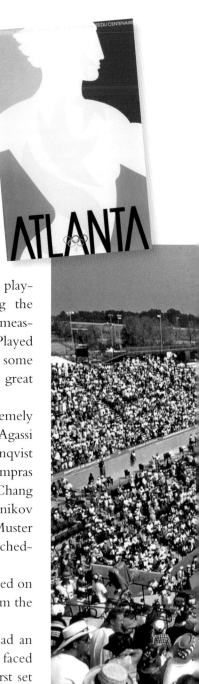

At the Centenary Games the United States players excelled at the tennis tournament by winning the Men's and Ladies' Gold Medals and, for good measure, also captured the Ladies' Doubles crown. Played at the new lawn facility at Stone Mountain Park, some 16 miles outside the City, the contestants received great support from the very enthusiastic local crowds.

The entry for the Men's Singles was extremely disappointing, with only three players, Andre Agassi (USA), Goran Ivanisevic (Croatia) and Thomas Enqvist (Sweden), out of the world's top ten attending. Pete Sampras (USA) was injured, while Jim Courier and Michael Chang (USA), Boris Becker (Germany), Yevgeny Kafelnikov (Russia), Richard Krajicek (Netherlands) and Thomas Muster (Austria) decided not to compete as their tournament schedules were too tight.

To ensure that the tournament would be concluded on time, the Men's Singles and Doubles were reduced from the best of five sets to three sets, except for the finals.

The only match in which the winner, Agassi, had an easy passage was in the final. In the opening round he faced Jonas Bjorkman of Sweden who had points for the first set and several in the second. In the third round the American was down 6–2 3–1 to Italy's Andrea Gaudenzi before recovering, but it was in the quarter-final versus Wayne Ferreira that he was pushed to the limit. The South African recovered from the loss of the first set to eventually serve for the match at 5–4, but Agassi managed to survive. During this last set the American was issued with a warning and given a penalty point for losing his temper and swearing. He was extremely fortunate not to be disqualified.

At the bottom of the draw, Ivanisevic, seeded No.2 was completely out of form to fall to Marcus Odruska of South Africa. This opened the way for many, but eventually Sergi Bruguera of Spain met Fernando Meligeni from Brazil to contest the semi-final, which was won by the former, 7–6(11–9) 6–2. Earlier, Meligeni had

The Centre Court at Stone Mountain Park, 16 miles outside Atlanta

a fine run defeating Carlos Costa of Spain, 7–6(7–5) 6–4, and Mark Philippoussis (Australia) in a very long match, 7–6(9–7) 4–6 8–6. After defeating the Indian, Leander Paes, Agassi met Bruguera for the title. The Spaniard felt the full force of his opponent who, in devastating style, dropped just six games to win, 6–2 6–3 6–1.

With the third place play-offs for the Bronze Medal reinstated, Paes successfully edged through against Meligeni 3–6 6–2 6–4. Great Britain had two players competing. Tim Henman lost to Todd Woodbridge (Australia) in the second round, 7–6(8–6) 7–6(7–5), while Greg Rusedski was beaten in the third round by Bruguera, 7–6(9–7) 6–3.

All the leading ladies competed in the Singles except two, Steffi Graf (Germany) and Chandra Rubin (USA), who both withdrew at the last moment, owing to injury. Seeded No. 1, American Monica Seles had a smooth run until the quarter-final, when she fell at the hands of Jana Novotna, of the Czech Republic, in a long hard tussle, 7–5 3–6 8–6. The victor's progress was short-lived by the persistence of Spain's Arantxa Sanchez-Vicario, who took command at the end, 6–4 1–6 6–3.

Meanwhile a lighter and much fitter Lindsay Davenport (USA) seeded No. 9, steadily weaved her way through the draw to the semi-final, dropping just one set to the German, Anke Huber, in the third round. She then accounted for her fellow countrywoman, Mary Jo Fernandez in two sets, the second being a well-fought

14–point tie-break. In the previous round, Mary Jo Fernandez's moment of glory came with the dispatch of the No.2 seed, Conchita Martinez of Spain, 3–6 6–2 6–3.

In the final, Lindsay Davenport had Arantxa Sanchez-Vicario on the run for much of the time and together with her telling ground strokes, deserved the Gold Medal, 7–6(10–8) 6–4.

Britain's only competitor in the singles was Clare Wood, who lost in the opening round to Italy's Silvia Farina, 6–2 6–2.

The Men's doubles Gold Medal went to Woodbridge and his Australian partner, Mark Woodforde, who were too strong for Henman and his compatriot,Neil Broad in the final, 6–4 6–4 6–2. The two Australians had faced two match points in beating The Netherland's Jacco Eltingh and Paul Haarhuis in the semi-final, 6–2 5–7 18–16, after three and a quarter hours play.

Mary Jo Fernandez and Gigi Fernandez (USA) beat the Czech pair, Jana Novotna and Helena Sukova, in the final of the Ladies' Doubles to retain the title they won four years earlier in Barcelona. The Americans had eliminated Britain's Valda Lake and Clare Wood at the quarter-final stage, 6–2 6–1.

Left: The Men's singles medal winners: Silver – Sergei Brugera (Spain), gold – Andre Agassi (USA), and bronze – Leander Paes (India)

Right: American Lindsay Davenport (middle) won the Ladies' singles gold medal. She is flanked by left, Jana Novotna (CZE) – bronze and Arantxa Sanchez-Vicario (ESP) – silver

Below: Wimbledon champions, Australians Todd Woodbridge and Mark Woodforde are delighted to win the Men's doubles gold medal

2000

27th Olympic Games – Sydney, Australia

19–29 September

Nine nations share medals

The tennis tournament was staged at the new spacious and well designed New South Wales Tennis Centre in the Homebush area, some 10 minutes from the Olympic Village. The circular Centre Court, seating 10,000 people, was equipped with a roof, which provided shade for about three-quarters of the spectators. There were also nine other match courts and six practice courts. The surface of the courts was Rebound Ace. Evening sessions of play were held during the first five days. The transport arrangements were excellent in conveying the crowds to and from the City. The weather was warm throughout, apart from the occasional worrying wind.

Seven of the top men and ladies were present, but there were some notable names missing, such as Pete Sampras and Andre Agassi (USA), Martina Hingis (Switzerland), Mary Pierce and Nathalie Tauziat of France and Anna Kournikova of Russia, for various reasons. For the first time ATP computer ranking points were awarded to the men.

In the Men's Singles, Marat Safin, the newly crowned US Open champion, was placed as the top seed, but was promptly eliminated by Fabrice Santoro of France, 1–6 6–1 6–4. However, another Russian, Yevgeny Kafelnikov, seeded at No.5, took up the cause to win through five matches without the loss of a set and finally defeat Tommy Haas of Germany, over the full distance to take the Gold Medal, 7–6(7–4) 3–6 6–2 4–6 6–3. This was so different to earlier in the year when Kafelnikov failed to win a tournament. He had good wins over Mark Philippoussis (Australia), Gustavo Kuerten (Brazil), seeded at No.2 and, in the semi-final, the Frenchman Arnaud Di Pasquale, who had become a giant killer in disposing of Nicolas Kiefer (Germany), Vladimir Voltchkov (Russia), Magnus Norman (Sweden) and Juan Carlos Ferrero (Spain).

Surprisingly no Australian or American reached the quarter-finals, with names like Lleyton Hewitt and Pat Rafter (Australia) and Todd Martin (USA) falling by the wayside. Great Britain's Tim Henman and Greg Rusedski failed to pass the opening round, losing to Karol Kucera (Slovakia) and Arnaud Clement (France), respectively, both managing to win only five games. A young Roger Federer of Switzerland reached the semi-final, but failed to clinch a Bronze Medal.

In the Ladies' Singles, Venus Williams became the third American in succession to win the Olympic title. Seeded at No.2, she comfortably won her first three matches,

Inset: Russia's Yevgeny Kafelnikov, seeded No.5, was the surprise winner of the Men's singles gold medal

Tommy Haas of Germany reached the Men's singles final unseeded, and then fell in five sets

before encountering stiff opposition from Arantxa Sanchez-Vicario of Spain in the quarter-final and Monica Seles (USA) in the semi-final, where both opponents captured a set.

At the top of the draw, defending champion and No. 1 seed, Lindsay Davenport (USA) was forced to withdraw after her first match, owing to a foot injury. This considerably opened up the field and eased the path of the home favourite, Jelena Dokic who, in great form, reached the last four to face the No. 6 seed, Elena Dementieva of Russia. This match was regarded as the best of the event, where the outcome

was in the balance right up to the very end with the Russian edging out, 2–6 6–4 6–4. In the final a ruthless Venus Williams held control throughout to win the Gold Medal, 6–2 6–4. The Bronze Medal was taken by Monica Seles, who defeated Jelena Dokic, 6–1 6–4.

There was a big surprise in the final of the Men's Doubles, when the winners of four years earlier, Australians Todd Woodbridge and Mark Woodforde, were defeated by the Canadians Sebastian Lareau and Daniel Nestor, 5–7 6–3 6–4 7–6 (7–2). Venus Williams won a second medal in partnership with her sister, Serena, to bring back memories of Helen Wills (USA) performing the double way back in 1924. (Serena Williams did not play in the singles as competitors were limited to three per nation).

Left: The New South Wales Tennis Centre at Homebush, with a capacity of 10,000 people

Venus Williams (centre) became the third American in a row to capture the Ladies' singles gold medal. Left is Monica Seles (USA) – bronze, and right is Elena Dementieva (Russia) – silver

2004

28th Olympic Games – Athens, Greece

15–22 August

AΘHNA 2004

Nicolas Massu wins first Olympic gold medal for Chile

The Olympic Tennis Centre, as part of the Olympic complex, provided 16 courts. The Main Court seated 8,600 people, but only 6,000 seats were available to the public, while two other courts held 4,300 with only 3,200 available. (The Main Court in particular was extremely large by usual tennis standards so, the top seats, far away from the court, were left vacant). The other 13 side courts each seated 200 spectators. The courts used a Deco Turf II cushioned acrylic surface.

There were many upsets at the tournament. The big surprise was the winning of the Men's Singles by the 10th seed, Nicolas Massu of Chile, in a field which contained many top players, including Switzerland's Roger Federer and Andy Roddick of the United States. In addition, Massu won a second Gold Medal when he paired with fellow countryman Fernando Gonzales to capture the Men's Doubles.

With the shock exit of top-seeded Federer in the second round to the Czech, Tomas Berdych, 4–6 7–5 7–5 and a round later, Roddick, placed at No.2, to Gonzales, 6–4 6–4, Massu made his way through the draw meeting just one seed en route, the No.3 Carlos Moya of Spain, whom he passed, 6–2 7–5. After defeating Taylor Dent (USA) in the last four, 7–6 6–1, he found himself two sets to one down in the final to Mardy Fish of the United States but, with great resolve, he summoned up sufficient energy to win through, 6–3 3–6 2–6 6–3 6–4. This was quite a feat as he and Gonzales had only concluded the doubles final around 3am that morning, winning a marathon match against the Germans Nicolas Kiefer and Rainer Schuettler, 6–2 4–6 3–6 7–6(9–7) 6–4, after saving four match points. The Chileans were national heroes, securing their country's first ever Gold Medals. Gonzales gained a second medal by winning the singles play-off against Dent, but not before they had played a marathon deciding set, 16–14.

The main court in the Olympic Tennis Centre

Much was expected of Britain's Tim Henman, seeded at No.4, but he was well beaten by Jiri Novak of the Czech Republic in the opening round, 6–3 6–3.

The Ladies' Singles ran truer to form, with top-seeded Justin Henin-Hardenne of Belgium defeating the No.2, Amelie Mauresmo of France in the final, 6–3 6–3, to take the Gold Medal. In the round before, both faced tough opposition with Justine Henin-Hardenne pushed to the limit by the No.3 seed, Anastasia Myskina of Russia, 7–5 5–7 8–6, while the French lady was stretched by Australian, Alicia Molik, 7–6(10–8) 6–3. Alicia Molik had a great tournament, by-passing Russia's Elena Dementieva, the No.4 seed, Katarina Srebotnik of Slovenia, Lisa Raymond of the USA and Ai Sugiyama from Japan. Her reward came when she won the Bronze

Right: A delighted Justine Henin-Hardenne (Belgium) won the Ladies' singles gold medal, overcoming Amelie Mauresmo of France in the final

Below: Nicolas Massu of Chile was the unexpected winner of the gold medal in the Men's singles. He was seeded No.10

Above: Tian Tian Sun and Ting Li of China beat three seeded pairs to win the Ladies' doubles gold medal. Between them is Francesco Ricci Bitti, President of the International Tennis Federation

Left: Nicolas Massu won a second gold medal in partnership with his fellow-countryman, Fernando Gonzales

Medal from Anastasia Myskina. WTA computer ranking points were awarded for the first time.

No British players took part in the Ladies' Singles nor in the Men's and Ladies' Doubles. In the latter event, Ting Li and Tian Tian Sun of China, seeded at No.8, surprised all by winning the Gold Medal. After eliminating the No.4 and No.7 seeds, they defeated the No. 2 pair, Conchita Martinez and Virginia Ruano Pascual of Spain in the final, 6–3 6–3. Martina Navratilova and Lisa Raymond entered the event but lost in the quarter final.

2008

29th Olympic Games – Beijing, China

10–17 August

Spain and Russia to the fore

The new Olympic Tennis Centre provided top-class facilities for the eight-day event, Sunday to Sunday. The venue had a Centre Court designed in the shape of a lotus flower, which seated 10,000 people, and a No.1 and No.2 Court, holding 4,000 and 2,000 spectators, respectively. In addition there were seven other courts, each with 200 seats, and six practice courts. The surface of the courts was Deco Turf II.

The standard of entry was very high with most leading players participating. Only America's Andy Roddick declined to enter from the men's top ten list, while in the ladies' division, all were present with the exception of Russia's Maria Sharapova, who earlier had withdrawn with an injured shoulder. Unfortunately, after the draw the world's No.1, Anna Ivanovic of Serbia, pulled out with a thumb injury. Another casualty was Tatiana Golovin of France with a strained back.

Great interest was taken in whether the two 'greats' of the game, Roger Federer of Switzerland and Spain's Rafael Nadal, would clash for the Gold Medal in the final of the Men's Singles. Most of the year Federer's play had substantially declined and, with the Spaniard winning the Grand Slams at Paris and Wimbledon, the outcome of a third meeting between the two was eagerly awaited. But it was not to be. Although Federer won through his first three rounds without dropping a set, he was far from his best and in the quarter-final against James Blake, the American No.8 seed, he struggled from the start and eventually fell, 6–2 7–6(7–2). Blake's great moment was short-lived, for the following day in the semi-final, a marathon match saw the No.12 seed, Fernando Gonzales of Chile, edge through 4–6 7–5 11–9, after saving three match points.

In the meantime Nadal progressed, but not without some concern as early on he dropped a set to Potito Starace of Italy and later to Serbia's Novak Djokovic in a

Right: A triumphant Elena Dementieva of Russia celebrates winning the Ladies' singles gold medal, bettering her runner-up position of 2000

Below: Rafael Nadal of Spain won the Men's singles gold medal to add to his triumphs earlier in the year in Paris and Wimbledon

tight semi-final, 6–4 1–6 6–4. However the Spaniard was on good form in the final against Gonzales and won in straight sets, 6–3 7–6(7–2) 6–3 to capture the Gold Medal and so add to his triumphs earlier in the year. The day following the tournament, Federer, who had been the world's No.1 for 237 weeks, became the No.2, exchanging with Nadal.

Gonzales, by taking the Silver Medal, added to the two medals he won four years earlier in Athens. The play-off for the Bronze Medal resulted in Djokovic defeating Blake, 6–3 7–6(7–4).

The shock of the week occurred in the opening round when Britain's only singles contestant, Andy Murray, seeded at No.6, lost to the No.77 player in the world, Lu Yen-Hsun of Chinese Taipei, 7–6(7–5) 6–4. Other upsets saw Paul-Henri

The Centre Court,
designed in the shape
of a lotus flower, seated
10,000 spectators

The Swiss pair, Roger Federer and Stanislas Wawrinka played well during the week
to win the Men's doubles gold medal

Mathieu eliminate Russia's Nikolay Davydenko, seeded No.4, in the second round and another Frenchman, Gael Monfils unseeded, dispatching David Nalbandian of Argentina, the following day.

The Ladies' Singles was dominated by Russian players, three of whom progressed to sweep the board and capture all medals at stake. The fourth player, Svetlana Kuznetsova, the No.3 seed, unexpectedly fell in the opening round to unseeded Na Li of China, 7–6(7–5) 6–4, who went on to join the Russians in the semi-final. At this stage Elena Dementieva, the No.5 seed, defeated Vera Zvonareva, seeded No.9, 6–3 7–6(7–3) while Dinara Safina, seeded No.6, accounted for Na Li, 7–6(7–3) 7–5. The match for the Gold Medal ended when Elena Dementieva overcame a first set deficit, before gradually gaining control to trumph, 3–6 7–5 6–3. This bettered her performance of reaching the final in 2000. Vera Zvonareva won the Bronze Medal from Na Li, 6–0 7–5.

The quarter-final stage of the event provided the surprises. Both Williams sisters departed – Serena to Elena Dementieva 3–6 6–4 6–3 and Venus to Na Li, 7–5 7–5, Jelena Jankovic of Serbia, the No.2 seed, but wearing the No.1 mantle, fell to Dinara Safina in a fluctuating contest, 6–2 5–7 6–3. Sadly no British ladies took part in the event.

The Williams sisters, Venus and Serena (USA) repeated their success of 2000 by winning the Ladies' doubles gold medal

Competing at his third Games, a delighted Federer, together with his fellow-countryman, Stanislas Wawrinka, managed to win his first medal defeating the Swedish pair, Simon Aspelin and Thomas Johansson, in the final of the Men's Doubles, 6–3 6–4 6–7(4–7) 6–3 to take the Gold Medal. The Swiss pair, seeded No.4, had played well during the week, overcoming the top seeds, Bob and Mike Bryan in the semi-final, 7–6(8–6) 6–4 and earlier, the experienced Mahesh Bhupathi and Leander Paes from India, 6–2 6–4. In the other semi-final, the Swedish combination defeated the Frenchmen, Arnaud Clement and Michael Llodra, 7–6(8–6) 4–6 19–17, to record the longest ever men's three set match at the Olympics, decided over 4 hours 46 minutes. Bryan and Bryan won the Bronze Medal. Andy Murray paired with his brother Jamie, but their progress was halted in the second round by Clement and Llodra, 6–1 6–3.

In the Ladies' Doubles, the winners of 2000, Serena and Venus Williams, repeated their victory by easily beating the Spanish pair, Anabel Medina Garrigues and Virginia Ruano Pascual, in the final, 6–2 6–0. In the round before, they overcame the loss of the first set to dismiss the Bondarenko sisters, Alona and Kateryna, from the Ukraine, 4–6 6–4 6–1, while the Spanish duo edged past Zi Yan and Jie Zheng of China, 6–4 7–6(7–5). The latter combination won the Bronze Medal.

Competitors Participating

Year	Venue	Date	Nations	Men's Singles	
			P	E	P
1896	Athens	8-11 April	6	15	13
1900	Paris	6-11 July	4	15	13
1904	St Louis	29 August – 3 September	2	34	27
1906★	Athens	23-26 April	6	29	18
1908	London (CC)	6-11 May	2	10	7
1908	London (G)	6-11 July	9	45	31
1912	Stockholm (CC)	5-12 May	6	25	22
1912	Stockholm (HC)	28 June – 5 July	13	67	50
1920	Antwerp	15-24 August	14	44	41
1924	Paris	13-20 July	27	92	82
1988	Seoul	19 September – 2 October	39	64	64
1992	Barcelona	28 July – 8 August	47	64	64
1996	Atlanta	23 July – 3 August	55	64	64
2000	Sydney	19 September – 1 October	52	64	64
2004	Athens	15-22 August	51	64	64
2008	Beijing	10-17 August	48	64	64

E – Entries; P – Participants
CC – Covered courts; G – Grass; HC – Hard courts
1906★ – Intercalated Games

Ladies' Singles		Men's Doubles (Pairs)		Ladies' Doubles (Pairs)		Mixed Doubles (Pairs)	
E	P	E	P	E	P	E	P
—	—	6	6	—	—	—	—
6	6	8	8	—	—	6	6
—	—	15	15	—	—	—	—
8	5	12	7	—	—	5	5
9	7	5	5	—	—	—	—
12	5	21	12	—	—	—	—
10	8	11	8	—	—	10	8
12	8	31	21	—	—	13	6
21	18	26	22	9	9	21	17
38	31	45	39	17	11	27	21
48	48	32	31	14	14	—	—
64	64	32	30	32	31	—	—
64	64	32	31	31	28	—	—
64	64	29	29	31	31	—	—
64	64	32	30	32	32	—	—
64	64	32	32	32	31	—	—

Nations Participating

Year	Venue	Nations	Participating Nations
1896	Athens	6	Australia, British Isles, France, Germany, Greece, Hungary
1900	Paris	4	Bohemia, British Isles, France, USA
1904	St Louis	2	Germany, USA
1906★	Athens	6	Bohemia, France, Greece, Holland, Hungary, USA (British Isles withdrew)
1908	London (CC)	2	British Isles, Sweden (Australasia withdrew)
1908	London (G)	9	Austria, Bohemia, British Isles, Canada, France, Germany, Holland, Hungary, South Africa
1912	Stockholm (CC)	6	Australasia, Bohemia, British Isles, Denmark, France, Sweden
1912	Stockholm (HC)	13	Austria, Belgium, Bohemia, Denmark, France, Germany, Holland, Hungary, Norway, Russia, South Africa, Sweden, USA
1920	Antwerp	14	Australia, Belgium, Czechoslovakia, Denmark, British Isles, France, Greece, Italy, Japan, Norway, South Africa, Spain, Sweden, Switzerland (Holland withdrew)
1924	Paris	27	Argentina, Australia, Belgium, Chile, Czechoslovakia, Denmark, Finland, France, Great Britain, Greece, Holland, Hungary, India, Ireland, Italy, Japan, Luxembourg, Mexico, Norway, Portugal, Romania, South Africa, Spain, Sweden, Switzerland, USA, Yugoslavia (China withdrew)

CC – Covered courts; G – Grass courts; HC – Hard courts
1906★ – Intercalated Games

Year	Venue	Nations	Participating Nations
1988	Seoul	39	Algeria, Argentina, Australia, Austria, Bermuda, Brazil, Bulgaria, Canada, China, Colombia, Czechoslovakia, Denmark, Federal Republic of Germany, France, Great Britain, Greece, Haiti, Hungary, India, Indonesia, Ireland, Israel, Ivory Coast, Italy, Japan, Korea, Mexico, Netherlands, New Zealand, Nigeria, Paraguay, Poland, Spain, Sweden, Switzerland, USA, USSR, Yugoslavia, Zimbabwe
1992	Barcelona	47	Argentina, Australia, Austria, Bahamas, Belgium, Brazil, Bulgaria, Canada, Chile, China, Commonwealth of Independent States, Croatia, Czechoslovakia, Denmark, France, Germany, Great Britain, Greece, Hungary, India, Indonesia, Ireland, Israel, Italy, Japan, Korea, Latvia, Madagascar, Morocco, Mexico, Netherlands, Norway, Paraguay, Peru, Poland, Portugal, Puerto Rico, Romania, San Marino, Slovenia, South Africa, Spain, Sweden, Switzerland, Thailand, USA, Yugoslavia
1996	Atlanta	55	Argentina, Armenia, Australia, Austria, Bahamas, Belarus, Belgium, Brazil, Bulgaria, Canada, Chile, China, Chinese Taipei, Croatia, Czech Republic, Denmark, Dominican Republic, Ecuador, France, Germany, Great Britain, Greece, Haiti, Hungary, India, Indonesia, Ireland, Italy, Ivory Coast, Japan, Korea, Luxembourg, Madagascar, Morocco, Mexico, Netherlands, New Zealand, Nigeria, Norway, Poland, Portugal, Romania, Russia, Slovak Republic, Spain, South Africa, Sweden, Switzerland, Thailand, Tunisia, Uruguay, USA, Uzbekistan, Venezuela, Zimbabwe
2000	Sydney	52	Argentina, Armenia, Australia, Austria, Bahamas, Belgium, Benin, Belarus, Bolivia, Brazil, Canada, Chile, China, Chinese Taipei, Colombia, Costa Rica, Croatia, Czech Republic, Denmark, France, Great Britain, Germany, Greece, Haiti, Hungary, Indonesia, India, Italy, Japan, Korea, Luxembourg, Morocco, Mexico, Netherlands, Norway, Paraguay, Portugal, Romania, Russia, Slovak Republic, Slovenia, South Africa, Spain, Sweden, Switzerland, Thailand, Uzbekistan, Ukraine, USA, Venezuela, Yugoslavia, Zimbabwe

Year	Venue	Nations	Participating Nations
2004	Athens	51	Algeria, Argentina, Armenia, Australia, Austria, Bahamas, Belgium, Belarus, Bosnia & Herzegovina, Brazil, Bulgaria, Canada, Chile, China, Chinese Taipei, Colombia, Croatia, Czech Republic, Cyprus, Ecuador, Estonia, Finland, France, Germany, Greece, Hungary, Indonesia, India, Israel, Italy, Japan, Korea, Luxembourg, Madagascar, Morocco, Peru, Poland, Romania, Russia, Serbia & Montenegro, Slovak Republic, Slovenia, Puerto Rico, Spain, Sweden, Switzerland, Thailand, Ukraine, USA, Venezuela, Zimbabwe
2008	Beijing	48	Argentina, Australia, Austria, Bahamas, Belgium, Belarus, Brazil, Bulgaria, Canada, Chile, China, Chinese Taipei, Croatia, Czech Republic, Denmark, Ecuador, El Salvador, Estonia, Finland, France, Germany, Great Britain, Greece, Hungary, India, Israel, Italy, Japan, Korea, Latvia, New Zealand, Poland, Romania, Russia, Serbia, Slovak Republic, South Africa, Spain, Sweden, Switzerland, Thailand, Togo, Tunisia, Ukraine, USA, Uzbekistan, Venezuela, Zimbabwe

Alphabetical List
of Medallists

Men

Name	Country	Year of win	Event	Born	Died
Agassi, Andre Kirk	USA	1996	Singles 1	24 Apr 1970	
Albarran, Pierre Henry Maurice	FRA	1920	Doubles 3	1893	24 Feb 1960
Ancic, Mario	CRO	2004	Doubles 3	30 Mar 1984	
Arrese, Jordi	ESP	1992	Singles 2	28 Aug 1964	
Aspelin, Simon Olof Karl	SWE	2008	Doubles 2	11 May 1974	
Ballis, Ioannis	GRE	1906	Doubles 2		
Barrett, Herbert Roper	BRI	1908	*Doubles 1*	24 Nov 1873	27 Jul 1943
		1912	*Mixed 2*		
Beamish, Alfred Ernest	BRI	1912	*Doubles 3*	6 Aug 1879	28 Feb 1944
Becker, Boris Franz	GER	1992	Doubles 1	22 Nov 1967	
Bell, Alphonzo Edward	USA	1904	Singles 3	29 Sep 1875	27 Dec 1947
		1904	Doubles 2		
Boland, John Mary Pius	BRI	1896	Singles 1	16 Sep 1870	17 Mar 1958
		1896	Doubles 1		
Borotra, Jean Robert	FRA	1924	Doubles 3	13 Aug 1898	17 Jul 1994
Bostrom, Wollmar	SWE	1908	*Doubles 3*	15 Jun 1878	7 Nov 1956
Broad, Neil	GBR	1996	Doubles 2	20 Nov 1966	
Brugnon, Jacques	FRA	1924	Doubles 2	11 May 1895	20 Mar 1978
Bruguera, Sergi	ESP	1996	Singles 2	16 Jan 1971	
Bryan, Michael Carl	USA	2008	Doubles 3	29 Apr 1978	
Bryan, Robert Charles	USA	2008	Doubles 3	29 Apr 1978	

Events shown in *italics* indicate Covered Courts
Event – 1 = Gold, 2 = Silver, 3 = Bronze

Name	Country	Year of win	Event	Born	Died
Canet, Albert H	FRA	1912	Doubles 3	17 Apr 1878	27 Jul 1930
		1912	Mixed 3		
Caridia, Georges Aristides	BRI	1908	*Singles* 2	20 Feb 1869	21 Apr 1937
		1908	*Doubles* 2		
Casal, Sergio	ESP	1988	Doubles 2	8 Sep 1962	
Cazalet, Clement Haughton Langston	BRI	1908	Doubles 3	16 Jul 1879	23 Mar 1950
Cherkasov, Andres	CIS	1992	Singles 3	2 Feb 1966	
Cochet, Henri Jean	FRA	1924	Singles 2	14 Dec 1901	1 Apr 1987
		1924	Doubles 2		
Corretja, Alex	ESP	2000	Doubles 3	11 Apr 1974	
Costa, Albert	ESP	2000	Doubles 3	25 Jun 1975	
de la Chapelle, Georges	FRA	1900	Doubles 3		
de Garmendia, Basil Spalding	USA	1900	Doubles 2	28 Feb1860	9 Nov 1932
de Morpurgo, Uberto Luigi	ITA	1924	Singles 3	12 Jan 1896	26 Feb 1961
Decugis, Maxime Omer	FRA	1900	Doubles 2	24 Sep 1882	6 Sep 1978
		1906	Singles 1		
		1906	Doubles 1		
		1906	Mixed 1		
		1920	Doubles 3		
		1920	Mixed 1		
Di Pasquale, Arnaud	FRA	2000	Singles 3	11 Feb 1979	
Dixon, Charles Percy	BRI	1908	Doubles 3	7 Feb 1873	29 Apr 1939
		1912	*Singles* 2		
		1912	*Doubles* 3		
		1912	*Mixed* 1		
Djokovic, Novak	SRB	2008	Singles 3	22 May 1987	
Doherty, Hugh Laurence	BRI	1900	Singles 1	8 Oct 1875	21 Aug 1919
		1900	Doubles 1		
		1900	Mixed 3		
Doherty, Reginald Frank	BRI	1900	Singles 3	14 Oct 1872	29 Dec 1910
		1900	Doubles 1		
		1900	Mixed 1		
		1908	Doubles 1		
Eaves, Wilberforce Vaughan	BRI	1908	Singles 3	10 Dec 1867	12 Feb 1920
Edberg, Stefan Bengt	SWE	1988	Singles 3	9 Jan 1966	
		1988	Doubles 3		

Name	Country	Year of win	Event	Born	Died
Federer, Roger	SUI	2008	Doubles 1	8 Aug 1981	
Ferreiro, Wayne	RSA	1992	Doubles 2	15 Sep 1971	
Fish, Mardy	USA	2004	Singles 2	9 Dec 1981	
Flach, Kenneth Eliot	USA	1988	Doubles 1	24 May 1963	
Flack, Edwin Harold	AUS	1896	Doubles 3	5 Nov 1873	10 Jan 1935
Frana, Javier Alberto	ARG	1992	Doubles 3	25 Dec 1966	
Froitzheim, Otto	GER	1908	Singles 2	24 Apr 1884	29 Oct 1962
Gamble, Clarence Oliver	USA	1904	Doubles 3	16 Aug 1881	13 Jun 1952
Germot, Maurice	FRA	1906	Singles 2	17 Nov 1882	6 Aug 1958
		1906	Doubles 1		
		1912	*Doubles 1*		
Gilbert, Bradley N	USA	1988	Singles 3	9 Aug 1961	
Gobert, Andre Henri	FRA	1912	*Singles 1*	30 Sep 1890	6 Dec 1951
		1912	*Doubles 1*		
Goellner, Marc-Kevin	GER	1996	Doubles 3	22 Sep 1970	
Gonzales, Fernando Francisco	CHI	2004	Singles 3	29 Jul 1980	
		2004	Doubles 1		
		2008	Singles 2		
Gore, Arthur Wentworth	BRI	1908	*Singles 1*	2 Jan 1868	1 Dec 1928
		1908	*Doubles 1*		
Haas, Thomas Mario	GER	2000	Singles 2	3 Apr 1978	
Henman, Timothy Henry	GBR	1996	Doubles 2	6 Sep 1974	
Hillyard, George Whiteside	BRI	1908	Doubles 1	6 Feb 1864	24 Mar 1943
Hunter, Francis Townsend	USA	1924	Doubles 1	28 Jun 1894	2 Dec 1981
Ivanisevic, Goran Simun	CRO	1992	Singles 3	13 Sep 1971	
		1992	Doubles 3		
Jarryd, Anders Pierre	SWE	1988	Doubles 3	13 Jul 1961	
Johnasson, Thomas Karl	SWE	2008	Doubles 2	24 Mar 1975	
Kafelnikov, Yevgeny	RUS	2000	Singles 1	18 Feb 1974	
Kasdaglis, Dionysios	GRE	1896	Singles 2		
		1896	Doubles 2		
Kasdaglis, Xenophon	GRE	1906	Doubles 2	27 Feb 1880	2 May 1943
		1906	Mixed 3		
Kashio, Seiichiro	JPN	1920	Doubles 2	2 Jan 1892	6 Sep 1962
Kempe, Carl	SWE	1912	*Doubles 2*	8 Dec 1884	8 Jul 1967
Kiefer, Nicolas	GER	2004	Doubles 2	5 Jul 1977	
Kitson, Harold Austin	RSA	1912	Singles 2	17 Jun 1874	30 Nov 1951
		1912	Doubles 1		

Name	Country	Year of win	Event	Born	Died
Kreuzer, Oscar	GER	1912	Singles 3	14 Jun 1887	3 May 1968
Kumagai, Ichiya	JPN	1920	Singles 2	10 Sep 1890	16 Aug 1968
		1920	Doubles 2		
Lacoste, Jean Rene	FRA	1924	Doubles 3	2 Jul 1904	12 Oct 1996
Lareau, Sebastian	CAN	2000	Doubles 1	27 Apr 1973	
Leonard, Edgar Welch	USA	1904	Singles 3	19 Jun 1881	7 Oct 1948
		1904	Doubles 1		
Le Roy, Robert	USA	1904	Singles 2	7 Feb 1885	7 Sep 1946
		1904	Doubles 2		
Ljubicic, Ivan	CRO	2004	Doubles 3	19 Mar 1979	
Mahony, Harold Sergerson	BRI	1900	Singles 2	13 Feb 1867	27 Jun 1905
		1900	Doubles 3		
		1900	Mixed 2		
Massu, Nicolas Alejandro	CHI	2004	Singles 1	10 Oct 1979	
		2004	Doubles 1		
Mayotte, Timothy Spence	USA	1988	Singles 2	3 Aug 1960	
Mecir, Miloslav	TCH	1988	Singles 1	19 May 1964	
		1988	Doubles 3		
Meny, Edouard Marie Marc	FRA	1912	Doubles 3	30 Nov 1882	23 Jan 1960
Miniussi, Christian	ARG	1996	Doubles 3	5 Jul 1967	
Nadal, Rafael	ESP	2008	Singles 1	3 Jun 1986	
Nestor, Daniel Mark	CAN	2000	Doubles 1	4 Sep 1972	
Norris, Anthony B J	BRI	1900	Singles 3		
		1900	Doubles 3		
Norval, Piet	RSA	1992	Doubles 2	7 Apr 1970	
Paes, Leander Adrian	IND	1996	Singles 3	17 Jun 1973	
Parke, James Cecil	BRI	1908	Doubles 2	26 Jul 1881	27 Feb 1946
Paspatis, Konstantinos	GRE	1896	Singles 3	5 Jun 1878	14 Mar 1903
Petrokokkinos, Dimitrios	GRE	1896	Doubles 2	17 Apr 1878	
Piepes, Felix	AUT	1912	Doubles 2	15 Apr 1887	
Prevost, Andre	FRA	1900	Doubles 3		
Prinosil, David	GER	1996	Doubles 3	9 Mar 1973	
Prpic, Goran	CRO	1992	Doubles 3	4 May 1964	
Raymond, Louis Bosman	RSA	1920	Singles 1	28 Jun 1895	30 Jan 1962
Richards, Vincent	USA	1924	Singles 1	20 Mar 1903	28 Sep 1959
		1924	Doubles 1		
		1924	Mixed 2		

Name	Country	Year of win	Event	Born	Died
Ritchie, Major Josiah George	BRI	1908	Singles 1	18 Oct 1870	28 Feb 1955
		1908	Doubles 2		
		1908	*Singles* 3		
Robertson, George Stuart	BRI	1896	Doubles 3	25 May 1872	29 Jan 1967
Rosset, Marc	SUI	1992	Singles 1	7 Oct 1970	
Sanchez, Emilio	ESP	1988	Doubles 2	29 May 1965	
Schomburgk, Heinrich	GER	1912	Mixed 1	30 Jun 1885	29 Mar 1965
Schuettler, Rainer	GER	2004	Doubles 2	25 Apr 1976	
Seguso, Robert Arthur	USA	1988	Doubles 1	1 May 1963	
Setterwall, Gunnar	SWE	1908	*Doubles* 3	18 Aug 1881	26 Feb 1928
		1912	Mixed 2		
		1912	*Doubles* 2		
		1912	Mixed 3		
Simiriotis, Georgios	GRE	1906	Mixed 2	1886	
Simond, George Mieville	BRI	1908	*Doubles* 2	23 Jan 1867	8 Apr 1941
Srejber, Milan	TCH	1988	Mixed 3	30 Dec 1963	
Stich, Michael Detlef	GER	1992	Doubles 1	18 Oct 1968	
Tapavica, Moracilo	HUN	1896	Singles 3	14 Oct 1872	10 Jan 1949
Timmer, Hendrick	NED	1924	Mixed 3	8 Feb 1904	13 Nov 1998
Traun, Friedrich Adolph	GER	1896	Doubles 1	29 Mar 1876	11 Jul 1908
Turnbull, Oswald Graham Noel	BRI	1920	Doubles 1	20 Dec 1890	17 Dec 1970
Warden, Archibald Adam	BRI	1900	Mixed 3	11 May 1869	7 Oct 1943
Wawrinka, Stanislas	SUI	2008	Doubles 1	28 Mar 1985	
Wear, Arthur Yancey	USA	1904	Doubles 3	1 Mar 1880	6 Nov 1918
Wear, Joseph Walker	USA	1904	Doubles 3	27 Nov 1876	4 Jun 1941
West, Allen Tarwater	USA	1904	Doubles 3	2 Aug 1872	31 Aug 1952
Wilding, Anthony Frederick	AUL	1912	*Singles* 3	31 Oct 1883	9 May 1915
Williams, Richard Norris	USA	1924	Mixed 1	29 Jan 1891	2 Jun 1968
Winslow, Charles Lyndhurst	RSA	1912	Singles 1	1 Aug 1888	15 Sep 1963
		1912	Doubles 1		
		1920	Singles 3		
Woodbridge, Todd Andrew	AUS	1996	Doubles 1	2 Apr 1971	
		2000	Doubles 2		
Woodforde, Mark Raymond	AUS	1996	Doubles 1	23 Sep 1965	
		2000	Doubles 2		
Woosnam, Maxwell	BRI	1920	Doubles 1	6 Sep 1892	14 Jul 1965
		1920	Mixed 2		

Name	Country	Year of win	Event	Born	Died
Wright, Beals Coleman	USA	1904	Singles 1	19 Dec 1879	23 Aug 1961
		1904	Doubles 1		
Zborzil, Arthur	AUT	1912	Doubles 2	15 Jul 1885	15 Oct 1937
Zemla, Ladislav (Razny)	BOH	1906	Doubles 3	6 Nov 1887	17 Jun 1955
	TCH	1920	Mixed 3		
Zemla, Zdenek (Jansky)	BOH	1906	Singles 3		
		1906	Doubles 3		

Ladies

Name	Country	Year of win	Event	Born	Died
Adlerstrahle, Mrs Martha	SWE	1908	*Singles* 3	16 Jun 1868	4 Jan 1956
Aitchison, Miss Francis Helen	BRI	1912	*Mixed* 2	6 Dec 1881	26 May 1947
Barron, Mrs Dorothy Cunliffe	GBR	1924	Doubles 3	24 Nov 1897	20 Feb 1953
Beamish, Mrs Winifred Geraldine	GBR	1920	Doubles 2	23 Jun 1885	10 May 1972
Bjurstedt, Miss Anna Margrethe (Molla)	NOR	1912	Singles 3	6 Mar 1884	22 Nov 1959
Boogert, Miss Kristie	NED	2000	Doubles 2	16 Dec 1973	
Boothby, Miss Penelope Dora Harvey	BRI	1908	Singles 2	2 Aug 1881	22 Jul 1970
Bouman, Miss Kornelia (Kea)	NED	1924	Mixed 3	23 Nov 1903	17 Nov 1998
Broquedis, Miss Marie Marguerite	FRA	1912	Singles 1	17 Apr 1893	23 Apr 1983
		1912	Mixed 3		
Callens, Miss Els	BEL	2000	Doubles 3	20 Aug 1970	
Capriati, Miss Jennifer Marie	USA	1992	Singles 1	23 Mar 1976	
Castenschiold, Miss Thora Gerda Sofie	DEN	1912	*Singles* 2	1 Feb 1882	30 Jan 1979
Chambers, Mrs Dorothea Katharine	BRI	1908	Singles 1	3 Sep 1978	7 Jan 1960
Colyer, Miss Evelyn Lucy	GBR	1924	Doubles 3	16 Aug 1902	4 Nov 1930
Cooper, Miss Charlotte Reinagle	BRI	1900	Singles 1	22 Sep 1870	10 Oct 1966
		1900	Mixed 1		
Covell, Mrs Phyllis Lindrea	GBR	1924	Doubles 2	22 May 1895	28 Oct 1982
d'Ayen, Miss Elizabeth Pauline Sabine Marie	FRA	1920	Doubles 3	27 Oct 1898	7 Dec 1969

Name	Country	Year of win	Event	Born	Died
Davenport, Miss Lindsay Ann	USA	1996	Singles 1	8 Jun 1976	
Decugis, Mrs Marie	FRA	1906	Mixed 1	7 Aug 1884	4 May 1969
Dementieva, Miss Elena	RUS	2000	Singles 2	15 Oct 1981	
		2008	Singles 1		
Eastlake-Smith, Miss Gladys Shirley	BRI	1908	Singles 1	14 Aug 1883	18 Sep 1941
Fernandez, Miss Bertriz Cristina (Gigi)	USA	1992	Doubles 1	22 Feb 1964	
		1996	Doubles 1		
Fernandez, Miss Maria Jose (Mary Joe)	USA	1992	Singles 3	19 Aug 1971	
		1992	Doubles 1		
		1996	Doubles 1		
Fick, Mrs Sigrid	SWE	1912	Mixed 2	28 Mar 1887	4 Jun 1979
		1912	*Mixed* 3		
Garrison, Miss Zina Lynna	USA	1988	Singles 3	16 Nov 1963	
		1988	Doubles 1		
Graf, Miss Stefanie Maria	FRG	1988	Singles 1	14 Jun 1969	
		1988	Doubles 3		
	GER	1992	Singles 2		
Greene, Miss Alice Norah Gertrude	BRI	1908	*Singles* 2	15 Oct 1879	
Hannam, Miss Edith Margaret	BRI	1912	*Singles* 1	22 Nov 1878	16 Jan 1951
		1912	*Mixed* 1		
Henin-Hardenne, Mrs Justine	BEL	2004	Singles 1	1 Jun 1982	
Holman, Miss Edith Dorothy	BRI	1920	Singles 2	18 Jul 1883	15 Jun 1968
		1920	Doubles 2		
Jessup, Mrs Marion Hall	USA	1924	Mixed 2	2 May 1897	13 Aug 1980
Jones, Miss Marion	USA	1900	Singles 3	2 Nov 1879	14 Mar 1965
		1900	Mixed 3		
Kohde-Kilsch, Miss Claudia Gertrud	FRG	1988	Doubles 3	11 Dec 1963	
Koring, Miss Dorothea (Dora)	GER	1912	Singles 2	11 Jul 1880	13 Feb 1945
		1912	Mixed 1		
Lenglen, Miss Suzanne Rachel Flore	FRA	1920	Singles 1	24 May 1899	4 Jul 1938
		1920	Doubles 3		
		1920	Mixed 1		

Name	Country	Year of win	Event	Born	Died
Li, Miss Ting	CHN	2004	Doubles 1	5 Jan 1980	
Maleeva, Miss Manuela					
Georgieva	BUL	1988	Singles 3	14 Feb 1967	
Marinou, Miss Sophia	GRE	1906	Singles 2	1884	
		1906	Mixed 2		
Martinez, Miss Immaculada					
Concepion (Conchita)	ESP	1992	Doubles 2	16 Apr 1972	
		1996	Doubles 3		
		2004	Doubles 2		
Matsa, Miss Aspasia	GRE	2006	Mixed 3	1885	
Mauresmo, Miss Amelie	FRA	2004	Singles 2	5 Jul 1979	
McKane, Miss Kathleen	BRI	1920	Singles 3	7 May 1896	19 Jun 1992
		1920	Doubles 1		
		1920	Mixed 2		
	GBR	1924	Singles 3		
		1924	Doubles 2		
McNair, Mrs Winifred					
Margaret	BRI	1920	Doubles 1	9 Aug 1877	28 Mar 1954
McQuillian, Miss Rachel	AUS	1992	Doubles 3	2 Dec 1971	
Medina Garrigues, Miss Anabel	ESP	2008	Doubles 2	31 Jul 1982	
Meskhi, Miss Leila	CIS	1992	Doubles 3	5 Jan 1968	
Molik, Miss Alicia Helena	AUS	2004	Singles 3	27 Jan 1981	
Novotna, Miss Jana	TCH	1988	Doubles 2	2 Oct 1968	
	CZE	1996	Singles 3		
		1996	Doubles 2		
Oremans, Miss Miriam	NED	2000	Doubles 2	19 Sep 1972	
Parton, Mrs Mabel Bramwell	BRI	1912	*Singles* 3	22 Jul 1881	12 Aug 1962
Paspati, Miss Euphrosine	GRE	1906	Singles 3	1880	
Prevost, Miss Helene	FRA	1900	Singles 2		
		1900	Mixed 2		
Provis, Miss Nicole					
Anne-Louise	AUS	1992	Doubles 3	22 Sep 1969	
Rosenbaum, Miss Hedwig	BOH	1900	Singles 3		
		1900	Mixed 3		
Ruano Pascual, Miss Virginia	ESP	2004	Doubles 2	21 Sep 1973	
		2008	Doubles 2		
Sabatini, Miss Gabriela Beatriz	ARG	1988	Singles 2	16 May 1970	

Name	Country	Year of win	Event	Born	Died
Safina, Miss Dinara	RUS	2008	Singles 2	27 Apr 1986	
Sanchez-Vicario, Miss Arantxa Isabel Maria	ESP	1992	Singles 3	29 May 1965	
		1992	Doubles 2		
		1996	Singles 2		
		1996	Doubles 3		
Seles, Miss Monica	USA	2000	Singles 3	2 Dec 1973	
Shriver, Miss Pamela Howard	USA	1988	Doubles 1	4 Jul 1962	
Simiriotou, Miss Esmee	GRE	1906	Singles 1	1884	
Skrbkova, Miss Milada	TCH	1920	Mixed 3	30 May 1897	3 Oct 1935
Smylie, Mrs Elizabeth Marie	AUS	1988	Doubles 3	11 Apr 1963	
Suarez, Miss Paola	ARG	2004	Doubles 3	23 Jun 1976	
Sukova, Miss Helena	TCH	1988	Doubles 2	23 Feb 1965	
	CZE	1996	Doubles 2		
Sun, Miss Tian Tian	CHN	2004	Doubles 1	12 Oct 1981	
Tarabini, Miss Patricia	ARG	2004	Doubles 3	6 Aug 1968	
Turnbull, Miss Wendy May	AUS	1988	Doubles 3	26 Nov 1952	
Van Roost, Miss Dominique	BEL	2000	Doubles 3	31 May 1973	
Vlasto, Miss Julie Penelope (Diddie)	FRA	1924	Singles 2	8 Aug 1903	8 Feb 1985
Wightman, Mrs Hazel Virginia	USA	1924	Doubles 1	20 Dec 1886	5 Dec 1974
		1924	Mixed 1		
Williams, Miss Serena Jamika	USA	2000	Doubles 1	26 Sep 1981	
		2008	Doubles 1		
Williams, Miss Venus Ebone Starr	USA	2000	Singles 1	17 Jun 1980	
		2000	Doubles 1		
		2008	Doubles 1		
Wills, Miss Helen Newington	USA	1924	Singles 1	6 Oct 1905	1 Jan 1998
		1924	Doubles 1		
Winch, Mrs Ruth Jean	BRI	1908	Singles 3		
Yan, Miss Zi	CHN	2008	Doubles 3	12 Nov 1984	
Zheng, Miss Jie	CHN	2008	Doubles 3	5 Jul 1983	
Zvereva, Miss Natalia Maratovna	CIS	1992	Doubles 3	22 Sep 1969	
Zvonareva, Miss Vera	RUS	2008	Singles 3	7 Sep 1984	

Tournament Scores

1896 – Athens

Velodrome Stadium, 8,9,11 April

Men's Singles – First Round:
Aristidis Akratopoulos (GRE) bt Edwin Flack (AUS),
Konstantinos Paspatis (GRE) bt George Robertson (BRI),
John Boland (BRI) bt Freidrich Traun (GER), Evangelos
Rallis (GRE) bt Dimitrios Petrokokkinos (GRE), Frank
Marshall (BRI) v George Marshall (BRI) (both withdrew),
Momcilo Tapavicza (HUN) bt J. Fragopoulos (GRE),
Dionysios Kasdaglis (GRE) bt J. Defert (FRA)

Quarter-final:
Paspatis bt A. Akratopoulos, Boland bt Rallis 6–0 2–6 6–2, Tapavicza w.o., Kasdaglis bt
Konstantinos Akratopoulos (GRE)

Semi-final:
Boland bt Paspatis, Kasdaglis bt Tapavicza

Final:
Boland (Silver) bt Kasdaglis (Copper) 6–2 6–2

Men's Doubles – First Round:
Dionysios Kasdaglis & Dimitrios Petrokokkinos (GRE) bt Konstantinos Paspatis &
Evangelos Rallis (GRE), Edwin Flack (AUS) & George Robertson (BRI) bt Frank
Marshall & George Marshall (BRI)

Semi-final:

Kasdaglis & Petrokokkinos bt Flack & Robertson, John Boland (BRI) & Freidrich Traun (GER) bt Aristidis Akratopoulos & Konstantinos Akratopoulos (GRE)

Final:

Boland & Traun (Silver) bt Kasdaglis & Petrokokkinos (Copper) 5–7 6–3 6–3

(Scores of earlier rounds not available)

1900 – Paris

Puteaux Club, 6–11 July

Men's Singles – First Round:
Basil de Garmendia (USA) bt Charles Voigt (FRA) 6–1 6–3, Laurence Doherty (BRI) bt Paul Lebreton (FRA) 6–2 6–3, Reginald Doherty (BRI) bt E. Durand (FRA) 6–1 6–3, Paul Lecaron (FRA) bt A. Lippman (BRI) 6–0 6–1, Archibald Warden (BRI) bt Wylie Grant (USA) w.o., Anthony Norris (BRI) bt Andre Prevost (FRA) 6–4 6–4, Harold Mahony (BRI) bt Charles Sands (USA) 6–2 6–3

Quarter-final:
L. Doherty bt de Garmendia 6–2 8–6, R.Doherty bt Lecaron 6–2 6–1, Norris bt Warden 6–4 6–2, Mahony bt Maxime Decugis (FRA) w.o.

Semi-final:
L. Doherty bt R. Doherty w.o., Mahony bt Norris 8–6 6–1

Final:
L. Doherty bt Mahony 6–4 6–2 6–3

Ladies' Singles – First Round:
Charlotte Cooper (BRI) bt Miss Fourrier (FRA) 6–2 6–0, Helene Prevost (FRA) bt Georgina Jones (USA) 6–0 6–1

Semi-final:
Charlotte Cooper bt Marion Jones (USA) 6–2 7–5, Helene Prevost bt Hedwig Rosenbaum (BOH) 6–1 6–1

Final:

Charlotte Cooper bt Helen Prevost 6–1 6–4

Men's Doubles – First Round:

Georges de la Chapelle & Andre Prevost (FRA) bt Viscomte Elie de Lastours & Baron G. Lejeune (FRA) 6–3 7–9 6–2, Maxime Decugis (FRA) & Basil de Garmendia (USA) bt Charles Sands (USA) & Archibald Warden(BRI) 6–3 7–5, Laurence Doherty & Reginald Doherty (BRI) bt Paul Lebreten & Paul Lecaron (FRA) 6–2 6–3, Harold Mahony & Anthony Norris (BRI) bt E. Durand & A. Fauchier-Magnan (FRA) 6–8 6–1 6–3

Semi-final:

Decugis & de Garmendia bt de la Chapelle & Prevost 6–2 6–4, Doherty & Doherty bt Mahony & Norris 6–4 6–1 6–4 (Best of 5 sets)

Final:

Doherty & Doherty bt Decugis & de Garmendia 6–1 6–1 6–0 (Best of 5 sets)

Mixed Doubles – First Round:

Archibald Warden (BRI) & Hedwig Rosenbaum (BOH) bt P. Verdi-Delisle & Kate Gillou (FRA) 6–3 3–6 6–2, Laurence Doherty (BRI) & Marion Jones (USA) bt Charles Sands & Georgina Jones (USA) 6–1 7–5

Semi-final:

Harold Mahony (BRI) & Helene Prevost (FRA) bt Warden & Hedwig Rosenbaum 6–3 6–0, Reginald Doherty & Charlotte Cooper (BRI) bt L. Doherty & Marion Jones 6–2 6–4

Final:

R. Doherty & Charlotte Cooper bt Mahony & Helene Prevost 6–2 6–4

(Referee: Charles Voigt, USA)

1904 – St. Louis

Francis Field, 29 August-3 September

Men's Singles – Preliminary Round:
W.E. Blatherwick bt Melville Bergfeld w.o., Nathaniel
Semple bt George Stadel 6–2 6–1

First Round:
Charles Cresson bt Frank Wheaton 6–2 6–4, M.H. Holland v
Rahn (both withdrew), Robert Le Roy bt T. Holland w.o.,
Fred Sanderson bt J. Elliott w.o., Edgar Leonard bt Chris
Forney 6–1 6–1, Ralph McKittrick bt William Easton 6–2 6–2,
Blatherwick bt Semple 4–6 6–4 6–1, J. Cunningham bt J. Berger
w.o., Beals Wright bt Forest Montgomery 6–3 6–1, Hugo Hardy (GER) bt Frank Eberhardt
w.o., John Neely bt Malcolm McDonald 6–1 6–1, F.R.Felthans bt Joseph Charles 8–6 6–1,
Alphonzo Bell bt Orion Vernon 6–3 6–2, Dwight Davis bt James Tritle 6–2 6–1, Semp
Russ bt Douglas Turner 6–2 6–1, H. McKittrick Jones bt Andrew Drew 6–4 6–1

Second Round:
Cresson w.o., Le Roy bt Sanderson 6–3 6–3, Leonard bt McKittrick 6–4 6–4, Blatherwick
bt Cunningham 6–2 0–6 6–4, Wright bt Hardy 6–2 6–1 Neely bt Felthans 6–0 6–2, Bell bt
Davis w.o. Russ bt Jones 6–1 6–2

Quarter-final:
Le Roy bt Cresson 6–4 8–6, Leonard bt Blatherwick 6–2 6–0, Wright bt Neely 6–0 6–2,
Bell bt Russ 6–3 6–1

Semi-final:
Le Roy bt Leonard 6–3 6–3, Wright bt Bell 6–3 6–4

Final:
Wright (Gold) bt Le Roy (Silver) 6–4 6–4

Third Place:
Both defeated semi-finalists were awarded Bronze medals

Men's Doubles – First Round:
Clarence Gamble & Arthur Wear bt N.M. Smith & Joseph Charles 6–3 7–5, Edgar
Leonard & Beals Wright bt W.E. Blatherwick & Orion Vernon 6–3 7–5, Charles Cresson

& Semp Russ bt Forest Montgomery & James Tritle 7–5 6–2, Dwight Davis & Ralph McKittrick bt Nathaniel Semple & Malcolm MacDonald 6–1 6–1, Alphonzo Bell & Robert LeRoy bt Paul Gleason & Hugo Hardy (GER) 6–3 6–1, McKittrick Jones & Harold Kauffman bt Frederick Semple & George Stadel 6–1 8–6, Joseph Wear & Allen West bt Andrew Drew & Douglas Turner 6–3 6–4

Quarter-final:

Gamble & A.Y. Wear bt Frank Wheaton & Frances Hunter 6–1 6–4, Leonard & Wright bt Cresson & Russ 6–2 5–7 6–3, Bell & Le Roy bt Davis & McKittrick 9–7 6–4, J.W. Wear & West bt Jones & Kauffman 6–3 4–6 6–4

Semi-final:

Leonard & Wright bt Gamble & A.Y. Wear 6–1 6–2, Bell & Le Roy bt J.W. Wear & West 2–6 6–1 6–2

Final:

Leonard & Wright (Gold) bt Bell & Le Roy (Silver) 6–4 6–4 6–2

Third Place:

Both defeated semi-finalists were awarded Bronze medals

(All competitors were from the United States with the exception of Hugo Hardy, Germany)

1906 – Athens

Lawn Tennis Club, 23–26 April

Men's Singles – First Round:

J. Whittal (BRI) v A. Georgiadis (GRE) (both withdrew), P. Manesis (GRE) v Dionysios Kasdaglis (GRE) (both withdrew), Guus Kessler (HOL) bt Ioannis Ketseas (GRE) w.o., Jaroslav Zemla (BOH) bt K. Vitous (HUN) 6–4 7–5, Leonidas Zariphis (GRE) bt D. Whittal (BRI) w.o., Maxime Decugis (FRA) bt Nikolaos Karydias (GRE) 6–0 6–0, Xenophon Kasdaglis (GRE) bt He. Melis (GRE) w.o., Zdenek Zemla (BOH) bt J. Millet (FRA) w.o., Maurice Germot (FRA) bt M. Agelastos (GRE) w.o., Jacques Giraud (FRA) bt Gino De Martino (ITA) w.o., Karl Beukema (HOL) bt Ladislav Zemla (BOH) 6–0 6–4, Gerard Scheurleer (HOL) bt Nikolaos Zariphis (GRE) 6–0 3–6 6–2, Ioannis Ballis (GRE) bt Homer Byington(USA) 6–1 6–2

Second Round:

E. Giraud (FRA) w.o., Kessler w.o., L. Zariphis bt J. Zemla w.o., Decugis bt X. Kasdaglis 6–1 6–0, Germot bt Z. Zemla 3–6 6–1 6–2, Beukema bt J. Giraud 6–4 3–6 7–5, Scheurleer bt Ballis 6–1 6–4, Georgios Simiriotis (GRE) bt Robert Schauffler (USA) 6–1 2–6 6–2

Quarter-final:

Kessler bt E. Giraud w.o., Decugis bt L. Zariphis 6–1 6–0, Germot bt Beukema 6–4 6–2, Scheurleer bt Simiriotis 6–3 8–6

Semi-final:

Decugis bt Kessler 6–0 6–0, Germot bt Scheurleer 6–4 6–1

Final:

Decugis (Silver) bt Germot 6–1 7–9 6–4 6–1

Third place:

Awarded to Z. Zemla

Ladies' Singles – First Round:

Euphrosine Paspati (GRE) bt Domini Eliadi (GRE) w.o., Sophia Marinou (GRE) bt Ioannia Tissamenou (GRE) 6–0 6–1, Aspasia Matsa (GRE) bt Marie Decugis (FRA) w.o., Esmee Simiriotou (GRE) bt V. Melis (GRE) w.o.

Semi-final:

Sophia Marinou bt Euphrosine Paspati 6–0 4–6 6–3, Esmee Simiriotou bt Aspasia Matsa 7–5 6–2

Final:

Esmee Simiriotou (Silver) bt Sophia Marinou 2–6 6–3 6–3

Third Place Play- off:

Euphrosine Paspati bt Aspasia Matsa 6–0 6–4

Men's Doubles – First Round:

Ladislav Zemla & Zdenek Zemla (BOH) bt A. Georgiadis & D. Syriotis (GRE) w.o., Homer Byington & Robert Schauffler (USA) bt Jacques Giraud (FRA) & J. Whittal (BRI) w.o.,He. Melis & P. Manesis (GRE) v H. Giraud (FRA) & D. Whittal (BRI) match not played, Ioannis Ballis & Xenophon Kasdaglis (GRE) bt Jaroslav Zemla (BOH) & K. Vitous (HUN) w.o.

Quarter-final:

Maxime Decugis & Maurice Germot (FRA) bt Karl Beukema & Gerard Scheurleer (HOL) 6–4 6–0, Ladislav Zemla & Zdenek Zemla bt Byington & Schauffler 6–3 6–3, Ballis & Kasdaglis w.o., Georgios Simiriotis & Nikolaos Zariphis (GRE) bt Ioannis Ketseas & Georgios Skouzis (GRE) 9–7 6–1

Semi-final:

Decugis & Germot bt L. Zemla & Z. Zemla 6–3 6–4, Ballis & Kasdaglis bt Simiriotis & Zariphis 7–5 6–4

Final:

Decugis & Germot (Silver) bt Ballis & Kasdaglis 6–3 9–7 3–6 0–6 6–0

Third Place Play-off:

L. Zemla & Z. Zemla bt Simiriotis & Zariphis 6–2 6–3

Mixed Doubles – First Round:

Georgios Simiriotis & Sophia Marinou (GRE) bt Dionysios Kasdaglis & Euphrosine Paspati (GRE) 6–2 6–2

Semi-final:

Maxime Decugis & Marie Decugis (FRA) bt Simiriotis & Sophia Marinou 8–6 6–3, Xenophon Kasdaglis & Aspasia Matsa (GRE) bt Nikolaos Zariphis & Esme Simiriotou (GRE) 6–1 6–4

Final:

Decugis & Marie Decugis (Silver) bt X. Kasdaglis & Aspasia Matsa 6–3 7–5

The event jury decided that Simiriotis and Sophia Marinou had achieved a better result than X. Kasdaglis and Aspasia Matsa against the winners and awarded them second place. X.Kasdaglis and Aspasia Matsa were placed third.

1908 London

Queen's Club (Covered Courts) 6–11 May

Men's Singles – First Round:
Major Ritchie (BRI) bt Roper Barrett (BRI) w.o., Gunnar Setterwall (SWE) bt Lionel Escombe (BRI) 6–2 6–3 6–1

Quarter-final:
Arthur Gore (BRI) bt Anthony Wilding (AUL) w.o., Ritchie bt Leslie Poidevin (AUS) w.o., George Caridia (BRI) bt Setterwall 6–2 6–1 6–1, Wilberforce Eaves (BRI) bt Wollmar Bostrom (SWE) 7–5 6–2 9–7

Semi-final:
Gore bt Ritchie 4–6 6–3 5–7 6–1 6–4, Caridia bt Eaves 7–5 retd

Final:
Gore (Gold) bt Caridia (Silver) 6–3 7–5 6–4

Third Place:
Ritchie (Bronze) w.o.

Ladies' Singles – First Round:
Alice Greene (BRI) bt Ruth Winch (BRI) w.o.

Quarter-final:
Marthe Adlerstrahle (SWE) bt Dorothea Chambers (BRI) w.o., Alice Greene bt Dora Boothby (BRI) 6–2 6–2, Else Wallenberg (SWE) bt Mildred Coles (BRI) 11–9 4–6 4–5 retd, Gladys Eastlake-Smith (BRI) bt Violet Pinckney (BRI) 7–5 7–5

Semi-final:
Alice Greene bt Marthe Adlerstrahle 6–1 6–3, Gladys Eastlake-Smith bt Else Wallenberg 6–4 6–4

Final:
Gladys Eastlake-Smith (Gold) bt Alice Greene (Silver) 6–2 4–6 6–0

Third Place Play-off:
Marthe Adlerstrahle (Bronze) bt Else Wallenberg 1–6 6–3 6–2

Men's Doubles – First Round:

George Caridia & George Simond (BRI) bt Wilberforce Eaves & George Hillyard (BRI) 2–6 7–9 6–4 10–8 6–4

Semi-final:

Caridia & Simond bt Wollmar Bostrom & Gunnar Setterwall (SWE) 6–4 9–7 2–6 6–2, Roper Barrett & Arthur Gore (BRI) bt Lionel Escombe & Major Ritchie (BRI) 0–6 6–4 6–3 6–3

Final:

Barrett & Gore (Gold) bt Caridia & Simond (Silver) 6–2 2–6 6–3 6–3

Third Place Play-off:

Bostrom & Setterwall (Bronze) bt Escombe & Ritchie 4–6 6–3 1–6 6–0 6–3

(Referee: Bonham Carter Evelegh, BRI)

1908 London

All England Lawn Tennis Club (Grass Courts) 6–11 July

Men's Singles – First Round:

Charles Dixon (BRI) bt Friedrich-Wilhelm Rahe (GER) 6–2 7–5 6–4, J. Cerny (BOH) bt Odon Schmid (HUN) w.o. Jeno Zsigmondy (HUN) bt L. Ivanaka (HUN) w.o. Baron Moritz von Bissing (GER) bt George Ball-Greene (BRI) w.o., Arthur Zborzil (AUT) bt Arthur Gore (BRI) w.o., Curt von Wesseley (AUT) bt Roper Barrett (BRI) w.o., Wilberforce Eaves (BRI) bt Rolf Kinzl (AUT) 6–3 6–1 6–0, Ede Toth (HUN) bt Josef Micovsky (BOH) 6–3 2–1 retd, James Parke (BRI) bt Josef Roessler-Orowsky (BOH) w.o., Oskar Kreuzer (GER) bt Felix Piepes (AUT) 6–3 6–1 6–4, Otto Froitzheim (GER) bt Kenneth Powell (BRI) 6–3 6–1 6–4, Robert Powell (CAN) bt Christiaan von Lennep (HOL) 6–4 6–1 6–2, Ladislav Zemla (BOH) bt Laurence Doherty (BRI) w.o.

Second Round:

C.K. Vitous (BOH) bt H.M. Suckling (CAN) w.o., Maurice Germot (FRA) bt Heinrich Schomburgk (GER) 7–5 6–4 6–2, Major Ritchie (BRI) bt Victor R. Gauntlett (RSA) 6–1 6–4 6–1. Walter Crawley (BRI) bt George Hillyard (BRI) w.o., Dixon bt Dezso Lauber (HUN) 6–1 6–0 6–0, Cerny bt Zsigmondy 7–5 6–4 3–6 6–0, Von Bissing bt Zborzil 6–1 6–4 6–4, Eaves bt von Wesseley w.o., Parke bt Toth 6–1 6–3 6–2, Froitzheim bt Kreuzer 6–2 6–3 6–3, Robert Powell bt L. Zemla 2–6 6–0 6–4 6–1, George Caridia

(BRI) bt Harold Kitson (RSA) 6–1 6–3 6–1, Capt James Foulkes (CAN) bt Roelof van Lennep (HOL) 6–2 6–4 6–3, Rev John Richardson (RSA) bt Maxime Decugis (FRA) w.o., D. Slava (BOH) bt Jaroslav Zemla (BOH) w.o., Capt C.R. Brown (CAN) bt Zdenek Zemla (BOH) w.o.

Third Round:
Germot bt Vitous w.o., Ritchie bt Crawley 6–1 6–4 6–1, Dixon bt Cerny 6–1 6–2 6–3, Eaves bt von Bissing 8–6 7–5 7–5, Froitzheim bt Parke 6–4 11–9 6–4, Caridia bt R.B. Powell 6–4 3–6 6–4 6–2, Richardson bt Foulkes 6–2 6–4 6–3, Brown bt Slava 6–2 6–1 6–2

Quarter-final:
Ritchie bt Germot 6–0 4–0 retd, Eaves bt Dixon 6–3 7–5 6–3, Froitzheim bt Caridia 6–4 6–1 5–7 6–1, Richardson bt Brown 6–3 6–1 6–0

Semi-final:
Ritchie bt Eaves 2–6 6–1 6–4 6–1, Froitzheim bt Richardson 2–6 6–1 6–4 6–4

Final:
Ritchie (Gold) bt Froitzheim (Silver) 7–5 6–3 6–4

Third Place Play-off:
Eaves (Bronze) bt Richardson 6–2 6–2 6–3

Ladies' Singles – First Round:
Agnes Morton (BRI) bt Alice Greene (BRI) 8–6 6–2, Katalin Czery (HUN) bt Frida Pietrikowski (AUT) w.o., Ruth Winch (BRI) bt E. Mattuch (AUT) w.o., Kate Fenwick (FRA) bt Marie Amende (AUT) w.o.

Quarter-final:
Dorothea Chambers (BRI) bt Agnes Morton 6–2 6–3, Ruth Winch bt Katalin Czery w.o., Kate Fenwick bt Charlotte Sterry (BRI) w.o., Dora Boothby (BRI) bt Blanche Hillyard (BRI) w.o.

Semi-final:
Dorothea Chambers bt Ruth Winch 6–1 6–1, Dora Boothby bt Kate Fenwick w.o.

Final:
Dorothea Chambers (Gold) bt Dora Boothby (Silver) 6–1 7–5

Third Place:

Ruth Winch (Bronze) w.o.

Men's Doubles – First Round:

Clement Cazalet & Charles Dixon (BRI) bt Rolf Kinzl & Kurt von Wesseley (AUT) w.o., Otto Froitzheim & Heinrich Schomburgk (GER) bt Oskar Kreuzer & Friedrich-Wilhelm Rahe (GER) 6–1 6–3 6–3, Victor Gauntlett & Harold Kitson (RSA) bt J. Cerny & D. Slava (BOH) 6–0 6–4 6–3, L. Ivanka & Dezso Lauber (HUN) bt Roper Barrett & Arthur Gore (BRI) w.o., Felix Piepes & Arthur Zborzil (AUT) bt Josef Micovsky & Josef Roessler Orowsky (BOH) w.o.,

Second Round:

Walter Crawley & Kenneth Powell (BRI) bt Capt James Foulkes & Robert Powell (CAN) 7–6 6–3 6–2, Reginald Doherty & George Hillyard (BRI) bt C.K. Vitous & Jaroslav Zemla (BOH) w.o., Cazalet & Dixon bt Christiaan van Lennep & Roelof van Lennep (HOL) 6–4 6–0 3–6 6–2, Gauntlett & Kitson bt Froitzheim & Schomburgk 3–6 6–2 7–5 6–3, Piepes & Zborzil bt Ivanka & Lauber w.o., James Parke & Major Ritchie (BRI) bt Jeno Zsigmondy & Ede Toth (HUN) 6–1 6–0 6–3, Capt C.R. Brown & H.M. Suckling (CAN) bt Ladislav Zemla & Zdenek Zemla (BOH) w.o., Maxime Decugis & Maurice Germot (FRA) bt George Ball-Greene & Wilberforce Eaves (BRI) w.o.

Quarter-final:

Doherty & Hillyard bt Crawley & Powell 10–8 6–1 7–9 7–5, Cazalet & Dixon bt Gauntlett & Kitson 6–2 5–7 2–6 6–3 6–3, Parke & Ritchie bt Piepes & Zborzil 7–5 6–4 6–2, Decugis & Germot bt Brown & Suckling w.o.

Semi-final:

Doherty & Hillyard bt Cazalet & Dixon 5–7 2–6 6–4 17–15 6–4, Parke & Ritchie bt Decugis & Germot w.o.

Final:

Doherty & Hillyard (Gold) bt Parke & Ritchie (Silver) 9–7 7–5 9–7

Third Place:

Cazalet & Dixon (Bronze) w.o.

(Referee: William Herbert Collins, BRI)

1912 – Stockholm

Royal Club, (Covered Courts) 5–12 May

Men's Singles – First Round:
Jaroslav Just (BOH) bt Maxime Decugis (FRA) w.o.,
Thorsten Gronfors (SWE) bt Josef Sebek (BOH) w.o.,
Anthony Wilding (AUL) bt Lennart Silverstolpe (SWE)
6–0 6–1 6–1, George Caridia (BRI) bt Frans Moller (SWE)
6–2 7–5 5–7 6–4, Arthur Gore (BRI) bt Hakon Leffler
(SWE) 7–5 6–4 7–5, Arthur Lowe (BRI) bt Wollmar
Bostrom (SWE) 5–7 6–4 6–4 6–4, Maurice Germot (FRA)
bt Alfred Beamish (BRI) 4–6 6–2 4–6 6–2 6–4, Andre
Gobert (FRA) bt Erik Larson (DEN) 8–6 6–1 5–7 8–6, Carl
Kempe (SWE) bt Jaromir Haintz (BOH) 6–1 6–4 3–6 6–3

Second Round:
Charles Dixon (BRI) bt Theodore Mavrogordato (BRI) 6–2 9–7 4–6 10–8, Karel Fuchs
(BOH) bt Just w.o., Wilding bt Gronfors 6–3 6–3 6–3, Caridia bt Gore 6–2 9–7 7–5,
A. Lowe bt Germot 6–4 3–6 6–1 6–4, Gobert bt Kempe 6–1 6–2 7–5, Gunnar Setterwall
(SWE) bt Roper Barrett (BRI) 4–6 6–1 6–4 6–8 6–4, Gordon Lowe (BRI) bt Charles
Wennergren (SWE) 6–4 6–1 6–4

Quarter-final:
Dixon bt Fuchs 6–2 6–4 6–1, Wilding bt Caridia 6–3 6–1 6–2, Gobert bt A. Lowe 6–1 6–1
6–3, G. Lowe bt Setterwall 6–4 1–6 6–3 8–6

Semi-final:
Dixon bt Wilding 6–0 4–6 6–4 6–4, Gobert bt G. Lowe 6–4 10–8 2–6 2–6 6–2

Final:
Gobert (Gold) bt Dixon (Silver) 8–6 6–4 6–4

Third Place Play off:
Wilding (Bronze) bt G. Lowe 4–6 6–2 7–5 6–0

Ladies' Singles – First Round:
Mabel Parton (BRI) bt Margarete Cederschoild (SWE) 6–0 6–1, Sigrid Fick (SWE) bt Elsa
Magnusson (SWE) w.o.

Quarter-final:

Edith Hannam (BRI) bt Edit Arnheim 7–5 6–1, Mabel Parton bt Marie Decugis (FRA) w.o., Sigrid Fick bt Annie Holmstrom (SWE) 6–1 6–1, Sophie Castenschiold (DEN) bt Helen Aitchison (BRI) 2–6 6–2 6–1

Semi-final:

Edith Hannam bt Mabel Parton 7–5 6–2, Sophie Castenschiold bt Sigrid Fick 6–4 6–4

Final:

Edith Hannam (Gold) bt Sophie Castenschiold (Silver) 6–4 6–3

Third Place Play-off:

Mabel Parton (Bronze) bt Sigrid Fick 6–3 6–3

Men's Doubles – First Round:

Arthur Lowe & Gordon Lowe (BRI) bt Carl Nylen and Charles Wennergren (SWE) 9–7 11–9 6–2, Maurice Germot & Andre Gobert (FRA) bt Jaromir Haintz & Josef Sebek (BOH) w.o., Carl Kempe & Gunnar Setterwall (SWE) bt George Caridia & Theodore Mavrogordato (BRI) 6–4 4–6 6–8 6–2 6–3

Quarter-final:

Alfred Beamish & Charles Dixon (BRI) bt Karel Fuchs & Jaroslav Just (BOH) w.o., Germot & Gobert bt Lowe & Lowe 3–6 6–8 6–4 6–2 6–3, Kempe & Setterwall bt Frans Moller & Thorsten Gronfors (SWE) w.o., Roper Barrett & Arthur Gore (BRI) bt Wollmar Bostrom & Curt Benckert (SWE) 7–5 6–4 6–1

Semi-final:

Germot & Gobert bt Beamish & Dixon 6–3 6–1 6–2, Kempe & Setterwall bt Barrett & Gore 4–6 3–6 6–1 6–4 6–3

Final:

Germot & Gobert (Gold) bt Kempe & Setterwall (Silver) 4–6 14–12 6–2 6–4

Third Place Play-off:

Beamish & Dixon (Bronze) bt Barrett & Gore 6–2 0–6 6–2 4–6 6–3

Mixed Doubles – First Round:

Roper Barrett & Helen Aitchison (BRI) bt Carl O. Nylen & Edit Arnheim (SWE) 6–4 6–1, Theodore Mavrogordato & Mabel Parton (BRI) bt Franz Moller & E.Hay (SWE) 6–3 6–0

Quarter-final:
Gunnar Setterwall & Sigrid Fick (SWE) bt Josef Sebek & M. Sebkova (BOH) w.o., Barrett
& Helen Aitchison bt Erik Larsen & Sophie Castenschiold (DEN) 6–0 6–3, Charles
Dixon & Edith Hannam bt Mavrogordato & Mabel Parton 2–6 6–4 6–3, Carl Kempe &
Margarete Cederschiold (SWE) bt Maxime Decugis & Marie Decugis (FRA) w.o.

Semi-final:
Barrett & Helen Aitchison bt Setterwall & Sigrid Fick 3–6 6–1 6–2, Dixon & Edith
Hannam bt Kempe & Margarete Cederschiold 6–2 6–2

Final:
Dixon & Edith Hannam (Gold) bt Barrett & Helen Aitchison (Silver) 6–4 3–6 6–2

Third Place Play-off:
Setterwall & Sigrid Fick (Bronze) bt Kempe & Margarete Cederschiold w.o.

1912 – Stockholm

Idrottsplatz, (Hard Courts) 28 June-5 July

Men's Singles – First Round:
Lionel Tapscott (RSA) bt Jiri Kodl (BOH) 6–4 6–1 6–2, Felix Piepes (AUT) bt
Paul Lindpaintner (GER) 6–2 6–3 6–3, Axel Thayssen (DEN) bt Karel Ardelt (BOH) w.o.

Second Round:
Harold Kitson (RSA) bt Hakon Leffler (SWE) 6–2 6–1 6–0, Frans Moller (SWE) bt Jean-
Pierre Samazeuilh (FRA) w.o., Robert Spies (GER) bt Jaroslav Just (BOH) 2–6 6–3 3–6
6–3 6–1, Heinrich Schombugk (GER) bt J. Montariol (FRA) w.o. Wollmar Bostrom
(SWE) bt Trygve Smith (NOR) 6–2 6–4 6–1, Count Ludwig Salm (AUT) bt Richard
Petersen (NOR) 6–1 7–5 6–3, Charles Wennergren (SWE) bt Jaromir Zeman (BOH) 6–1
6–0 6–0, Leif Rovsing bt Paul Segner (HUN) w.o., V.G. Hansen (DEN) bt Odon Schmid
(HUN) w.o., Bela von Kehrling (HUN) bt Carl Kempe (SWE) w.o., Jeno Zsigmondy
(HUN) bt H. Liebisch (AUT) w.o., Otto von Muller (GER) bt O. Fredriksen (DEN) 6–4
6–1 6–2, Rudolf Bertrand (AUT) bt H. Planner von Plaun (AUT) w.o., Ladislav Zemla
(BOH) bt Adolf Hammacher (GER) w.o., Jean-Francois Blanchy (FRA) bt Bohuslav
Hyks (BEL) 5–7 6–1 6–2 6–1, Tapscott bt Piepes 3–6 7–5 4–6 7–5 7–5, Thayssen bt
Aage Madsen (DEN) 6–1 6–3 3–6 6–3, Charles Winslow (RSA) bt P. Frigast (DEN) 7–5
6–3 6–2, Thorsten Gronfors (SWE) bt Ede Toth (HUN) w.o., Vagn Ingerslev (DEN)
bt Jorgen Arenholdt (DEN) 6–2 1–6 6–0 6–4, Luis Heyden (GER) bt Eduard Meny de

Marangue (FRA) 7–9 4–6 6–2 7–5 6–1, Aurel von Keleman (HUN) bt Leo von Barath (HUN) 6–1 6–3 6–4, Albert Canet (FRA) bt Conrad Langaard (NOR) 6–3 6–3 6–1, T.Roosevelt Pell (USA) bt P. Gyula (HUN) w.o., Noble Stibolt (NOR) bt Daniel Lawton (FRA) w.o., Josef Sebek (BOH) bt Otto Froitzheim (GER) w.o., Karel Fuchs (BOH) bt Kurt von Wessely (AUT) w.o., Albert Zborzil (AUT) bt Curt Benckert (SWE) 6–2 6–4 1–6 6–3, Gunnar Setterwall (SWE) bt Otto Blum (HOL) 6–3 6–3 8–6, Count Mikhail Soumarokoff-Elston (RUS) bt Aleksandr Alenitzyn (RUS) w.o., Bjame Angell (NOR) bt Otto Relly (AUT) w.o., Oskar Kreuzer (GER) bt Herman Bjorklund (NOR) 6–0 6–0 6–1

Third Round:
Kitson bt Moller 6–1 6–2 6–0, Schomburgk bt Spies 8–6 6–1 retd, Salm bt Bastrom 7–5 8–6 6–1, Wennergren bt Rovsing 4–6 9–7 6–8 6–1 6–1, von Kehrling bt Hansen 6–4 6–1 6–8 6–4, von Muller bt Zsegmondy 6–1 6–2 6–0, Zemla bt Bertrand w.o., Tapscott bt Blanchy 1–6 5–7 6–3 6–4 6–4, Winslow bt Thayssen 6–4 3–6 6–4 9–7, Ingersley bt Gronfors 6–1 6–2 6–2, Heyden bt von Kelemen 6–3 4–6 7–5 7–5, Pell bt Canet 6–2 6–3 6–4, Sebek bt Stibolt 6–1 6–3 6–3, Zborsil bt Fuchs 6–4 6–2 6–1, Soumarakoff bt Setterwall 6–3 6–3 11–13 6–2, Kreuzer bt Angell 6–0 6–0 6–1

Fourth Round:
Kitson bt Schomburgk 6–2 6–2 6–3, Salm bt Weneergren 6–3 8–10 7–5 6–1, von Muller bt von Kehrling 6–2 6–1 6–1, Zemla bt Tapscott 1–6 4–6 6–2 6–4 6–2, Winslow bt Ingersley 6–4 8–6 6–4, Heyden bt Pell 2–6 7–5 8–6 7–5, Zborzil bt Sebek 6–1 6–0 3–6 6–2, Kreuzer bt Soumarokoff 6–2 10–12 6–4 6–0

Quarter-final:
Kitson bt Salm 6–2 6–2 6–4, Zemla bt von Muller 6–4 7–5 6–4, Winslow bt Heyden 6–1 6–4 8–10 4–6 6–3, Kreuzer bt Zborzil 6–4 6–3 6–2

Semi-final:
Kitson bt Zemla 2–6 6–3 6–2 4–6 6–3, Winslow bt Kreuzer 9–7 7–5 6–1

Final:
Winslow (Gold) bt Kitson (Silver) 7–5 4–6 10–8 8–6

Third Place Play-off:
Kreuzer (Bronze) bt Zemla 6–2 3–6 6–3 6–1

Ladies' Singles – First Round:
Dora Koring (GER) bt Sigrid Fick (SWE) 7–5 6–3, Valborg Bjurstedt (NOR) bt Micken Rieck (GER) w.o., Margarete Cederschoild (SWE) bt Ellen Brusewitz (SWE) 8–6 8–6, Marguerite Broquedis (FRA) bt Princess J. de Lobowicz (BOH) w.o.

Quarter-final:

Edit Arnheim (SWE) bt Annie Holmstrom (SWE) 4–6 6–4 6–1, Dora Koring bt Valborg Bjurstedt w.o., Marguerite Broquedis bt Margarete Cederschoild 6–1 6–4, Margrethe Bjurstedt (NOR) bt Gertrud Kaminski (GER) w.o.

Semi-final:

Dora Koring bt Edit Arnheim 6–4 6–3, Marguerite Broquedis bt Margrethe Bjurstedt 6–3 2–6 6–4

Final:

Marguerite Broquedis (Gold) bt Dora Koring (Silver) 4–6 6–3 6–4

Third Place Play-off:

Margrethe Bjurstedt (Bronze) bt Edit Arnheim 6–2 6–2

Men's Doubles – First Round:

Heinrich Schomburgk & Otto von Muller (GER) bt Leo von Barath & Aurel von Kelemen (HUN) 6–0 6–0 6–2, Albert Canet & Eduard Meny de Marangue (FRA) bt Daniel Lawton & Jean-Pierre Samazeuilh (FRA) w.o., Aleksandr Alenitzyn & Count Mikhail Soumarakoff-Elston (RUS) bt Jean-Francois Blanchy & J.Montariol (FRA) w.o., V.G. Hansen & Leif Rovsing (DEN) bt Karel Ardelt & K. Vodl (BOH) w.o., Curt Benckert & Wollmar Bostrom (SWE) bt Otto Froitzheim & Oskar Kreuzer (GER) w.o., Adolf Hammacher & Paul Lindpaintner (GER) bt P. Gyula & Odon Schmid (HUN) w.o., Ludwig Salm & H. Planner von Plaun (AUT) bt Carl Kempe & Gunnar Setterwall (SWE) w.o., Arthur Zborzil & Felix Piepes (AUT) bt Herman Bjorklund & Trygve Smith (NOR) 6–0 6–2 6–0, Aage Madsen & Axel Thayssen (DEN) bt Bohuslav Hyks & Josef Sebek (BOH) 6–3 6–4 6–4, Carl Nylen & Charles Wennergren (SWE) bt Paul Segner & Ede Toth (HUN) w.o., Bela von Kehrling & Jeno Zsigmondy (HUN) bt Karel Fuchs & Jaromir Zeman (BOH) 3–6 6–1 6–4 6–4, Harold Kitson & Charles Winslow (RSA) bt Jorgen Arenholdt & Vagn Ingerslev (DEN) 6–4 6–1 6–4, Jaroslav Just & Ladislav Zemla (BOH) bt Bjame Angell & Noble Stibolt (NOR) 6–1 6–2 6–0, Conrad Langaard & Richard Peterson (NOR) bt Rudolf Bertrand & Kurt von Wessely (AUT) w.o., Luis Heyden & Robert Spies (GER) bt Thorsten Gronfors & Frans Moller (SWE) 3–6 6–4 6–2 6–1

Second Round:

Canet & Meny de Marangue bt Schomburgk & von Muller 6–8 6–3 6–2 6–3, Alenitzyn & Soumarokoff bt Hansen & Rovsing 2–6 6–3 7–5 6–3, Benckert & Bostrom bt Hammacher & Lindpaintner w.o., Piepes & Zborzil (AUT) bt Salm & von Plaun w.o., Nylen & Wennergren bt Madsen & Thayssen 6–1 6–2 6–4, Kitson & Winslow bt von Kehrling & Zsegmondy 6–3 6–3 7–9 6–2, Just & Zemla bt Langaard & Petersen 6–1 6–2 6–4, Heyden & Spies bt O. Fredriksen & E.P. Frigast (DEN) 6–2 7–5 6–1

Quarter-final:

Canet & Meny de Marangue bt Alenitzyn & Soumarokoff 6–8 6–3 6–2 6–3, Piepes & Zborzil bt Benckert & Bostrom 6–3 4–6 6–1 6–1, Kitson & Winslow bt Nylen & Wennergren 6–3 7–5 6–1, Just & Zemla bt Heyden & Spies 6–0 8–6 6–4

Semi-final:

Piepes & Zborzil bt Canet & Meny de Marangue 7–5 3–6 10–8 10–8, Kitson & Winslow bt Just & Zemla 4–6 6–1 7–5 6–4

Final:

Kitson & Winslow (Gold) bt Piepes & Zborzil (Silver) 4–6 6–1 6–2 6–2

Third Place Play-off:

Canet & Meny de Marangue (Bronze) bt Just & Zemla 13–11 6–3 8–6

Mixed Doubles – First Round:

Albert Canet & Marguerite Broquedis (FRA) bt Carl Nylen & Edit Arnheim (SWE) 6–2 6–4, Jaroslav Just & Princess J.M. Lobkowicz (BOH) bt A. Kubes & J. Kubesova (BOH) w.o., Heinrich Schomburgk & Dora Koring (GER) bt Trygve Smith & Valborg Bjurstedt (NOR) w.o., Gunnar Setterwall & Sigrid Fick (SWE) bt Josef Sebek & A. Sebkova (BOH) w.o., Thorsten Gronfors & A. Holmstrom (SWE) bt Conrad Langaard & Margrethe Bjurstedt (NOR) 6–4 4–6 7–5

Quarter-final:

Canet & Marguerite Broquedis bt Just & Princess Lobkowicz w.o., Schomburgk & Dora Koring bt Carl Kempe & Margarete Cederschiold (SWE) w.o., Oskar Kreuzer & Micken Rieck (GER) bt O. von Muller & Gertrud Kaminski (GER) w.o., Setterwall & Sigrid Fick bt Gronfors & A. Holmstrom 8–6 10–8

Semi-final:

Schomburgk & Dora Koring bt Canet & Marguerite Broquedis 6–2 6–3, Setterwall & Sigrid Fick bt Kreuzer & Micken Rieck w.o.

Final:

Schomburgk & Dora Koring (Gold) bt Setterwall & Sigrid Fick (Silver) 6–4 6–0

Third Place Play-off:

Canet & Marguerite Broquedis (Bronze) w.o.

1920 – Antwerp

Beerschot Tennis Club, 15–24 August

Men's Singles – First Round:

Eduardo Flaquer (ESP) bt Albert Lindquist (SWE) 0–6 6–2 6–3 6–2, Mino Balbi di Robecco (ITA) bt Gerald Patterson (AUS) w.o., Karel Ardelt (TCH) bt L. Nypels (HOL) w.o., Alfred Beamish (BRI) bt. Otto Wojek (TCH) 6–1 6–3 6–4, Manuel Alonso-Areyzaga (ESP) bt Jaroslav Just (TCH) 6–3 2–6 6–0 6–2, Maxwell Woosnam (BRI) bt Frans Moller (SWE) 3–6 6–1 6–3 6–3, Carl-Erik von Braun (SWE) bt Alberto Bonacossa (ITA) 4–6 6–1 7–5 6–2, Albert Lammens (BEL) bt Hans Syz (SUI) 6–3 6–4 3–6 7–5, Ichiya Kumagae (JPN) bt Jose-Maria Alonso-Areyzaga (ESP) 7–5 6–3 6–2, Victor de Laveleye (BEL) bt Conrad Langaard (NOR) 6–2 2–6 6–3 6–3, George Dodd (RSA) bt Jean-Francois Blanchy (FRA) 2–6 6–2 6–1 9–7, Maxime Decugis (FRA) bt Brian Norton (RSA) 6–4 12–10 2–6 8–6

Second Round:

Charles Simon (SUI) bt Enrique de Satrustequi (ESP) 3–6 8–6 6–2 6–8 6–2, Sune Malmstrom (SWE) bt Leonidas Zemla (TCH) 4–6 6–2 6–3 7–5, Louis Raymond (RSA) bt Maurice van den Bemden (BEL) 7–5 6–1 4–6 6–1, Jacques Brugnon (FRA) bt Alberto Chiesa (SUI) 6–4 7–5 6–4, Noel Turnbull (BRI) bt J. Scholler (SUI) w.o., Balbi di Robecco bt Flaquer 6–2 6–4 6–1, Beamish bt Ardelt 6–2 6–4 6–3, M. Alonso-Areyzaga bt Woosnam 6–1 2–6 6–1 6–3, Lammens bt von Braun 6–2 6–1 6–1, Kumagae bt de Laveleye 6–0 6–1 6–0, Dodd bt Decugis 6–2 6–1 6–1, Seiichiro Kashio (JPN) bt Erik Tegner (DEN) 6–3 6–1 6–2, Cesare Colombo (ITA) bt Jack Nielson (NOR) 6–2 6–3 6–1, Gordon Lowe (BRI) bt Augustos Zerlandi (GRE) 14–12 8–10 5–7 6–4 6–4, Jean Washer (BEL) bt Ronald Thomas (AUS) 6–1 6–3 3–6 6–4, Charles Winslow (RSA) bt Jean-Pierre Samazeuilh (FRA) 7–5 2–6 6–3 6–2

Third Round:

Malmstrom bt Simon 6–3 6–2 6–0, Raymond bt Brugnon 3–6 6–2 6–0 6–1, Turnbull bt Balbi di Robecco 3–6 6–3 6–0 6–8 6–2, Alonso-Areyzaga bt Beamish 6–1 5–7 5–7 6–3 6–1, Kumagae bt Lammens 7–5 6–1 6–4, Dodd bt Kashio 6–3 4–6 6–2 3–6 6–1, Lowe bt Colombo 6–4 6–0 2–6 7–5, Winslow bt Washer 8–6 6–4 6–1

Quarter-final:

Raymond bt Malmstrom 6–3 6–1 6–1, Turnbull bt Alonso-Areyzaga 0–6 7–5 4–6 6–3 7–5, Kumagae bt Dodd 7–5 6–1 6–1, Winslow bt Lowe 6–4 3–6 6–4 4–6 6–2

Semi-final:

Raymond bt Turnbull 2–6 1–6 6–2 6–2 6–1, Kumagae bt Winslow 6–2 6–2 6–2

Final:

Raymond (Gold) bt Kumagae (Silver) 5–7 6–4 7–5 6–4

Third Place Play-off:

Winslow (Bronze) bt Turnbull w.o.

Ladies' Singles – First Round:

Elsebeth Brehm (DEN) bt Marthe Dupont (BEL) 6–3 6–4, Winifred McNair (BRI) bt Francesca Subirana (ESP) w.o., Suzanne Lenglen (FRA) bt Marie Storms (BEL) 6–0 6–0, Rosetta Gagliardi (ITA) bt Maggie Lindberg (SWE) 6–0 retd, Kathleen McKane (BRI) bt Jeanne Vaussard (FRA) 6–4 6–4

Second Round:

Anne de Borman (BEL) bt Milada Skrobkova (TCH) w.o., Sigrid Fick (SWE) bt Caro Dahl (NOR) 7–5 6–2, Lily Stromberg (SWE) bt Elsebeth Brehm 7–5 6–3, Suzanne Lenglen bt Winifred McNair 6–0 6–0, Kathleen McKane bt Rosetta Gagliardi 6–1 1–6 6–2, Elisabeth d'Ayen (FRA) bt Amoury Folmer-Hansen(DEN) 6–2 6–3, Fernande Arendt (BEL) bt Giulia Ferelli (ITA) w.o., Dorothy Holman (BRI) bt Geraldine Beamish (BRI) 8–6 6–2

Quarter-final:

Sigrid Fick bt Anne de Borman 6–4 8–6, Suzanne Lenglen bt Lily Stromberg 6–0 6–0, Kathleen McKane bt Elisabeth d'Ayen 6–2 6–3, Dorothy Holman bt Elisabeth Arendt 6–2 6–3

Semi-final:

Suzanne Lenglen bt Sigrid Fick 6–0 6–1, Dorothy Holman bt Kathleen McKane w.o.

Final:

Suzanne Lenglen (Gold) bt Dorothy Holman (Silver) 6–3 6–0

Third Place Play-off:

Kathleen McKane (Bronze) bt Sigrid Fick 6–2 6–0

Men's Doubles – First Round:

Conrad Langaard & Jack Nielsen (NOR) bt Alberto Chiesa & J. Scholler (SUI) w.o., Albert Lammens & Jean Washer (BEL) bt Sume Malstrom & Carl-Erik von Braun (SWE) 6–2 6–4 6–3, Seiichiro Kashio & Ichiya Kumagae (JPN) bt Cesare Colombo & Alberto

Suzzl (ITA) w.o.,Karel Ardelt & Ladislav Zemla (TCH) bt Andre Laloux & Rene Laloux (BEL) 6–2 6–4 6–4, Brian Norton & Louis Raymond (RSA) bt Jose-Maria Alonso-Areyzaga & Manuel Alonso-Areyzaga (ESP) 6–3 7–5 6–0, Daniel Lawton & Jean-Pierre Samazeuilh (FRA) bt Eugene Grisar & Maurice van den Bemden (BEL) 6–4 6–2 6–3, Cecil Blackbeard & George Dodd (RSA) bt Alfred Beamish & Gordon Lowe (BRI) 6–1 10–8 6–3, Eduardo Flaquer & Enrique de Satrustegui (ESP) bt Stephan Halot & Victor de Laveleye (BEL) 7–5 6–3 1–6 6–4, Pierre Albarran & Maxime Decugis (FRA) bt J. Bures & J. Popelka (TCH) w.o., Frantisek Tyr & Otti Wojek (TCH) bt Gerald Patterson & Ronald Thomas (AUS) w.o.

Second Round:

Jean-Francois Blanchy & Jacques Brugnon (FRA) bt Bohuslav Hyks & Jaroslav Just (TCH) 6–1 6–2 6–4, Langaard & Nielsen bt Olle Andersson & Frans Moller (SWE) 6–1 6–8 6–1 6–4, Kashio & Kumagae bt Lammens & Washer 6–1 6–4 6–4, Norton & Raymond bt Ardelt & Zemla 6–1 8–6 8–6, Blackbeard & Dodd bt Lawton & Samazeuilh 6–3 6–0 9–7, Albarran & Decugis bt Flaquer & Satrustegui 6–2 3–6 6–0 6–4, Noel Turnbull & Maxwell Woosnam (BRI) bt Tyr & Woffek 6–1 6–2 6–3, Mino Balbi Di Robecco & Cesare Colombo (ITA) bt Charles Simon & Hans Syz (SWI) 6–3 7–5 3–6 6–4

Quarter-final:

Blanchy & Brugnon bt Langaard & Nielsen 6–1 6–1 6–3, Kashio & Kumagae bt Norton & Raymond 6–3 6–2 4–6 6–3, Albarran & Decugis bt Blackbeard & Dodd 3–6 6–4 6–4 7–5, Turnbull & Woosnam bt Balbi & Colombo 6–2 6–8 6–1 6–3

Semi-final:

Kashio & Kumagae bt Blanchy & Brugnon 6–4 4–6 6–3 6–1, Turnbull & Woosnam bt Albarran & Decugis 4–6 6–4 6–3 10–8

Final:

Turnbull & Woosnam (Gold) bt Kashio & Kumagae (Silver) 6–2 5–7 7–5 7–5

Third Place Play-off:

Albarran & Decugis (Bronze) bt Blanchy & Brugnon w.o.

Ladies' Doubles – First Round:

J Chaudoir & Marthe Dupont (BEL) bt Jones & Laurenan (BEL) 6–3 2–6 6–2

Quarter-final:

Elisabeth d'Ayen and Suzanne Lenglen (FRA) bt Sigrid Fick & Lily Stromberg (SWE) 6–4 6–3, Kathleen McKane & Winifred McNair (BRI) bt J. Chaudoir & Marthe Dupont

6–2 7–5, Geraldine Beamish & Dorothy Holman (BRI) bt Anne de Borman & Lucienne Tschagenny (BEL) 6–2 6–4, Fernande Arendt & Marie Storms (BEL) bt Elsebeth Brehm & Amoury Folmer-Hansen (DEN) 6–1 6–1

Semi-final:
Kathleen McKane & Winifred McNair bt Elisabeth d'Ayen & Suzanne Lenglen 2–6 6–3 8–6, Geraldine Beamish & Dorothy Holman bt Fernande Arendt & Marie Storms 6–4 6–3

Final:
Kathleen McKane & Winifred McNair (Gold) bt Geraldine Beamish & Dorothy Holman (Silver) 8–6 6–4

Third Place Play-off:
Elisabeth d'Ayen & Suzanne Lenglen (Bronze) bt Fernande Arendt & Marie Storms w.o.

Mixed Doubles – First Round:
Albert Lammens & J.Chaudoir (BEL) bt Manuel Alonso & Francesca Subarina (ESP) w.o., Maxime Decugis & Suzanne Lenglen (FRA) bt Jose-Maria Alonso Areyzaga & Maria Rospide (ESP) w.o., Alfred Beamish & Geraldine Beamish (BRI) bt Noel Turnbull & Winifred McNair (BRI) 4–6 6–4 7–5, Pierre Hirsch & Elisabeth d'Ayen (FRA) bt Albert Lindqvist & Sigrid Fick (SWE) 7–5 8–6, Maxwell Woosnam & Kathleen McKane (BRI) bt Gordon Lowe & Dorothy Holman (BRI) 6–4 6–2

Second Round:
Erik Tegner & Amoury Folmer-Hansen (DEN) bt Jean Washer & Anne de Borman (BEL) 4–6 8–6 6–3, Sune Malmstrom & Lily Stromberg bt Olle Andersson & Maggie Lindberg (SWE) w.o., Lammens & J. Chaudoir bt Jean-Francois Blancy & Jeanne Vaussard (FRA) 4–6 7–5 6–3, Decugis & Suzanne Lenglen bt Beamish & Geraldine Beamish 6–2 6–0, Woosnam & Kathleen McKane bt Hirsch & Elisabeth d'Ayen 6–4 6–2, Conrad Langaard & Caro Dahl (NOR) bt Mino Balbi Di-Robecco & Giulia Ferelli (ITA) w.o., Ladislav Zemla & Milada Skrobkova (TCH) bt Francois Laloux & Marthe Dupont (BEL) 7–5 6–4, Stephan Halot & Marie Storms (BEL) bt Cesare Colombo & Rosetta Gagliardi (ITA) 8–6 6–3

Quarter-final:
Tegner & Amoury Folmer-Hansen bt Malmstrom & Lily Stromberg 0–6 6–1 6–2, Decugis & Suzanne Lenglen bt Lammens & J. Chaudoir 3–6 6–1 6–1, Woosnam & Kathleen McKane bt Langaard & Caro Dalh w.o., Zemla & Milada Skrobkova bt Halot & Marie Storms 7–5 6–3

Semi-final:

Decugis & Suzanne Lenglen bt Tegner & Amoury Folmer-Hansen 6–0 6–1, Woosnam & Kathleen McKane bt Zemla & Milada Skrobkova 9–7 6–3

Final:

Decugis & Suzanne Lenglen (Gold) bt Woosnam & Kathleen McKane (Silver) 6–4 6–2

Third Place Play-off:

Zemla & Milada Skrobkova (Bronze) bt Tegner & Amoury Folmer-Hansen 8–6 6–4

(Referee: Paul de Borman, BEL)

1924 – Paris

Colombes, 13–20 July

Men's Singles – First Round:

Henning Muller (SWE) bt L. Wei (CHN) w.o., Algernon Kingscote (GBR) bt Friedrich von Rohrer (TCH) 6–3 6–4 4–6 3–6 6–3, Jean Borotra (FRA) bt A. Honda (JPN) 6–3 6–3 7–5, Luis Torralva-Ponsa (CHI) bt Antonio Casanovas (POR) w.o., Jack Nielsen (NOR) bt Ivan Balas (YUG) w.o., Erik Tegner (DEN) bt Aurel Kelemen (HUN) 6–4 6–4 6–1, Maurice Ferrier (SUI) bt Ernst Schybergson (FIN) 6–4 6–4 6–3, Sydney Jacob (IND) bt Raidmundo Morales-Marques (ESP) 6–2 6–4 6–4, Stephan Halot (BEL) bt W.G. Ireland (IRL) 8–6 6–1 6–4, Aubrey Willard (AUS) bt Louis Raymond (RSA) 2–6 6–4 6–4 2–6 6–4, Christiaan van Lennep (HOL) bt Sze-Cheung Wu (CHN) w.o., Americo-Hector Cattaruzza (ARG) bt Panagiotis Papadopoulos (GRE) 7–5 7–5 6–1, Watson Washburn (USA) bt Clemente Serventi (ITA) 6–4 6–3 6–4, Gheorghe Lupu (ROM) bt Felix del Canto (MEX) 6–4 6–4 6–4, Arturo Hortal (ARG) bt Rodrigo Castro-Pereira (POR) 6–1 6–4 6–2, Francis Hunter (USA) bt Arne Grahm (FIN) 6–3 6–0 6–2, Eduardo Flaquer (ESP) bt Domingo Torralva-Ponsa (CHI) 6–4 3–6 6–0 6–0, Jean Washer (BEL) bt Nicolae Misha (ROM) 6–2 6–4 6–2, Augustos Zerlendi (GRE) bt Sze-Kwang Ng (CHN) w.o., Athar-Ali Fyzee (IND) bt Conrad Langaard (NOR) 6–4 6–2 6–3, Pablo Debran (SUI) bt D'Arcy McCrea (IRL) 6–4 6–4 6–0, Uberto de Morpurgo (ITA) bt M.C. Wolff (LUX) 6–1 6–1 6–0, Gerard Leembruggen (HOL) bt Hooi-Hye Khoo (CHN) w.o., Brian Gilbert (GBR) bt A. Durdjenski (YUG) 8–6 6–1 2–6 6–2, J. Bayley (AUS) bt Boris Schildt (FIN) 6–1 6–3 6–4, E. Bache (DEN) bt Mariano Lozano-Alatorre (MEX) 2–6 8–6 9–7 6–4, Maurice Cousin

(FRA) bt Jack Condon (RSA) 4–6 6–3 6–2 6–4, Charles Wennergren (SWE) bt Kalman Kirchmayer (HUN) 8–6 6–2 6–4

Second Round:

Pavel Macenauer (TCH) bt Albert Lammens (BEL) 6–0 6–1 6–0, Richard Williams (USA) bt Saeed-Mohamed Hadi (IND) 6–0 6–2 6–1, Bela von Kehrling (HUN) bt A. Roman (ROM) 6–1 6–1 6–2, Charles Aeschliman (SUI) bt Carlos Dumas (ARG) 7–5 6–4 6–0, Hendrik Timmer (HOL) bt Einer Ulrich (DEN) 6–3 2–6 1–6 6–2 6–3, Masanosuke Fukuda (JPN) bt Patrick Wheatley (GBR) 6–2 6–4 6–3, Ivie Richardson (RSA) bt Francisco Sindreu (ESP) 6–4 6–4 6–3, Henri Cochet (FRA) bt Cesare Colombo (ITA) w.o., Runar Granholm (FIN) bt Norman Brookes (AUS) w.o., Kingscote bt Muller 6–2 7–5 6–2, Borotra bt Torralva 9–7 7–5 7–5, Nielsen bt Tegner 5–7 6–4 6–4 9–7, Jacob bt Ferrier 5–7 6–3 6–1 6–1, Willard bt Halot 8–6 6–2 6–2, van Lennep bt Cattaruzza 6–3 6–3 6–1, Washburn bt Luppu 6–2 6–3 6–4, Hunter bt Hortal 6–3 6–3 6–1, Washer bt Flaquer 6–1 6–4 7–5, Zerlendi bt Fyzee 6–3 1–6 6–3 6–4, de Morpurgo bt Debran 6–2 6–3 6–3, Gilbert bt Leembruggen 6–1 12–10 6–1, Bayley bt Bache 6–2 6–1 6–2, Cousin bt Wennergren 6–4 6–3 6–2, Takeichi Harada (JPN) bt Ladislav Zemla (TCH) 6–3 3–6 6–2 6–2, Rene Lacoste (FRA) bt Lajos Goncz (HUN) 6–0 6–0 6–1, Jan Kozeluh (TCH) bt Sunao Okamoto (JPN) 4–6 7–5 10–8 4–6 6–4, Patrick Spence (RSA) bt Hans Syz (SUI) 6–3 6–2 7–5, Maxwell Woosnam (GBR) bt Bjorn Thalbitzer (DEN) 6–1 6–1 6–2, Vincent Richards (USA) bt Victor de Laveleye (BEL) 6–2 6–4 6–0, Manuel Alonso-Areyzaga (ESP) bt Riccardo Sabbadini (ITA) w.o., Guillermo Robson (ARG) bt Misu Stern (ROM) w.o.,

Third Round:

Williams bt Macenauer 6–2 4–6 3–6 6–2 6–1, von Kehrling bt Aeschliman 4–6 6–8 7–5 6–2 6–3, Fukuda bt Timmer 8–6 6–4 5–7 6–4, Cochet bt Richardson 6–3 6–3 6–4, Kingscote bt Granholm 6–2 6–0 6–0, Borotra bt Nielsen 6–0 6–1 6–2, Jacob bt Willard 6–1 6–2 6–8 2–6 6–3, Washburn bt van Lennep 2–6 6–1 6–1 6–2, Washer bt Hunter 2–6 1–6 6–2 6–1 6–4, de Morpurgo bt Zerlendi 6–0 6–2 6–4, Gilbert bt Bayley 7–5 9–7 6–1, Spence bt Woosnam 4–6 10–8 6–3 3–6 6–3, Richards bt Sleem 8–6 2–6 6–4 4–6 6–2, M. Alonso bt Robson 7–9 6–4 6–0 6–4

Fourth Round:

Williams bt von Kehrling 6–4 3–6 6–3 4–6 6–3, Cochet bt Fukuda 6–2 6–1 6–3, Borotra bt Kingscote 6–1 6–3 6–1, Jacob bt Washburn 6–1 6–4 8–10 6–2, de Morpurgo bt Washer 2–6 6–4 1–6 6–2 8–6, Harada bt Gilbert 10–8 2–6 11–9 6–2, Lacoste bt Spence 6–2 6–0 6–1, Richards bt Alonso 7–5 10–8 2–6 10–8

Quarter-final:

Cochet bt Williams 5–7 6–3 6–2 6–4, Borotra bt Jacob 4–6 6–4 7–5 6–3, de Morpurgo bt Harada 6–4 6–1 6–1, Richards bt Lacoste 6–3 3–6 6–1 6–1

Semi-final:

Cochet bt Borotra 6–2 5–7 6–2 6–3, Richards bt de Morpurgo 6–3 3–6 6–1 6–4

Final:

Richards (Gold) bt Cochet (Silver) 6–4 6–4 5–7 4–6 6–2

Third Place Play-off:

de Morpurgo (Bronze) bt Borotra 1–6 6–1 8–6 4–6 7–5

Ladies' Singles – First Round:

Germaine Golding (FRA) bt Lily von Essen (SWE) 6–4 6–2, Ilona Peteri (HUN) bt A. Janssens (BEL) 6–4 6–1, Phyllis Covell (GBR) bt Hilda Wallis (IRE) 3–6 6–0 6–2, Rosetta Gagliardi (ITA) bt Elsebeth Brehm (DEN) 6–0 6–2, Phoebe Blair-White (IRE) bt Rita Le Gallais (LUX) w.o., Dorothy Shepherd- Barron (GBR) bt Isabel Fonrodona (ESP) w.o.

Second Round:

Helen Wills (USA) bt Maria-Luisa Marnet (ESP) w.o., Phyllis Satterthwaite (GBR) bt Maria Forlanini (ITA) w.o., Kornelia Bouman (NED) bt Marthe Dupont (BEL) 8–6 6–4, Margrethe Mallory (USA) bt Jeanne Vassard (FRA) 6–2 6–3, N.Polley (IND) bt Lena Valaroiti-Scaramanga (GRE) 1–6 6–3 6–2, Lili de Alvarez (ESP) bt Lilian Scharman (USA) 6–2 6–2, Germaine Golding bt Paola Bologna (ITA) 6–0 6–3, Phyllis Covell bt Ilona Peteri 6–1 6–3, Rosetta Gagliardi bt Phoebe Blair-White 4–6 7–5 6–2, Dorothy Shepherd-Barron bt Marie Storms (BEL) 6–1 6–1, Eleanor Goss (USA) bt Helene Contostavlos (GRE) w.o., Diddie Vlasto (FRA), bt Caro Dahl (NOR) 6–1 6–0, Rosa Torras (ESP) bt Guilia Perelli (ITA) 6–4 4–6 8–6. Marion Jessup (USA) bt Suzanne Lenglen (FRA) w.o., Sigrid Fick (SWE) bt Medy Krencsey (HUN) w.o., Kathleen McKane (GBR) bt Anne de Borman (BEL) 6–0 6–2

Third Round:

Helen Wills bt Phyllis Satterthwaite 6–1 6–2, Margrethe Mallory bt Kornelia Bouman 9–7 6–0, Lili de Alvarez bt N. Polley 6–0 6–3, Germaine Golding bt Phyllis Covell 6–3 3–6 6–2, Dorothy Shepherd-Barron bt Rosetta Gagliardi 6–1 6–0, Diddie Vlasto bt Eleanor Goss 6–3 2–6 6–4, Marion Jessup bt Rosa Torras 6–2 6–0, Kathleen McKane bt Sigrid Fick 6–1 6–1

Quarter-final:

Helen Wills bt Margrethe Mallory 6–2 6–3, Germaine Golding bt Lili de Alvarez 7–5 6–3, Diddie Vlasto bt Dorothy Shepherd-Barron 6–4 6–2, Kathleen McKane bt Marion Jessup 6–2 6–0

Semi-final:

Helen Wills bt Germaine Golding 6–2 6–1, Diddie Vlasto bt Kathleen McKane 0–6 7–5 6–1

Final:

Helen Wills (Gold) bt Diddie Vlasto (Silver) 6–2 6–2

Third Place Play-off:

Kathleen McKane (Bronze) bt Germaine Golding 5–7 6–3 6–0

Men's Doubles – First Round:

Domingo Torralva-Ponsa & Luis Torralva-Ponsa (CHI) bt Gheorge Luppu & A. Roman (ROM) 7–5 6–2 6–3, Masanosuke Fukuda & A. Honda (JPN) bt Christiaan van Lennep & Hendrik Timmer (NED) 6–4 1–6 6–3 1–6 6–2, Eduardo Flaquer & Raimundo Saprisa (ESP) bt Antonio Casanovas & Rodrigo Castro-Pereira (POR) w.o., Ernst Gottlieb & Friedrich von Rohrer (TCH) bt Leslie Godfree & Maxwell Woosnam (GBR) 6–3 6–4 6–2, Watson Washburn & Richard Williams (USA) bt Lajos Goncz & Kalman Kirchmayer (HUN) 6–1 6–0 6–0, Erik Tegner & Einer Ulrich (DEN) bt Sydney Jacob & Mohammed Salim (IND) 6–3 6–4 4–6 6–4, Pablo Debran & Hans Syz (SUI) bt D'Arcy McCrea & W.G. Ireland (IRE) 4–6 6–2 6–2 1–6 6–4, Charles Aeschliman & Maurice Ferrier (SUI) bt Louis Raymond & Patrick Spence w.o., Jan Kozeluh & Ladislav Zemla (TCH) bt Marinus van der Freen & Gerard Leembruggen (NED) 6–3 6–2 6–3, J.M. Bayley & Aubrey Willard (AUS) bt Bela von Kehrling & Aurel Kelemen (HUN) 6–8 11–9 3–6 6–3 6–2, Francis Hunter & Vincent Richards (USA) bt Nicolae Misu & Misu Stern (ROM) w.o., Jose-Maria Alonso-Areyzaga & Manuel Alonso-Areyzaga (ESP) bt Algernon Kingscote & Patrick Wheatley (GBR) 6–4 6–3 6–1, Takeichi Harada & Sunao Okamoto (JPN) bt E. Bache & Bjorn Thalbitzer (DEN) 6–0 6–0 6–1

Second Round:

Henning Muller & Charles Wennergren (SWE) bt Americo-Hector Cattaruzza & Jorge Williams (ARG) 6–2 6–0 6–3, Runar Granholm & Boris Schildt (FIN) bt G. Sze Kwong & L. Wei (CHN) w.o., Uberto de Morpurgo & Clemente Serventi (ITA) bt Victor de Lavelege & Jean Washer (BEL) 6–4 6–4 7–5, Jacques Brugnon & Henri Cochet (FRA) bt Ivan Balas & A. Durdjensky (YUG) w.o., Jack Condon & Ivie Richardson (RSA) bt Torralva-Ponsa & Torralva-Ponsa 6–2 6–1 4–6 6–2, Flaquer & Saprisa bt Fukuda & Honda 6–2 6–3 6–3, Washburn & Williams bt Gottlieb & von Rohrer 6–3 6–2 6–1, Tegner & Ulrich bt Debran & Syz 3–6 6–0 6–0 6–1, Kozeluh & Zemla bt Aeschliman & Ferrier 6–4 3–6 6–4 6–4, Hunter & Richards bt Bayley & Willard 6–1 6–2 6–2, Alonso-Areyzaga & Alonso-Areyzaga bt Harado & Okamoto 6–4 4–6 6–4 6–4, Panagiotis Papadopoulos & Augustos Zerlendi (GRE) bt Felix Del Canto & V.A. Loyano (MEX) 6–2 6–3 4–6 6–2, Cesare Colombo & Riccardo Sabbadini (ITA) bt Hooi-Hye Khoo & Sze-Chaung (CHN) w.o., Saeed-Mohamed Hadi & D.R. Rutman (IND) bt Conrad Langaard & Jack Nielsen (NOR) 6–2 6–3 6–0, Jean Borotra & Rene Lacoste (FRA) bt Stephan Halot & Albert Lammens (BEL) 6–3 6–0 6–2, Carlos Dumas & Guillermo Robson (ARG) bt Arne Grahn & Ernst Schybergson (FIN) 6–1 6–3 6–0

Third Round:
Muller & Wennergren bt Granholm & Schildt 6–3 6–1 6–4, Brugnon & Cochet bt de Morpurgo & Serventi 6–2 6–4 6–2, Condon & Richardson bt Flaquer & Saprisa 6–2 6–3 6–1, Washburn & Williams bt Tegner & Ulrich 6–4 6–4 12–10, Hunter & Richards bt Kozeluh & Zemla 6–2 6–3 6–4, Alonso-Areyzaga & Alonso-Areyzaga bt Papadopoulos & Zerlendi 6–2 9–7 6–4, Hadi & Rutnam bt Colombo & Sabbadini w.o., Borotra & Lacoste bt Dumas & Robson 6–4 6–1 6–3

Quarter-final:
Brugnon & Cochet bt Muller & Wennergren 6–4 6–1 6–3, Condon & Richardson bt Washburn & Williams 4–6 11–9 4–6 6–4 6–4, Hunter & Richards bt Alonso-Areyzaga & Alonso-Areyzaga 6–4 6–4 6–3, Borotra & Lacoste bt Hadi & Rutnam 6–2 6–2 6–3

Semi-final:
Brugnon & Cochet bt Condon & Richardson 5–7 6–3 7–5 6–2, Hunter & Richards bt Borotra & Lacoste 6–2 6–3 0–6 5–7 6–3

Final:
Hunter & Richards (Gold) bt Brugnon & Cochet (Silver) 4–6 6–2 6–3 2–6 6–3

Third Place Play-off:
Borotra & Lacoste (Bronze) bt Condon & Richardson 6–3 10–8 6–3

Ladies' Doubles – First Round:
Phyllis Covell & Kathleen McKane (GBR) bt Marion Jessup & Eleanor Goss (USA) 6–1 6–2

Second Round:
Rosetta Gagliardi & Guilia Perelli (ITA) bt Helen Contostavlos & Lena Valaroiti-Scaramanga (GRE) w.o., Marguerite Billout & Yvonne Bourgeois (FRA) bt Rosa Torras & Lili De Alvarez (ESP) 4–6 6–3 6–4, Sigrid Fick & Lily Stromberg von Essen (SWE) bt Hilda Wallis & Phoebe Blair-White (IRE) 6–2 5–7 6–2, Phyllis Covell & Kathleen McKane bt Anne de Borman & Marie Storms (BEL) 6–1 6–2, Dorothy Shepherd-Barron & Evelyn Colyer (GBR) bt G. Janssen & Marthe Dupont (BEL) w.o., Germaine Golding & Jeanne Vaussard (FRA) bt Maria Forlanini & Paola Bologna (ITA) w.o., Hazel Wightman & Helen Wills (USA) bt Margrethe Mallory & Caro Dahl (NOR) w.o. Ilona Peteri & Medy Krencsey (HUN) bt Maria-Luisa Marnet & Isabel Fonrodona (ESP) w.o.

Quarter-final:
Marguerite Billout & Yvonne Bourgeois bt Rosetta Gagliardi & Guilia Perelli 7–5 6–4, Phyllis Covell & Kathleen McKane bt Sigrid Fick & Lily Stromberg von Essen 6–2 6–3,

Dorothy Shepherd-Barron & Evelyn Colyer bt Germaine Golding & Jeanne Vaussard 6–2 6–2, Hazel Wightman & Helen Wills bt Ilona Peteri & Medy Krencsy w.o.

Semi-final:
Phyllis Covell & Kathleen McKane bt Marguerite Billout & Yvonne Bourgeois 6–2 6–2, Hazel Wightman & Helen Wills bt Dorothy Shepherd-Barron & Evleyn Colyer 6–3 1–6 7–5

Final:
Hazel Wightman & Helen Wills (Gold) bt Phyllis Covell & Kathleen McKane (Silver) 7–5 8–6

Third Place Play-off:
Dorothy Shepherd-Barron & Evelyn Colyer (Bronze) bt Marguerite Billout & Yvonne Bourgeois 6–1 6–2

Mixed Doubles – First Round:
Vincent Richards & Marion Jessup (USA) bt Jean Borotra & Marguerite Billout (FRA) 1–6 6–3 6–3, Jack Nielsen & Margrethe Mallory (NOR) bt Jean Washer & Marthe Dupont (BEL) 1–6 6–3 6–3, Leslie Godfree & Phyllis Covell (GBR) bt W.G. Ireland & Phoebe Blair-White (IRE) 6–2 6–4, Panagiotis Papadopoulos & Helene Contostavlos (GRE) bt C. Wolff & Rita le Gallais (LUX) w.o., Aurel Kelemen & Ilona Peteri (HUN) bt Riccardo Sabbadini & Rosetta Gagliardi (ITA) w.o., Hendrik Timmer & Kornelia Bouman (HOL) bt Charles Wennergren & Lily Stromberg von Essen (SWE) 6–4 6–4, Stephan Halot & Anne de Borman (BEL) bt Erik Tegner & Elsebeth Brehm (DEN) 6–2 6–4, Henning Muller & Sigrid Fick (SWE) bt Bela von Kehrling & Medy Krencsey (HUN) w.o., Augustos Zerlendi & Lena Valaroiti Scaramanga (GRE) bt Conrad Langaard & Caro Dahl (NOR) 4–6 6–2 6–2, Richard Williams & Hazel Wightman (USA) bt Henri Cochet & Suzanne Lenglen (FRA) w.o., Uberto de Morpurgo & Guilia Perelli (ITA) bt Raimundo Saprisa & Rosa Torras (ESP) 6–3 10–8

Second Round:
Eduardo Flaquer & Lili de Alvarez (ESP) bt Mohammed Salim & M. Tata (IND) w.o., Richards & Marion Jessup bt Nielsen & Margrethe Mallory 6–3 6–2, Godfree & Phyllis Covell bt Papadopoulos & Helene Contostavlos w.o., Timmer & Kornelia Bouman bt Keleman & Ilona Peteri 6–4 6–2, Muller & Sigrid Fick bt Halot & Anne de Borman 6–0 6–3, Williams & Hazel Wightman bt Zerlendi & Lena Valaroiti Scaramanga 6–2 6–1, Brian Gilbert & Kathleen McKane (GBR) bt de Morpurgo & Guilia Perelli 9–7 1–6 7–5, D'Arcy McCrea & Hilda Wallis (IRE) bt Sydney Jacob & N. Polley (IND) 9–7 4–6 9–7

Quarter-final:
Richards & Marion Jessup bt Flaquer & Lili de Alvarez 6–3 6–1, Timmer & Kornelia Bouman bt Godfree & Phyllis Covell 6–1 7–5, Williams & Hazel Wightman bt Muller & Sigrid Fick 8–6 6–2, Gilbert & Kathleen McKane bt McCrea & Hilda Wallis 6–1 7–5

Semi-final:
Richards & Marion Jessup bt Timmer & Kornelia Bouman 6–3 6–0, Williams & Hazel Wightman bt Gilbert & Kathleen McKane 2–6 8–6 6–1

Final:
Williams & Hazel Wightman (Gold) bt Richards & Marion Jessup (Silver) 6–2 6–3

Third Place Play-off:
Timmer & Kornelia Bouman (Bronze) bt Gilbert & Kathleen McKane w.o.

(Referee: Pierre Gillou, FRA)

1988 – Seoul

Olympic Park, 19 September-2 October

Men's Singles – First Round:
Stefan Edberg (SWE)(1) bt Horst Skoff (AUT)(WC) 7–6(7–3) 6–2 6–3, Augustin Moreno (MEX) bt Toshihisa Tsuchihashi (JAP) 7–6(7–5) 6–2 6–4, Zeesham Ali (IND) bt Victor Caballero (PAR) 6–3 6–2 6–4, Jakob Hlasek (SUI)(10) bt Stephen Alger (BER) 6–3 6–4 6–2, Grant Connell (CAN) bt John Fitzgerald (AUS) (14) 6–4 4–6 6–2 6–2, Javier Sancez (ESP) bt Sadiq Abdullah (ALG) 6–2 7–5 6–3, Paolo Cane (ITA) bt Milan Srejber (TCH) 6–3 7–6(7–4) 4–6 6–3, Emilio Sanchez (ESP)(6) bt Shuzo Matsuoka (JAP) 6–3 6–4 6–3, Miloslav Mecir (TCH)(3) bt Eric Jelen (FRG) 5–7 6–1 6–2 7–6(8–6), Jeremy Bates (GBR) bt Gilad Bloom (ISR) 4–6 6–4 2–6 6–2 9–7, Guy Forget (FRA) bt Omar Camporese (ITA) 6–2 6–0 6–3, Slobodan Zivojinovic (YUG)(15) bt Morton Christensen (DEN) 7–5 6–2 6–4, Leonardo Lavalle (MEX) bt Ronald Agenor (HAI)(11)(WC) 3–6 6–3 6–2 2–1 retd, Sergio Casal (ESP) bt Mark Gurr (ZIM) 6–2 6–3 6–1, Tony Mmoh (NIG)bt Wojcieh Kowalski (POL) 6–2 6–4 6–4, Michel Schapers (NED) bt Andrei Chesnokov (URS)(8)(WC) 6–3 5–7 6–0 6–2, Bradley Gilbert (USA) (5)(WC) bt Michael Tauson (DEN) 6–2 1–6 6–1 6–2, Andrei Cherkasov (URS) bt Hugo Chapacu (PAR) 6–0 6–0 6–1, Robert Seguso (USA) bt Nduka Odizor (NIG)(WC) 6–4

6–2 6–3. Darren Cahill (AUS)(9) bt Alexander Antonitsch (AUT) 6–2 6–4 6–7(2–7) 6–2, Martin Jaite (ARG)(13) bt Chris Pridham (CAN) 6–1 6–3 6–2, Javier Frana (ARG) bt Sharar Perkiss (ISR) 6–2 4–6 6–4 6–4, Bong-Soo Kim (KOR) bt George Kalovelonis (GRE) 7–5 3–6 6–2 6–7(3–7) 6–3, Henri Leconte (FRA)(4) bt Vijay Amritraj (IND) 4–6 6–4 6–4 3–6 6–3, Anders Jarryd (SWE)(7)(WC) bt Martin Lauvendeau (CAN) 7–6(10–8) 4–6 7–5 7–5, Andrew Castle (GBR) bt Clement N'Goran (CIV) 6–7(7–9) 3–6 6–2 7–6(7–3) 7–5, Carl-Uwe Steeb (FRG) bt Alexander Volkov (URS) 7–5 6–4 6–3, Wally Masur (AUS) bt Luiz Mattar (BRA)(16) 6–4 6–4 4–6 6–7(7–9) 6–4, Amos Mansdorf (ISR)(12) bt Jin-Sun Yoo (KOR) 6–2 6–4 7–5, Kelly Evernden (NZL) bt Goran Ivanisevic (YUG) 7–6(7–0) 6–3 6–3, Diego Nargiso (ITA) bt Francisco Maciel (MEX) 4–6 2–6 7–6(7–2) 7–6(7–3) 8–6, Timothy Mayotte (USA)(2) bt Dong-Wook Song(KOR) 6–3 6–3 6–4

Second Round:

Edberg(1) bt Moreno 6–2 7–6(7–2) 6–0, Hlasek(10) bt Ali 6–4 7–5 7–5, J. Sanchez bt Connell 6–4 6–4 6–2, Cane bt E. Sanchez(6) 7–5 6–3 6–7(4–7) 6–4, Mecir(3) bt Bates 6–3 4–6 6–1 6–4, Forget bt Zivojinovic(15) 7–5 7–6(8–6) 6–2, Casal bt Lavalle 6–3 6–4 7–6(7–2), Schapers bt Mmoh 4–6 6–3 6–1 4–6 6–1, Gilbert(5) bt Cherkasov 6–4 1–6 6–1 6–2, Seguso bt Cahill(9) 6–3 7–6(7–3) 6–7(8–10) 6–2, Jaite(13) bt Frana 6–2 6–4 6–2, Kim bt Leconte(4) 4–6 7–5 6–3 3–6 7–5, Jarryd(7) bt Castle 6–0 6–3 6–1, Steeb bt Masur 6–3 5–7 6–3 1–6 7–5, Mansdorf(12) bt Evernden 6–4 3–6 6–1 7–5, Mayotte(2) bt Nargiso 2–6 6–2 6–4 6–0

Third Round:

Edberg(1) bt Hlasek(10) 6–4 7–5 7–5, Cane bt J. Sanchez 7–6(7–1) 6–1 6–2, Mecir(3) bt Forget 7–6(7–1) 6–3 7–5, Schapers bt Casal 6–4 4–6 2–6 6–3 6–4, Gilbert(5) bt Seguso 6–2 6–1 6–1, Jaite(13) bt Kim 6–4 6–1 6–3, Steeb bt Jarryd(7) 2–6 7–5 6–3 7–5, Mayotte(2) bt Mansdorf(12) 6–4 6–2 6–4

Quarter-final:

Edberg(1) bt Cane 6–1 7–5 6–4, Mecir(3) bt Schapers 3–6 7–6(7–2) 6–2 6–4, Gilbert(5) bt Jaite(13) 5–7 6–1 7–6(7–1) 6–3, Mayotte(2) bt Steeb 7–6(7–4) 7–5 6–3

Semi-final:

Mecir(3) bt Edberg(1) 3–6 6–0 1–6 4–6 6–2, Mayotte(2) bt Gilbert(5) 6–4 6–4 6–3

Final:

Mecir(3) (Gold) bt Mayotte(2) (Silver) 3–6 6–2 6–4 6–2

Third Place:

Both defeated semi-finalists were awarded Bronze Medals

Ladies' Singles – First Round:

Leila Meskhi (URS) bt Regina Rajchrtova (TCH) 7–5 7–5, Catherine Suire (FRA) bt Rahayu Basuki (INA) 6–3 3–6 6–0, Sara Gomer (GBR) bt Belinda Cordwell (NZL) 4–6 7–5 6–2, Il-Soon Kim (KOR) bt Etsuko Inoue (JAP)(WC) 6–3 3–6 7–5, Jill Hetherington (CAN) bt Ilina Berger (ISR) 6–1 6–4, Gisele Miro (BRA) bt Helen Kelesi (CAN) 7–5 7–5, Jana Novotna (TCH) bt Isabelle Demongeot (FRA) 6–4 6–3, Barbara Paulus (AUT) bt Bettina Fulco (ARG) 7–6(7–5) 6–4, Anne Minter (AUS) bt Xochitl Escobedo (MEX) 6–1 6–3, Wendy Turnbull (AUS) bt Clare Wood (GBR) 6–1 6–3, Tine Scheuer-Larsen (DEN) bt Oarda Bouchabou (ALG) 6–0 6–1, Sabrina Goles (YUG) bt Arantxa Sanchez (ESP) 6–4 6–2, Mercedes Paz (ARG) bt Olga Tsarbopoulou (GRE) 7–6(9–7) 6–3, Caterina Lindquist (SWE)(WC) bt Kumiko Okamoto (JPN) 7–6(6–3) 7–5, Nathalie Tauziat (FRA) bt Carling Bassett-Seguso (CAN) 7–6(7–5) 6–1, Raffaella Reggi (ITA) bt Elizabeth Smylie (AUS) 7–6(7–3) 6–0

Second Round:

Steffi Graf (FRG)(1) bt Leila Meskhi 7–5 6–1, Catherine Suire bt Jeong-Myung Lee (KOR) 7–5 4–6 7–5, Larisa Savchenko (URS)(11) bt Sara Gomer 6–7(3–7) 7–6(7–3) 9–7, Il-Soon Kim bt Helena Sukova (TCH)(5) 6–2 4–6 6–2, Pam Shriver (USA)(4) bt Jill Hetherington 6–2 6–3, Katerina Maleeva (BUL)(10) bt Gisele Miro 7–5 6–3, Barbara Paulus bt Jana Novotna 6–4 6–3, Zina Garrison (USA)(8) bt Claudia Hernandez (MEX) 6–1 6–4, Natalia Zvereva (URS)(6) bt Anne Minter 6–4 3–6 6–1, Tine Scheuer-Larsen bt Wendy Turnbull 6–4 6–3, Sylvia Hanika (FRG)(12) bt Julia Muir (ZIM) 6–1 6–1, Gabriela Sabatini (ARG)(3) bt Sabrina Goles 6–1 6–0, Manuela Maleeva (BUL)(7) bt Mercedes Paz 6–1 6–2, Caterina Lindquist bt Nathalie Tauziat 2–6 6–3 6–4, Raffaella Reggi bt Claudia Kohde-Kilsch (FRG)(9) 4–6 7–6(8–6) 6–3, Chris Evert-Mill (USA)(2) bt Maria Cecchini (ITA)(WC) 6–2 6–2

Third Round:

Steffi Graf(1) bt Catherine Suire 6–3 6–0, Larisa Savchenko(11) bt Il-Soon Kim 6–3 7–6(7–4), Pam Shriver bt Katerina Maleeva(10) 6–4 3–6 6–2, Zina Garrison(8) bt Barbara Paulus 7–5 6–2, Natalia Zvereva(6) bt Tine Scheuer-Larsen 6–1 6–2, Gabriela Sabatini(3) bt Sylvia Hanika (12) 1–6 6–4 6–2, Manuela Maleeva(7) bt Caterina Lindquist 6–1 6–0, Raffaella Reggi bt Chris Evert-Mill(2) 2–6 6–4 6–1

Quarter-final:

Steffi Graf(1) bt Larisa Savchenko(11) 6–2 4–6 6–3, Zina Garrison(8) bt Pam Shriver(4) 6–3 6–2, Gabriela Sabatini(3) bt Natalia Zvereva(6) 6–4 6–3, Manuela Maleeva(7) bt Raffaella Reggi 6–3 6–4

Semi-final:

Steffi Graf(1) bt Zina Garrison(8) 6–2 6–0, Gabriela Sabatini(3) bt Manuela Maleeva(7) 6–1 6–1

Final:

Steffi Graf(1)(Gold) bt Gabriela Sabatini(3)(Silver) 6–3 6–3

Third Place:

Both defeated semi-finalists were awarded Bronze Medals

Men's Doubles – First Round:

Kenneth Flach & Robert Seguso (USA)(1) bt Suharyadi Suharyadi & Donald Wailan Walalangi (INA) 6–3 6–1 7–5, Gabor Koeves & Laszlo Markovics (HUN) bt Leonardo Lavalle & Augustin Moreno (MEX) 3–6 6–3 6–7(10–12) 6–4 6–4, Galid Bloom & Amos Mansdorf (ISR) bt Owen Casey & Eoin Collins (IRE) 6–2 7–6(7–3) 4–6 7–5, Morten Christensen & Michael Tauson (DEN) bt Grant Connell & Glen Michibata (CAN)(6) 7–5 6–2 6–7(5–7) 7–5, Guy Forget & Henri Leconte (FRA) bt Tony Mmoh & Nduka Odizor (NIG) 6–3 6–2 6–7(5–7) 5–7 7–6(7–5), Ricardo Acioly & Luiz Mattar (BRA) bt Shuzo Matsuoka & Toshihisa Tscuchihashi (JAP) 4–6 6–4 6–2 6–2, Anand Amritraj & Vijay Amritraj (IND) bt Bong-Soo Kim & Jin-Sun Yoo (KOR) 6–3 7–6(7–5) 6–2, Miloslav Mecir & Milan Srejber (TCH)(8) bt Shuhua Liu & Keqin Ma (CHN) 7–5 6–1 6–4, Stefan Edberg & Anders Jarryd (SWE)(5) bt Eric Jelen & Carl-Uwe Steeb (FRG) 6–4 4–6 6–4 6–2, Mark Gurr & Peter Tuckniss (ZIM) bt Victor Caballero & Hugo Chapacu (PAR) 4–6 6–3 6–3 6–1, Bruce Derlin & Kelly Evernden (NZL) bt Javier Frana & Martin Jaite (ARG) 6–4 4–1 retd, Darren Cahill & John Fitzgerald (AUS)(3) bt Anastasis Bavelas & George Kalovelonis (GRE) 6–2 4–6 6–1 6–1, Goran Ivanisevic & Slobodan Zivojinovic (YUG) bt Jeremy Bates & Andrew Castle (GBR)(7) 7–5 2–6 6–3 7–6(7–4), Heinz Gunthardt & Jakob Hlasek (SUI) bt Omar Camporese & Diego Nargiso (ITA) 3–6 7–6(7–4) 6–3 7–6 (7–3), Alexander Antonitsch & Horst Skoff (AUT) bt Luis Arturo Gonzales & Alvaro Jordan (COL) w.o., Sergio Casal & Emilio Sanchez (ESP)(2) bt Andrei Olhovskiy & Alexander Volkov (URS) 6–3 6–3 6–1

Second Round:

Flack & Seguso(1) bt Koeves & Markovics 6–4 6–4 6–4, Christensen & Tauson bt Bloom & Mansdorf 7–5 6–3 6–2, Forget & Leconte (4) bt Acioly & Mattar 4–6 7–5 6–4 6–1, Mecir & Srejber(8) bt Amritraj & Amritraj 4–6 6–4 4–6 6–4 6–2, Edberg & Jarryd (5) bt Gurr & Tuckniss 6–0 6–1 6–4, Cahill & Fitzgerald(3) bt Derlin & Evernden 6–7(6–8) 6–4 6–2 3–6 6–1, Ivanisevic & Zivojinovic bt Gunthardt & Hlasek 6–3 7–6(8–6) 6–3, Casal & Sanchez(2) bt Antonitsch & Skoff 6–4 6–2 6–1

Quarter-final:

Flack & Seguso(1) bt Christensen & Tauson 6–4 7–5 6–2, Mecir & Srejber(8) bt Forget & Leconte(4) 3–6 4–6 7–5 6–3 9–7, Edberg & Jarryd(5) bt Cahill & Fitzgerald(3) 6–3 6–4 6–3, Casal & Sanchez(2) bt Ivanisevic & Zivojinovic 6–1 7–6(7–3) 6–3

Semi-final:

Flack & Seguso(1) bt Mecir & Srejber(8) 6–2 6–4 6–1, Casal & Sanchez (2) bt Edberg & Jarryd(5) 6–4 1–6 6–3 6–2

Final:

Flack & Seguso(1)(Gold) bt Casal & Sanchez(2)(Silver) 6–3 6–4 6–7(5–7) 6–7(1–7) 9–7

Third Place:

Both defeated semi-finalists were awarded Bronze Medals.

Ladies' Doubles – First Round:

Isabelle Demongeot & Natalie Tauziat (FRA) bt Sara Gomer & Clare Wood (GBR) 6–2 4–6 6–1, Larisa Savchenko & Natalia Zvereva (URS)(4) bt Xochiti Escobedo & Claudia Hernandez (MEX) 6–2 6–1, Elizabeth Smylie & Wendy Turnbull (AUS) bt Manuela Maleeva & Katerina Maleeva (BUL) 6–2 3–6 6–0, Elsuko Inoue & Kumiko Okamoto (JAP) bt Anna Maria Cecchini & Raffaella Reggi (ITA) 6–3 6–7(4–6) 8–6, Jana Novotna & Helena Sukova (TCH)(3) bt Il-Soon Kim & Jeong-Myung Lee (KOR) 6–2 7–6(7–4), Carling Bassett-Seguso & Jill Hetherington (CAN) bt Mercedes Paz & Gabriela Sabatini (ARG) 7–6(10–8) 5–7 20–18

Quarter-final:

Zina Garrison & Pam Shriver (USA)(1) bt Isabelle Demongeot & Natalie Tauziat 7–5 6–2, Elizabeth Smylie & Wendy Turnbull bt Larisa Savchenko & Natalia Zvereva 6–3 6–2, Jana Novotna & Helena Sukova bt Elsuko Inoue & Kumiko Okamoto 6–3 6–2, Steffi Graf & Claudia Kohde-Kilsch (FRG)(2) bt Carling Bassett-Seguso & Jill Hetherington 6–3 3–6 6–2

Semi-final:

Zina Garrison & Pam Shriver(1) bt Elizabeth Smylie & Wendy Turnbull 7–6(7–5) 6–4, Jana Novotna & Helena Sukova (3) bt Steffi Graf & Claudia Kohde-Kilsch(2) 7–5 6–3

Final:

Zina Garrison & Pam Shriver(1)(Gold) bt Jana Novotna & Helena Sukova(3)(Silver) 4–6 6–2 10–8

Third Place:

Both defeated semi-finalists were awarded Bronze Medals

(Referee: Peter Bellinger, AUS)

1992 – Barcelona

Vall d'Hebron Tennis Centre, 28 July-8 August

Men's Singles – First Round:
Jim Courier (USA)(1) bt Ramesh Krishnan (IND)(WC) 6–2
4–6 6–1 6–4, Gilad Bloom (ISR) bt Marian Vajda (TCH)
7–6(9–7) 6–1 6–0, Marc Rosset (SUI) bt Karim Alami (MAR)
6–2 4–6 2–1 retd, Wayne Ferreira (RSA)(9) bt Christo van
Rensburg (RSA) 7–5 6–2 2–6 6–4, Emilio Sanchez (ESP)
(12) bt Todd Woodbridge (AUS) 6–1 7–6(7–1) 6–2, Omar
Camporese (ITA) bt Juan-Oscar Rios (POR) 6–2 6–2 6–0,
Magnus Larsson (SWE)(WC) bt Horst Skoff (AUT) 6–2 6–2
6–3, Guy Forget (FRA)(7) bt Cristiano Caratti (ITA) 6–3 6–4 6–2, Goran Ivanisevic
(CRO)(4) bt Bernardo Motta (POR) 6–2 6–2 6–7(5–7) 4–6 6–3, Paul Haarhuis (NED) bt
Luiz Mattar (INA) 6–2 6–4 7–5, Jakob Hlasek (SUI)(15) bt Francisco Maciel (MEX) 6–3
6–4 4–6 6–2, Javier Frana (ARG) bt Pablo Arraya (PER) 6–2 6–0 6–7(3–7) 6–7(3–7) 6–2,
Fabrice Santoro (FRA) bt Cristian Miniussi (ARG) 6–1 7–6(7–3) 6–4, Younes El Aynaoui
(MAR) bt Chris Wilkinson (GBR) 6–4 6–1 7–5, Boris Becker (GER)(5) bt Christian
Ruud (NOR) 3–6 7–6(7–2) 5–7 7–6(7–2) 6–3, Michael Chang (USA)(6)(WC) bt Alberto
Mancini (ARG) 6–1 6–4 3–6 6–0, Jaime Oncins (BRA) bt Srdjan Muskatirovic (YUG)
7–6(7–3) 4–6 6–4 4–6 6–1, Mark Koevermans (NED) bt Sandor Noszaly (HUN) 6–2
6–3 2–6 6–2, Sergio Bruguera (ESP)(11) bt Andrew Castle (GBR) 6–1 6–2 6–3, Andrei
Cherkasov (CIS)(13) bt Roger Smith (BAH) 6–1 6–0 3–6 6–1, Goran Prpic (CRO) bt
Kenneth Carlsen (DEN) 6–4 4–6 6–3 7–5, Jaime Yzaga (PER) bt Leander Paes (IND)
1–6 7–6(7–4) 6–0 6–0, Pete Sampras (USA)(3) bt Wally Masur (AUS) 6–1 7–6(7–4) 6–4,
Michael Stich (GER) (8) bt Richard Fromberg (AUS) 6–3 3–6 6–1 3–6 6–3, Carl-Uwe
Steeb (GER)(WC) bt Andrei Pavel (ROM) 7–5 6–2 6–2, Leonardo Lavalle (MEX) bt Jan
Siemerink (NED) 6–4 6–4 6–2, Henri Leconte (FRA)(WC) bt Thomas Muster (AUT)(10)
7–6(7–5) 7–6(11–9) 6–4, Jordi Arrese (ESP)(16)(WC) bt Eui-Jong Chang (KOR) 6–4 6–2
6–2, Magnus Gustafsson (SWE) bt Owen Casey (IRE) 7– 6(10–8) 6–1 6–4, Renzo Furlan
(ITA)(WC) bt Shuzo Matsuoka (JPN) 6–4 6–3 3–6 6–4, Andrei Chesnokov (CIS)(WC) bt
Stefan Edberg (SWE)(2) 6–0 6–4 6–4

Second Round:
Courier(1) bt Bloom 6–2 6–0 6–0, Rosset bt Ferreira (9) 6–4 6–0 6–2, E. Sanchez(12)
bt Camporese 6–4 6–2 6–1, Larsson bt Forget(7) 6–3 6–3 6–1, Ivanisevic(4) bt Haarhuis
6–7(4–7) 6–2 1–6 6–3 6–2, Hlasek(15) bt Sznajder 4–6 6–4 6–3 7–6(7–1), Santoro bt Frana
4–6 6–2 6–1 6–1, Becker(5) bt El Aynaoui 6–4 5–7 6–4 6–0, Oncins bt Chang(6) 6–2
3–6 6–3 6–3, Koevermans bt Bruguera(11) 1–6 6–3 6–3 6–2, Cherkasov(13) bt Prpic 6–4

6–7(6–8) 6–4 6–3, Sampras(3) bt Yzaga 6–3 6–0 3–6 6–1, Steeb bt Stich(8) 6–4 6–2 4–6 6–3, Lavalle bt Leconte 6–4 3–6 4–6 6–3 10–8, Arrese(16) bt Gustafsson 6–2 4–6 6–1 3–6 9–7, Furlan bt Chesnokov 7–6(7–3) 6–4 6–4

Third Round:
Rosset bt Courier(1) 6–4 6–2 6–1, E. Sanchez(12) bt Larsson 6–4 7–6(7–3) 6–7(5–7) 6–4, Ivanisevic(4) bt Hlasek(15) 3–6 6–0 4–6 7–6(7–1) 9–7, Santoro bt Becker(5) 6–1 3–6 6–1 6–3, Oncins bt Koevermans 7–6(7–1) 6–0 7–6(7–2), Cherkasov(13) bt Sampras 6–7(7–9) 1–6 7–5 6–0 6–3, Lavalle bt Steeb 6–4 3–6 6–3 6–2, Arrese(16) bt Furlan 6–4 6–3 6–2

Quarter-final:
Rosset bt E. Sanchez(12) 6–4 7–6(7–2) 3–6 7–6(11–9), Ivanisevic(4) bt Santoro 6–7(5–7) 6–7(1–7) 6–4 6–4 8–6, Cherkasov(13) bt Oncins 6–1 6–4 6–7(3–7) 4–6 6–2, Arrese(16) bt Lavalle 6–1 7–6(8–6) 6–1

Semi-final:
Rosset bt Ivanisevic(4) 6–3 7–5 6–2, Arrese(16) bt Cherkasov(13) 6–4 7–6(7–4) 3–6 6–3

Final:
Rosset (Gold) bt Arrese (16) (Silver) 7–6(7–2)6–3 3–6 4–6 8–6

Third Place:
Both defeated semi-finalists were awarded Bronze Medals

Ladies' Singles – First Round:
Steffi Graf GER)(1) bt Guadalupe Novelo (MEX) 6–1 6–1, Brenda Schultz (NED) bt Fang Li (CHN) 7–5 6–7(4–7) 6–4, Magdalena Maleeva (BUL) bt Emanuela Zardo (SUI) 6–2 6–4, Kimiko Date (JPN)(14) bt Rene Simpson-Altet (CAN) 7–5 6–1, Sabine Appelmans (BEL)(16) bt Rachel McQuillan (AUS) 6–3 6–3, Nicole Provis (AUS) bt Katia Piccolini (ITA)(WC) 6–1 6–1, Eugenia Maniokova (CIS) bt Petra Ritter (AUT) 6–1 7–6(7–4), Katerina Maleeva (BUL)(8) bt Larisa Savchenko-Neiland (LAT) 7–6(7–3) 6–2, Mary Joe Fernandez (USA)(14) bt Li-Ling Chen (CHN) 6–2 6–3, Patricia Hy (CAN) bt Dally Randriantefy(MAD) 6–0 6–1, Samantha Smith (GBR) bt Sara Gomer (GBR) 2–6 6–3 6–1, Natalia Zvereva (CIS) bt Jana Novotna (TCH)(9) 6–1 6–0, Helena Sukova (TCH) (11) bt Natacha Randriantefy (MAD) 6–0 6–1, Angelica Gavaldon (MEX) bt Catarina Lindquist (SWE) 6–4 6–3, Raffaella Reggi-Concato (ITA) bt Jennifer Byrne (AUS)(WC) 6–4 7–6(7–2), Manuela Maleeva-Fragniere (SUI)(6) bt Andrea Vieira (BRA) 6–2 6–3, Anke Huber (GER)(7) bt Naoko Sawamatsu (JPN) 6–0 4–6 6–2, Barbara Paulus (AUT) bt Monique Javer (GBR) 6–7(9–11) 6–4 6–3, Nicole Muns-Jagerman (NED) bt Il-Soon Kim (KOR) 6–4 6–4, Julie Halard (FRA)(15) bt Katarzyna Nowak (POL) 6–4 7–6(7–1),

Mary Pierce (FRA)(13)(WC) bt Leila Meskhi (CIS) 7–6(7–5) 7–5, Yuyuk Basuki (INA) bt Mercedes Paz (ARG)(WC) 6–1 6–4, Patricia Tarabini (ARG) bt Mariaan de Swardt (RSA) 6–4 6–2, Jennifer Capriati (USA)(3) bt Elna Reinach (RSA)(WC) 6–1 6–0, Conchita Martinez (ESP)(5) bt Judith Wiesner (AUT) 4–6 6–1 6–2, Anna Marie Cecchini (ITA) bt Paulina Sepulveda (CHI) 6–2 6–3, Agnese Blumberga (LAT) bt Christina Padadaki (GRE) 4–6 6–1 6–2, Amanda Coetzer (RSA) bt Zina Garrison (USA)(12)(WC) 7–5 6–1, Nathalie Tauziat (FRA)(10) bt Radomira Zrubakova (TCH) 6–3 6–2, Barbara Rittner (GER)(WC), bt Florencia Labat (ARG) 6–3 6–3, Mana Endo (JPN) bt Elena Pampoulova-Wagner (BUL) 7–6(7–4) 7–6 (8–6), Arantxa Sanchez-Vicario (ESP)(2) bt Irina Spirlea (ROM) 6–1 6–3

Second Round:

Steffi Graf bt Brenda Schultz 6–1 6–0, Magdalena Maleeva bt Kimiko Date(14) 6–2 6–4, Sabine Appelmans(16) bt Nicole Provis 6–2 6–1, Eugenia Maniokova bt Katerina Maleeva(8) 7–6 (7–5) 4–6 6–0 Mary Joe Fernandez(4) bt Patricia Hy 6–2 1–6 12–10, Natalia Zvereva bt Samantha Smith 6–1 6–2, Angelica Gavaldon bt Helena Sukova(11) 4–6 6–3 5–3 retd, Manuela Maleeva-Fragniere(6) bt Raffaella Reggi-Concato 6–2 6–4, Anke Huber(7) bt Barbara Paulus 6–4 6–1, Nicole Muns-Jagerman bt Julie Halard(15) 7–6(7–3) 7–6(7–5), Yuyuk Basuki bt Mary Pierce(13) 0–6 6–3 10–8, Jennifer Capriati(3) bt Patricia Tarabini 6–4 6–1, Conchita Martinez(5) bt Anna Marie Cecchini 6–4 6–3, Amanda Coetzer bt Agnese Blumberga 6–2 6–4, Barbara Rittner bt Nathalie Tauziat(10) 6–3 6–2, Arantxa Sanchez-Vicario(2) bt Mana Endo 6–0 6–1

Third Round:

Steffi Graf(1) bt Magdalena Maleeva 6–3 6–4, Sabine Appelmans(16) bt Eugenia Maniokova 6–1 6–3, Mary Joe Fernandez(4) bt Natalia Zvereva 7–6(11–9) 6–1, Manuela Maleeva-Fragniere(6) bt Angelica Gavaldon 6–0 6–3, Anke Huber(7) bt Nicole Muns-Jagerman 7–5 7–6(7–3), Jennifer Capriati(3) bt Yuyuk Basuki 6–3 6–4, Conchita Martinez(5) bt Amanda Coetzer 6–4 6–3, Arantxa Sanchez –Vicario(2) bt Barbara Rittner 4–6 6–3 6–1

Quarter-final:

Steffi Graf(1) bt Sabine Appelmans(16) 6–1 6–0, Mary Joe Fernandez(4) bt Manuela Maleeva-Fragniere(6) 5–7 6–1 6–0, Jennifer Capriati(3) bt Anke Huber(7) 6–3 7–6(7–1), Arantxa Sanchez-Vicario(2) bt Conchita Martinez(5) 6–4 6–4

Semi-final:

Steffi Graf(1) bt Mary Joe Fernandez(4) 6–4 6–2, Jennifer Capriati(3) bt Arantxa Sanchez-Vicario(2) 6–3 3–6 6–4

Final:
Jennifer Capriati(3) (Gold) bt Steffi Graf(1) (Silver) 3–6 6–3 6–4

Third Place:
Both defeated semi-finalists were awarded Bronze Medals

Men's Doubles – First Round:
John Fitzgerald & Todd Woodbridge (AUS)(1) bt Mark Knowles & Roger Smith (BAH) 6–2 6–3 6–7(4–7) 4–6 6–3, Ramesh Krishnan & Leander Paes (IND) bt Iztok Bozic & Blaz Trupej (SLO) 6–3 6–2 6–2, Suharyadi Suharyadi & Bonit Wiryawan (INA) bt Eui-Jong Chang & Chi-Wan Kim (KOR), 6–1 6–7(6–8) 4–6 6–3 6–2, Goran Ivanisevic & Goran Prpic (CRO) bt Paul Haarhuis & Mark Koevermans (NED)(5) 2–6 6–4 6–2 6–2, Wayne Ferreira & Pieter Norval (RSA)(4) bt Bent-Ove Pedersen & Christian Ruud (NOR) 6–2 6–4 5–7 6–3, Brian Gyetko & Sebastian Leblanc (CAN) bt Kenneth Carlsen & Frederik Fetterlein (DEN) 6–3 7–6(7–4) 7–6(7–2), Gheorghe Cosac & Dinu Pescariu (ROM) bt Laszlo Markovits & Sandor Noszaly (HUN) w.o., Omar Camporese & Diego Nargiso (ITA)(8) bt Miguel Nido & Juan-Oscar Rios (POR) 6–1 6–2 6–3, Boris Becker & Michael Stich (GER)(6) bt Karim Alami & Younes El Aynaoui (MAR) w.o., Anastasios Bavelas & Konstantinos Efraimoglou (GRE) bt Christian Forcellini & Gabriel Francino (SAN) 6–1 6–2 6–2, Jim Courier & Pete Sampras (USA) bt Stefan Edberg & Anders Jarryd (SWE) 1–6 6–3 4–6 7–6(8–6) 6–4, Sergio Casal & Emilio Sanchez (ESP)(3) bt Luiz Mattar & Jaime Oncins (BRA) 6–3 3–6 6–7(4–7) 6–3 6–1, Javier Frana & Cristian Miniussi (ARG)(7) bt Andrew Castle & Chris Wilkinson (GBR) 6–3 6–4 7–6(7–1), Guy Forget & Henri Leconte (FRA) bt Emanuel Couto & Bernardo Motta (POR) 6–1 6–3 6–1, Owen Casey & Eoin Collins (IRL) bt Leonardo Lavalle & Francisco Maciel (MEX) 7–6(7–5) 6–4 retd, Jakob Hlasek & Mark Rosset (SUI)(2) bt Qiang-Hua Meng & Jian-Ping Xia (CHN) 7–5 6–1 6–2

Second Round:
Krishnan & Paes bt Fitzgerald & Woodbridge(1) 6–4 7–5 4–6 6–1, Ivanisevic & Prpic bt Suharyadi & Wiryawan 7–5 6–2 6–2, Ferreira & Norval(4) bt Gyetko & Leblanc 6–3 7–6(7–4) 6–4, Cosac & Pescariu bt Camporese & Nargiso(8) 6–1 4–6 4–6 6–4 6–2, Becker & Stich(6) bt Bavelas & Efraimoglou 6–3 6–1 6–4, Casal & Sanchez(3) bt Courier & Sampras 5–7 4–6 6–3 6–2 6–2, Frana & Miniussi(7) bt Forget & Leconte 4–6 6–7(3–7) 6–4 6–4 6–3, Hlasek & Rosset(2) bt Casey & Collins 7–6(7–4) 6–3 6–2

Quarter-final:
Ivanisevic & Prpic bt Krishnan & Paes 7–6(7–3) 5–7 6–4 6–3, Ferreira & Norval(4) bt Cosac & Pescarin 6–0 6–3 6–2, Becker & Stich(6) bt Casal & Sanchez(3) 6–3 4–6 7–6 (11–9) 5–7 6–3, Frana & Miniussi(7) bt Hlasek & Rosset (2)2–6 7–6(7–3) 3–6 6–2 6–2

Semi-final:

Ferreira & Norval(4) bt Ivanisevic & Prpic 7–6(7–5) 3–6 6–3 2–6 6–2, Becker & Stich(6) bt Frana & Miniussi(7) 7–6(7–3) 6–2 6–7(4–7) 2–6 6–4

Final:

Becker & Stich(6)(Gold) bt Ferreira & Norval(4)(Silver) 7–6(7–5) 4–6 7–6(7–5) 6–3

Third Place:

Both defeated semi-finalists were awarded Bronze Medals

Ladies' Doubles – First Round:

Conchita Martinez & Arantxa Sanchez-Vicario (ESP) (1) bt Dally Randriantefy & Natacha Randriantefy (MAD) 6–0 6–0, Manuela Maleeva-Fragniere & Emanuela Zardo (SUI) bt Tina Krizan & Karin Lusnic (SLO) 6–2 6–2, Patricia Hy & Rene Simpson-Alter (CAN) bt Suvimol Duangchang & Benjamas Sanagaram (THA) 6–4 6–4, Isabelle Demongeot & Nathalie Tauziat (FRA)(8) bt Rosana De Los Rios & Larissa Sohaerer (PAR) 6–1 7–6(7–3), Jana Novotna & Andrea Strnadova (TCH)(3) bt Rosana Dragomir & Irina Spirlea (ROM), 6–1 6–4, Kimiko Date & Maya Kidowaki (JAP) bt Il-Soon Kim & Jeong-Myung Lee (KOR) 5–2 retd, Claudia Chabalgoity & Andrea Vieira (BRA) bt Catarina Lindquist & Maria Lindstrom (SWE) 6–2 7–6(7–5), Rachel McQuillan & Nicole Provis (AUS)(5) bt Angelica Garaldon & Guadalupe Novelo (MEX) 5–7 6–3 6–1, Mercedes Paz & Patricia Tarabini (ARG)(7) bt Magdalena Mroz & Katarzyna Teodorowicz (POL) 6–4 4–6 6–3, Fang Li & Min Tang (CHN) bt Christina Papadaki & Christina Zachariadou (GRE) 7–6(7–5) 6–3, Petra Ritter & Judith Wiesner (AUT) bt Agnese Blumberga & Larisa Savchenko-Neiland (LAT) 6–4 5–7 6–3, Leila Meskhi & Natalia Zvereva (CIS)(4) bt Katerina Maleeva & Magdalena Maleeva (BUL) w.o., Mariaan de Swardt & Elna Reinach (RSA)(6) bt Sally-Anne McDonald & Julia Muir (ZIM) 6–0 6–3, Laura Garrone & Rafaella Reggi-Concato (ITA) bt Samantha Smith & Clare Wood (GBR) 5–7 6–1 6–3, Steffi Graf & Anke Huber (GER) bt Yuyuk Basuki & Suzanna Wibowo (INA) 6–2 6–3, Gigi Fernandez & Mary Joe Fernandez (USA)(2) bt Nicole Muns-Jagerman & Brenda Schultz (NED) 6–0 6–0

Second Round:

Conchita Martinez & Arantxa Sanchez-Vicario(1) bt Manuela Maleeva-Fragniere & Emanuela Zardo 6–0 6–1, Isabelle Demongeot & Natalie Tauziat(8) bt Patricia Hy & Rene Simpson-Alter 3–6 6–3 6–2, Jana Novotna & Andrea Strnadova(3) bt Kimiko Date & Maya Kidowaki 6–3 7–6(7–4), Rachel McQuillan & Nicole Provis(5) bt Claudia Chabalgoity & Andrea Vieira 6–2 6–1, Mercedes Paz & Patricia Tarabini bt Fang Li & Min Tang 6–0 6–1, Leila Meskhi & Natalia Zvereva(4) bt Petra Ritter & Judith Wiesner 6–1 6–1, Mariaan de Swardt & Elna Reinach(6) bt Laura Garrone & Rafaella Reggi-Concato 6–3 6–2, Gigi Fernandez & Mary Joe Fernandez(2) bt Steffi Graf & Anke Huber 7–6(7–3)6–4

Quarter-final:

Conchita Martinez & Arantxa Sanchez-Vicario(1) bt Isabelle Demongeot & Natalie Tauziat(8) 6–2 6–4, Rachel McQuillan & Nicole Provis(5) bt Jana Novotna & Andrea Strnadova(3) 6–3 6–3, Leila Meskhi & Natalia Zvereva(4) bt Mercedes Paz & Patricia Tarabini(7) 6–2 6–3, Gigi Fernandez & Mary Joe Fernandez(2) bt Mariaan de Swardt & Elna Reinach(6) 6–2 6–4

Semi-final:

Conchita Martinez & Arantxa Sanchez-Vicario(1) bt Rachel McQuillan & Nicole Provis(5) 6–1 6–2, Gigi Fernandez & Mary Joe Fernandez(2) bt Leila Meskhi & Natalia Zvereva(4) 6–4 7–5

Final:

Gigi Fernandez & Mary Joe Fernandez(2)(Gold) bt Conchita Martinez & Arantxa Sanchez-Vicario(1)(Silver) 7–5 2–6 6–2

Third Place Play-off:

Both defeated semi-finalists were awarded Bronze Medals

(Referee: Ken Farrar, CAN)

1996 – Atlanta

Stone Mountain Park Tennis Centre,
23 July – 3 August

Men's Singles – First Round:

Andre Agassi (USA)(1) bt Jonas Bjorkman (SWE) 7–6(8–6) 7–6(7–5); Karol Kucera (SVK) bt Dmitri Tomashevich (UZB)(WC) 6–3 2–6 6–0, Oscar Ortiz (MEX) bt Dinu Pescariu (ROM)(WC) 6–2 6–2, Andrea Gaudenzi (ITA) bt Carlos Costa (ESP)(15) 6–3 6–2, Todd Woodbridge (AUS) bt Jan Siemerink (NED)(9) 6–2 6–4, Tim Henman (GBR) bt Shuzo Matsuoka (JPN) 7–6(7–4) 6–3, Byron Black (ZIM) bt Guillaume Raoux (FRA) 6–3 3–6 6–2, Wayne Ferreira (RSA)(5) bt Gaston Etlis (ARG) (WC) 6–4 6–3, Thomas Enqvist (SWE)(3) bt Marc-Kevin Goellner(GER) 7–6(7–4) 4–6 6–4, Sargis Sargsian (ARM)(WC) bt Daniel Nestor (CAN)(WC) 6–4 6–4, Nicolas Pereira (VEN) bt Hernan Gumy (ARG) 6–4 6–0, Leander Paes (IND)(WC) bt Richey Reneberg (USA)(11) 6–7(2–7) 7–6(9–7) 1–0 retd, Renzo Furlan (ITA)(14) bt Jiri Novak (CZE) 4–6 6–4 6–3, Marcelo Filippini (URU) bt Luis Morejon (ECU)(WC) 6–7(3–7) 7–5 6–1,

Frederik Fetterlein (DEN) bt Jacco Eltingh (NED) 6–4 4–6 8–6, Marc Rosset (SUI)(8) bt Hicham Arazi (MAR)(WC) 6–2 6–3, Arnaud Boetsch (FRA) (7) bt Brett Steven (NZL) 6–2 7–6(7–2), Sergi Bruguera (ESP) bt Andrei Pavel (ROM)(WC) 2–6 6–1 8–6, Greg Rusedski (GBR) bt Javier Frana (ARG) 4–6 7–5 6–3, Magnus Gustafsson (SWE)(13) bt Ronald Agenor (HAI)(WC) 6–2 6–4, Jason Stoltenberg (AUS)(10) bt Sule Ladip (NGR) (WC) 7–6(7–4) 6–3, Kenneth Carlsen (DEN) bt Mark Knowles (BAH) 7–5 6–3, Oleg Ogorodov (UZB) bt Sandor Noszaly (HUN) 7–5 7–6(8–6), MaliVai Washington (USA)(4) bt Jan Kroslak (SVK) 6–3 7–6(7–3) , Alberto Costa (ESP) (6) bt Sebastien Lareau (CAN) (WC) 7–6(13–11) 6–4, Fernando Meligeni (BRA) bt Stefano Pescosolido (ITA) 6–4 6–2, Wayne Black (ZIM)(WC) bt Jimy Szymanski (VEN)(WC) 6–7(4–7) 6–4 6–3, Mark Philippoussis (AUS) bt Paul Haarhuis (NED)(12) 7–6(7–4) 7–6(7–2), Daniel Vacek (CZE) (16) bt David Prinosil (GER) 6–4 2–6 6–4, Andrei Olhovskiy (RUS) (WC) bt Nicolas Lapentti (ECU) 6–1 3–6 8–6, Christian Ruud (NOR) bt Alejandro Hernandez (MEX) (WC) 6–3 2–6 8–6, Marcos Ondruska (RSA) bt Goran Ivanisevic (CRO)(2) 6–2 6–4

Second Round:

Agassi(1) bt Kucera 6–4 6–4, Gaudenzi bt Ortiz 6–1 7–6(8–6), Woodbridge bt Henman 7–6(8–6) 7–6(7–5), Ferreira(5) bt Black 6–2 7–5, Enqvist(3) bt Sargsian 4–6 7–6(7–2) 6–4, Paes bt Pereira 6–2 6–3, Furlan(14) bt Filippini 7–5 6–2, Rosset(8) bt Fetterlein 7–6(7–5) 7–5, Bruguera bt Boetsch(7) 7–6(9–7) 4–6 6–2, Rusedski bt Gustafsson(13) 6–7(4–7) 7–6(7–3) 6–3, Carlsen bt Stoltenberg(10) 6–2 3–6 6–3, Washington(4) bt Ogorodov 6–3 6–4, Meligeni bt Costa(6) 7–6(7–5) 6–4, Philippoussis bt Black 6–4 6–2, Olhovskiy bt Vacek(16) 6–3 7–6(7–1), Ruud bt Ondruska 7–6(8–6) 7–6(7–1)

Third Round:

Agassi(1) bt Gaudenzi 2–6 6–4 6–2, Ferreira(5) bt Woodbridge 7–6(7–3) 7–6(7–5), Paes bt Enqvist(3) 7–5 7–6(7–3), Furlan(14) bt Rosset(8) 6–0 4–2 retd, Bruguera bt Rusedski 7–6(9–7) 6–3, Washington(4) bt Carlsen 6–7(8–10) 6–0 6–2, Meligeni bt Philippoussis 7–6(9–7) 4–6 8–6, Olhovskiy bt Ruud 6–4 6–3

Quarter-final:

Agassi(1) bt Ferreira(5) 7–5 4–6 7–5, Paes bt Furlan(14) 6–1 7–5, Bruguera bt Washington(4) 7–6(10–8) 4–6 7–5, Meligeni bt Olhovskiy 6–7(5–7) 7–5 6–3

Semi-final:

Agassi(1) bt Paes 7–6(7–5) 6–3, Bruguera bt Meligeni 7–6(11–9) 6–2

Final:

Agassi(1)(Gold) bt Bruguera (Silver) 6–2 6–3 6–1

Third Place Play-off:

Paes (Bronze) bt Meligeni 3–6 6–2 6–4

Ladies' Singles – First Round:

Monica Seles (USA)(1) bt Li Chen (CHN)(WC) 6–0 6–4, Patricia Hy-Boulais (CAN) bt Rita Grande (ITA) 6–4 6–4, Angelica Gavaldon (MEX) bt Christina Papadaki (GRE) 6–1 3–6 6–2, Gabriela Sabatini (ARG)(13) bt Nathalie Tauziat (FRA) 7–5 6–2, Martina Hingis (SUI)(15) bt Joelle Schad (DOM)(WC) 6–0 6–1, Ai Sugiyama (JPN) bt Katarina Studenikova (SVK) 6–2 6–3, Judith Wiesner (AUT) bt Andrea Temesvari (HUN) 7–6(7–5) 6–4, Jana Novotna (CZE)(6) bt Ruxandra Dragomir (ROM) 6–4 4–4 retd, Arantxa Sanchez-Vicario (ESP)(3) bt Dominique Van Roost (BEL) 6–1 7–5, Silvia Farina (ITA) bt Clare Wood (GBR) 6–2 6–2, Young-Ja Choi (KOR)(WC) bt Joanette Kruger (RSA) 6–7(5–7) 6–2 6–1, Brenda Schultz-McCarthy (NED)(11) bt Selima Sfar (TUN)(WC) 6–4 6–0, Magdalena Maleeva (BUL)(10) bt Rennae Stubbs (AUS)(WC) 6–2 6–1, Florencia Labat (ARG) bt Elena Makarova (RUS) 6–2 7–5, Virag Csurgo (HUN) bt Aleksandra Olsza (POL)(WC) 6–2 7–5, Kimiko Date (JPN)(8) bt Dally Randriantefy (MAD)(WC) 6–0 6–1, Anke Huber (GER)(5) bt Catalina Cristea (ROM)(WC) 2–6 6–4 6–2, Mariaan de Swardt (RSA) bt Helena Sukova (CZE) 7–6(7–4) 3–6 7–5, Naoko Sawamatsu (JPN) bt Sung-Hee Park (KOR) 6–3 4–6 6–3, Lindsay Davenport (USA)(9) bt Anne Kremer (LUX) (WC) 6–2 6–1, Karina Habsudova (SVK)(16) bt Yuyuk Basuki (INA) 6–3 6–3, Laurence Courtois (BEL) bt Anna Kournikova (RUS)(WC) 1–6 6–2 6–2, Virginia Ruano-Pascual (ESP) bt Magdalena Grzybowska (POL) 6–4 6–2, Iva Majoli (CRO)(4) bt Nicole Bradtke (AUS) 3–6 6–3 6–4, Mary Joe Fernandez (USA)(7) bt Elena Likhovtseva (RUS) 6–2 6–4, Shi-Ting Wang (TPE) bt Adriana Serra-Zanetti (ITA) 7–5 7–6(8–6), Ines Gorrochategui (ARG)(WC) bt Jing-Qian Yi (CHN) 6–2 1–6 6–1, Mary Pierce (FRA)(12) bt Olga Barabanschikova (BLR) 6–3 7–5, Amanda Coetzer (RSA)(14) bt Rachel McQuillan (AUS) (WC) 6–4 7–6(8–6), Natasha Zvereva (BLR) bt Sabine Appelmans (BEL) 7–5 6–3, Radka Zrubakova (SVK)(WC) bt Jana Nejedly (CAN)(WC) 6–3 6–2, Conchita Martinez (ESP)(2) bt Patty Schnyder (SUI)(WC) 6–1 6–2

Second Round:

Monica Seles(1) bt Patricia Hy-Boulais 6–3 6–2, Gabriela Sabatini(13) bt Angelica Gavaldon 6–4 6–0, Ai Sugiyama bt Martina Hingis(15) 6–4 6–4, Jana Novotna(6) bt Judith Wiesner 6–4 3–6 6–3, Arantxa Sanchez-Vicario(3) bt Silvia Farina 6–1 6–3, Brenda Schultz-McCarthy(11) bt Young-Ja Choi 6–2 6–4, Magdalena Maleeva(10) bt Florencia Labat 7–6(9–7) 6–1, Kimiko Date(8) bt Virag Csurgo 6–2 6–3, Anke Huber(5) bt Mariaan de Swardt 3–6 6–1 6–4, Lindsay Davenport(9) bt Naoko Sawamatsu 6–2 6–2, Karina Habsudova bt Laurence Courtois 7–5 6–2, Iva Majoli(4) bt Virginia Ruano-Pascual 7–5 6–3, Mary Joe Fernandez(7) bt Shi-Ting Wang 7–6(7–4) 2–6 6–1, Ines Gorrochategui bt Mary Pierce(12) 6–4 1–6 7–5, Natasha Zvereva bt Amanda Coetzer(14) 6–1 4–6 6–2, Conchita Martinez(2) bt Radka Zrubakova 6–1 6–4

Third Round:

Monica Seles(1) bt Gabriela Sabatini(13) 6–3 6–3, Jana Novotna(6) bt Ai Sugiyama 6–3 6–4, Arantxa Sanchez-Vicario (3) bt Brenda Schultz-McCarthy(11) 6–4 7–6(9–7), Kimiko Date(8) bt Magdalena Maleeva(10) 6–4 6–4, Lindsay Davenport(9) bt Anke Huber(5) 6–1 3–6 6–3, Iva Majoli(4) bt Karina Habsudova(16) 6–4 3–6 6–4, Mary Joe Fernandez(7) bt Ines Gorrochategui 6–0 6–3, Conchita Martinez(2) bt Natasha Zvereva 6–2 7–5

Quarter-final:

Jana Novotna(6) bt Monica Seles(1) 7–5 3–6 8–6, Arantxa Sanchez-Vicario(3) bt Kimiko Date(8) 4–6 6–3 10–8, Lindsay Davenport(9) bt Iva Majoli(4) 7–5 6–3, Mary Joe Fernandez(7) bt Conchita Martinez(2) 3–6 6–2 6–3

Semi-final:

Arantxa Sanchez-Vicario(3) bt Jana Novotna(6) 6–4 1–6 6–3, Lindsay Davenport(9) bt Mary Joe Fernandez(7) 6–2 7–6(8–6)

Final:

Lindsay Davenport(9) (Gold) bt Arantxa Sanchez-Vicario(3) (Silver) 7–6(8) 6–2

Third Place Play-off:

Jana Novotna(6) (Bronze) bt Mary Joe Fernandez(7) 7–6(10–8) 6–4

Men's Doubles – First Round:

Todd Woodbridge & Mark Woodforde (AUS)(1) bt Arnaud Boetsch & Guillaume Raoux (FRA) 6–2 3–6 6–3, Mahesh Bhupathi & Leander Paes (IND) bt Bing Pan & Jia-Ping Xia (CHN)(WC) 4–6 6–4 6–4, Satoshi Iwabuchi & Takao Suzuki (JPN) bt Juan Carlos Bianchi & Nicolas Pereira (VEN) 4–6 7–6(7–5) 8–6, Sergi Bruguera & Tomas Carbonell (ESP) bt Javier Frana & Luis Lobo(ARG)(7) 6–3 7–6(8–6), Jacco Eltingh & Paul Haarhuis (NED) (3) bt Andrei Pavel & Dinu Pescariu (ROM)(WC) 6–2 6–7(1–7) 6–4, Claude N'Goran & Clement N'Goran (CIV)(WC) bt Chih-Jung Chen & Yu-Hui Lien (TPE)(WC) 6–2 6–2, Andre Agassi & MaliVai Washington (USA) bt Alejandro Hernandez & Oscar Ortiz (MEX) 6–3 4–6 6–4, Ellis Ferreira & Wayne Ferreira (RSA)(6) bt Gabor Koves & Laszlo Markovits (HUN) 6–4 6–1, Byron Black & Wayne Black (ZIM)(8) bt Hyung-Taik Lee & Yong-Il Yoon (KOR)(WC) 6–4 6–2, Marc-Kevin Goellner & David Prinosil (GER) bt Andrea Gaudenzi & Diego Nargiso (ITA) 4–6 6–1 7–5, Mark Knowles & Roger Smith (BAH) bt Emanuel Couto & Bernardo Mota (POR) 7–6(8–6) 7–6(7–4), Sasa Hirszon & Goran Ivanisevic (CRO) bt Jonas Bjorkman & Nicklas Kulti (SWE)(4) 7–6(7–4) 7–6(7–4), Jiri Novak & Daniel Vacek (CZE)(5) bt Oleg Ogorodov & Dmitri Tomaschevich (UZB) (WC) w.o., Pablo Campana & Nicolas Lapentti (ECU) bt Kenneth Carlsen & Frederik Fetterlein (DEN) 6–4 3–6 6–3, Neil Broad & Tim Henman (GBR) bt Jan Kroslak & Karol

Kucera (SVK)(WC) 6–3 6–3, Grant Connell & Daniel Nestor (CAN)(2) bt Scott Barron & Owen Casey (IRE) (WC) 6–4 6–4

Second Round:

Woodbridge & Woodforde(1) bt Bhupathi & Paes 4–6 6–2 6–2, Bruguera & Carbonell bt Iwabuchi & Suzuki 6–7(1–7) 6–2 7–5, Eltingh & Haarhuis(3) bt N'Goran & N'Goran 6–4 6–4, Ferreira & Ferreira(6) bt Agassi & Washington 7–5 6–7(2–7) 6–0, Goellner & Prinosil bt Black & Black(8–6) 6–4 7–6(8–6), Hirszon & Ivanisevic bt Knowles & Smith 7–6(7–4) 6–3, Novak & Vacek(5) bt Campana & Lapentti 7–5 6–4, Broad &Henman bt Connell & Nestor(2) 7–6(7–5) 4–6 6–4

Quarter-final:

Woodbridge & Woodforde(1) bt Bruguera/Carbonell 6–4 6–1, Eltingh & Haarhuis(3) bt Ferreira & Ferreira(6) 7–6(7–4) 7–6(7–4), Goellner & Prinosil bt Hirszon & Ivanisevic 6–2 6–3, Broad & Henman bt Novak & Vacek(5) 7–6(7–4) 6–4

Semi-final:

Woodbridge & Woodforde(1) bt Eltingh & Haarhuis (3) 6–2 5–7 18–16, Broad & Henman bt Goellner & Prinosil 4–6 6–3 10–8

Final:

Woodbridge & Woodforde(1) (Gold) bt Broad & Henman (Silver) 6–4 6–4 6–2

Third Place Play-off:

Goellner & Prinosil (Bronze) bt Eltingh & Haarhuis (3) 6–2 7–5

Ladies' Doubles – First Round:

Mary Pierce & Nathalie Tauziat (FRA) bt Magdalena Grzybowska & Aleksandra Olsza (POL) 6–2 3–6 6–0, Valda Lake & Clare Wood (GBR) bt Katerina Maleeva & Magdalena Maleeva (BUL)(WC) 3–6 7–6(10–8) 6–3, Amanda Coetzer & Mariaan de Swardt (RSA) (7) bt Eun-Ha Kim & Sung-Hee Park (KOR)(WC) 6–1 6–3, Manon Bollegraf & Brenda Schultz-McCarthy (NED) bt Olga Lugina & Natalia Medvedeva (UKR) w.o., Virag Csurgo & Andrea Temesvari (HUN) bt Paula Cabezas & Barbara Castro (CHI)(WC) 6–4 1–6 6–3, Martina Hingis & Patty Schnyder (SUI) (WC) bt Karina Habsudova & Radka Zrubakova (SVK) 3–6 6–4 6–2, Sabine Appelmans & Laurence Courtois (BEL) bt Gabriela Sabatini & Patricia Tarabini (ARG)(6) 5–7 6–3 6–4, Li Chen & Jing-Qian Yi (CHN) bt Nicole Bradtke & Rennae Stubbs (AUS)(5) w.o., Benjamas Sangaram & Tamarine Tanasugarn (THA)(WC) bt Christina Papadaki & Christina Zachariadou (GRE) 6–2 6–7(3–7) 6–2, Iva Majoli & Maja Muric (CRO) bt Silvia Farina & Laura Golarsa (ITA) 7–6(7–2) 4–6 9–7, Conchita Martinez & Arantxa Sanchez-Vicario (ESP)(4) bt Dally

Randriantefy & Natacha Randriantefy (MAD) (WC) 6–1 6–3, Jill Hetherington & Patricia Hy-Boulais (CAN) bt Kyoko Nagatsuka & Ai Sugiyama (JPN)(8) 7–6(7–2) 6–1, Olga Barabanschikova & Natasha Zvereva (BLR)(WC) bt Miriam d'Agostini & Vanessa Menga (BRA) 6–2 6–3, Yuyuk Basuki & Romana Tedjakusuma (INA)(WC) bt Catalina Cristea & Ruxandra Dragomir (ROM) w.o., Jana Novotna & Helena Sukova (CZE)(2) bt Anna Kournikova & Elena Makarova (RUS) 6–2 6–2

Second Round:

Gigi Fernandez & Mary Joe Fernandez (USA) (1) bt Mary Pierce & Nathalie Tauziat 6–4 6–3, Valda Lake & Clare Wood bt Amanda Coetzer & Mariaan de Swardt(7) 7–5 7–5, Manon Bollegraf & Brenda Schultz-McCarthy bt Virag Csurgo & Andrea Temesvari 7–6(7–5) 7–6(7–5), Martina Hingis & Patty Schnyder bt Sabine Appelmans & Laurence Courtois 2–6 6–1 7–5, Benjamas Sangaram & Tamarine Tanasugarn bt Li Chen & Jing Qian Yi 2–6 6–4 6–4, Conchita Martinez & Arantxa Sanchez-Vicario(4) bt Iva Majoli & Maja Muric 6–2 6–1, Jill Hetherington & Patricia Hy-Boulais bt Olga Barabanschikova & Natasha Zvereva 2–6 6–4 6–1, Jana Novotna & Helena Sukova(2) bt Yuyuk Basuki & Romana Tedjakusuma 6–2 6–3

Quarter-final:

Gigi Fernandez & Mary Joe Fernandez (1) bt Valda Lake & Clare Wood 6–2 6–1, Manon Bollegraf & Brenda Schultz-McCarthy(3) bt Martina Hingis & Patty Schnyder 6–4 6–3, Conchita Martinez & Arantxa Sanchez-Vicario(4) bt Benjamas Sangaram & Tamarine Tanasugarn 6–2 6–1, Jana Novotna & Helena Sukova(2) bt Jill Hetherington & Patricia Hy-Boulais 6–2 6–4

Semi-final:

Gigi Fernandez & Mary Joe Fernandez(1) bt Manon Bollegraf & Brenda Schultz-McCarthy(3) 7–5 7–6(7–3), Jana Novotna & Helena Sukova(2) bt Conchita Martinez & Arantxa Sanchez-Vicario(4) 6–2 7–6(7–1)

Final:

Gigi Fernandez & Mary Joe Fernandez (1) (Gold) bt Jana Novotna & Helena Sukova(2) (Silver) 7–6(8–6) 6–4

Third Place Play-off:

Conchita Martinez & Arantxa Sanchez-Vicario(4) (Bronze) bt Manon Bollegraf & Brenda Schultz-McCarthy(3) 6–1 6–3

(Referee: Ken Farrar, CAN)

2000 – Sydney

New South Wales Tennis Centre,
19 September–1 October

Men's Singles – First Round:

Fabrice Santoro (FRA) bt Marat Safin (RUS)(1) 1–6 6–1
6–4, Fernando Vicente (ESP) bt Andrew Ilie (AUS) 6–3
6–3, Gianluca Pozzi (ITA) bt Jiri Novak (CZE) 6–1 6–2,
Karim Alami (MAR) bt Franco Squillari (ARG)(10) 6–4
7–6(7–5), Sebastien Lareau (CAN)(WC) bt Michael Chang
(USA)(16) 7–6(8–6) 6–3, Mikael Tillstrom (SWE) bt Leander
Paes (IND)(WC) 6–2 6–4, Roger Federer (SUI) bt David
Prinosil (GER) 6–2 6–2, Karol Kucera (SVK) bt Tim Henman (GBR)(7) 6–3 6–2, Max
Mirnyi (BLR) bt Lleyton Hewitt (AUS)(4) 6–3 6–3, Jiri Vanek (CZE) bt Wayne Black
(ZIM)(A) 5–7 6–1 6–1, Jeff Tarango (USA) bt Diego Camacho (BOL)(WC) 6–0 6–1,
Mariano Zabaleta (ARG) bt Marcelo Rios (CHI)(12) 6–7(8–10) 6–4 7–5, Tommy Haas
(GER) bt Wayne Ferreira (RSA)(14) 7–5 6–2, Andreas Vinciguerra (SWE) bt Christian
Ruud (NOR) 6–2 6–4, Arnaud Clement (FRA) bt Greg Rusedski (GBR) 6–2 6–3, Alex
Corretja (ESP)(6) bt Goran Ivanisevic (CRO) 7–6(7–3) 7–6(7–2), Juan Carlos Ferrero
(ESP)(8) bt Hyung-Taik Lee (KOR) 6–7(5–7) 7–6(8–6) 7–5, Nicolas Massu (CHI) bt Slava
Dosedel (CZE) 6–2 7–6(7–5), Daniel Nestor (CAN) bt Barry Cowan (GBR) 5–7 6–1 6–4,
Patrick Rafter (AUS)(13) bt Vincent Spadea (USA) 6–4 6–3, Arnaud Di Pasquale (FRA)
bt Nicolas Kiefer (GER)(9) 6–4 6–3, Vladimir Voltchkov (BLR) bt Gaston Gaudio (ARG)
7–6(7–4) 4–6 6–1, Paradorn Srichaphan (THA)(WC) bt Attila Savolt (HUN)(WC) 6–2
4–6 7–5, Magnus Norman (SWE)(3) bt Andrei Pavel (ROM) 6–7(1–7) 6–3 10–8, Yevgeny
Kafelnikov (RUS)(5) bt Juan Antonio Marin (CRC)(WC) 6–0 6–1, Juan Ignacio Chela
(ARG) bt Nicolas Escude (FRA) 6–7(5–7) 7–5 6–1, Kristian Pless (DEN)(WC) bt Sargis
Sargsian (ARM) 6–3 6–4, Mark Philippoussis (AUS)(11) bt Thomas Johansson (SWE) 7–6
(8–6) 6–4, Kevin Ullyett (ZIM) bt Albert Costa (ESP)(15) 6–3 3–6 11–9, Ivan Ljubicic
(CRO) bt Dominik Hrbaty (SVK) 6–1 1–6 6–3, Rainer Schuettler (GER) bt Todd Martin
(USA) 6–2 6–0, Gustavo Kuerten (BRA)(2) bt Christophe Pognon (BEN)(WC) 6–1 6–1

Second Round:

Santoro bt Vicente 6–1 6–7(2–7) 7–5, Alami bt Pozzi 6–2 4–6 8–6, Tillstrom bt Lareau
6–1 3–6 6–3, Federer bt Kucera 6–4 7–6(7–5) Mirnyi bt Vanek 6–7(4–7) 6–4 11–9,
Zabaleta bt Tarango 6–2 6–3, Haas bt Vinciguerra 4–6 6–4 6–2, Corretja(6) bt Clement
6–7(5–7) 6–4 6–4, Ferrero(8) bt Massu 6–4 7–6(8–6), Nestor bt Rafter(13) 7–5 7–6, Di
Pasquale bt Voltchkov 6–2 6–2, Norman(3) bt Srichaphan 7–5 6–2, Kafelnikov(5) bt

Chela 7–6(7–4) 6–4, Philippoussis(11) bt Pless 6–4 6–4, Ljubicic bt Ullyett 6–2 4–6 6–4, Kuerten(2) bt Schuettler 6–4 6–4

Third Round:

Alami bt Santoro 6–2 5–7 6–4, Federer bt Tillstrom 6–1 6–2, Mirnyi bt Zabaleta 7–6(7–4) 6–2, Haas bt Corretja(6) 7–6(9–7) 6–3, Ferrero(8) bt Nestor 7–6(7–4) 7–6(7–2), Kafelnikov(5) bt Philippoussis(11) 7–6 (7–4) 6–3, Kuerten (2) bt Ljubicic 7–6(7–2) 6–3

Quarter-final:

Federer bt Alami 7–6(7–2) 6–1, Haas bt Mirnyi 4–6 7–5 6–3, Di Pasquale bt Ferrero(8) 6–2 6–1, Kafelnikov(5) bt Kuerten(2) 6–4 7–5

Semi-final:

Haas bt Federer 6–3 6–2, Kafelnikov(5) bt Di Pasquale 6–4 6–4

Final:

Kafelnikov(5) (Gold) bt Haas (Silver) 7–6(7–4) 3–6 6–2 4–6 6–3

Third Place Play-off:

Di Pasquale (Bronze) bt Federer 7–6(7–5) 6–7(7–9) 6–3

Ladies' Singles – First Round:

Lindsay Davenport (USA)(1) bt Paola Suarez (ARG) 6–2 6–2, Rossana De Los Rios (PAR) (WC) bt Kveta Hrdlickova (CZE) 6–3 6–0, Rita Grande (ITA) bt Sylvia Plischke (AUT) 6–2 6–2, Jelena Dokic (AUS) bt Ai Sugiyama (JPN)(14) 6–0 7–6(7–1), Sabine Appelmans (BEL) (16) bt Sonya Jeyaseelan (CAN) 7–5 6–2, Maria Alejandra Vento (VEN)(WC) bt Amanda Hopmans (NED) 6–4 6–3, Anne Kremer (LUX) bt Iva Majoli (CRO)(WC) 6–2 6–4, Amanda Coetzer (RSA)(7) bt Rita Kuti Kis (HUN) 6–1 6–1, Conchita Martinez (ESP)(4) bt Petra Mandula (HUN)(WC)6–1 6–0, Karina Habsudova (SVK) bt Katarina Srebotnik (SLO)(WC) 6–3 7–6(9–7), Kristie Boogert (NED) bt Iroda Tulyaganova (UZB) (WC) 6–2 6–2. Elena Dementieva (RUS)(10) bt Miroslava Vavrinec (SUI)(WC) 6–1 6–1, Barbara Schett (AUT)(12) bt Alicia Molik(AUS)(WC) 7–6(9–7) 6–2, Maria Emilia Salerni (ARG)(WC) bt Natasha Zvereva (BLR) 6–3 4–6 6–2, Daniela Bedanova (CZE) bt Jing Qian Yi (CHN) 6–2 6–7(3–7) 6–3, Julie Halard-Decugis (FRA) bt Tathiana Garbin (ITA) 6–4 6–2, Dominique Van Roost (BEL)(8) bt Adriana Gersi (CZE) 6–1 6–1, Anastasia Myskina (RUS) bt Eleni Daniilidou (GRE)(WC) 6–1 7–5, Silvia Farina-Elia (ITA) bt Cara Black (ZIM) 6–2 3–6 6–3, Silvija Talaja (CRO)(13) bt Etienne Neyssa (HAI)(WC) 6–1 6–0, Nathalie Dechy (FRA)(11) bt Magui Serna (ESP) 6–1 6–2, Nicole Pratt (AUS) bt Ruxandra Dragomir (ROM) 6–3 6–3, Miriam Oremans (NED) bt Florencia Labat (ARG) 6–2 6–4, Monica Seles (USA)(3) bt Katalin Marosi-Aracama (HUN)(WC) 6–0

6–1, Arantxa Sanchez-Vicario (ESP)(5) bt Na Li (CHN)(WC) 6–1 7–5, Patricia Wartusch (AUT) bt Olga Barabanschikova (BLR) 6–4 6–2, Els Callens (BEL) bt Shinobu Asagoe (JPN)(WC) 6–0 6–4, Fabiola Zuluaga (COL) bt Amelie Mauresmo (FRA)(9) 6–3 3–6 6–2, Jana Kandarr (GER) bt Elena Likhovtseva (RUS)(15) 6–4 6–4, Emmanuelle Gagliardi (SUI) bt Wynne Prakusya (INA)(WC) 6–4 7–6(7–2), Tamarine Tanasugarn (THA) bt Tina Pisnik (SLO) 6–4 6–3, Venus Williams (USA) bt Henrieta Nagyova (SVK) 6–2 6–2

Second Round:
Rossana De Los Rios bt Lindsay Davenport(1) w.o., Jelena Dokic bt Rita Grande 5–7 6–3 6–3, Sabine Appelmans(16) bt Maria Alejandra Vento 6–2 6–2, Amanda Coetzer(7) bt Anne Kremer 4–6 6–3 6–4, Karina Habsudova bt Conchita Martinez(4) 1–6 6–0 6–4, Elena Dementieva(10) bt Kristie Boogert 6–2 4–6 7–5, Barbara Schett(12) bt Maria Emilia Salerni 7–6(7–5) 6–4, Julie Halard-Decugis bt Daniela Bedanova 6–3 6–4, Dominque Van Roost(8) bt Anastasia Myskina 6–2 6–3, Silvia Farina-Elia bt Silvija Talaja(13) 3–6 6–4 6–4, Nathalie Dechy(11) bt Nicole Pratt 6–3 6–1, Monica Seles(3) bt Miriam Oremans 6–1 6–1, Arantxa Sanchez-Vicario(5) bt Patricia Wartusch 6–2 6–4, Fabiola Zuluaga bt Els Callens 6–3 6–2, Jana Kandarr bt Emmanuelle Gagliardi 7–5 6–4, Venus William(2) bt Tamarine Tanasugarn 6–2 6–3

Third Round:
Jelena Dokic bt Rossana De Los Rios 7–6(7–5) 7–5, Amanda Coetzer(7) bt Sabine Appelmans(16) 6–3 6–1, Elena Dementieva(10) bt Karina Habsudova 6–2 6–1, Barbara Schett(12) bt Julie Halard-Decugis 2–6 6–2 6–1, Dominique Van Roost(8) bt Silvia Farina-Elia 6–1 7–5, Monica Seles(3) bt Nathalie Dechy(11) 6–3 6–2, Arantxa Sanchez-Vicario(5) bt Fabiola Zuluaga 6–2 6–0, Venus Williams(2) bt Jana Kandarr 6–2 6–2

Quarter-final:
Jelena Dokic bt Amanda Coetzer(7) 6–1 1–6 6–1, Elena Dementieva(10) bt Barbara Schett(12) 2–6 6–2 6–1, Monica Seles(3) bt Dominique Van Roost(8) 6–0 6–2, Venus Williams(2) bt Arantxa Sanchez-Vicario(5) 3–6 6–2 6–4

Semi-final:
Elena Dementieva(10) bt Jelena Dokic 2–6 6–4 6–4, Venus Williams(2) bt Monica Seles(3) 6–1 4–6 6–3

Final:
Venus Williams(2) (Gold) bt Elena Dementieva(10) (Silver) 6–2 6–4

Third Place Play-off:
Monica Seles(3) (Bronze) bt Jelena Dokic 6–1 6–4

Men's Doubles – First Round:

Mahesh Bhupathi & Leander Paes (IND) bt Andrei Pavel & Gabriel Trifu (ROM) 6–3 6–4, Dominik Hrbaty & Karol Kucera (SVK) bt Satoshi Iwabuchi & Thomas Shimada (JPN) 6–4 6–3, Massimo Bertolini & Cristian Brandi (ITA)(8) bt Gabor Koves & Attila Savolt (HUN)(WC) 3–6 6–2 6–2, Alex Corretja & Albert Costa (ESP) bt Juan Ignacio Chela & Mariano Zabaleta (ARG) 6–3 6–4, Arnaud Clement & Nicolas Escude (FRA) bt Dusan Vemic & Nenad Zimonjic (YUG) 6–3 6–3, Max Mirnyi & Vladimir Voltchkov (BLR)(WC) bt Nicklas Kulti & Mikael Tillstrom (SWE)(6) 6–3 6–4, Tommy Haas & David Prinosil (GER) bt Wayne Black & Kevin Ullyett (ZIM)(7) 6–1 6–4, Hyung-Taik Lee & Yoong-Il Yoon (KOR) bt Nicolas Massu & Marcelo Rios (CHI)(WC) 6–3 6–4, Jimy Szymanski & Jose De Armas (VEN)(WC) bt Mario Ancic & Goran Ivanisevic (CRO) (WC) 6–2 7–6(7–3), Sebastien Lareau & Daniel Nestor (CAN)(4) bt Gustavo Kuerten & Jaime Oncins (BRA) 6–1 6–4, David Adams & John-Laffnie De Jager (RSA)(5) bt Enrique Abaroa & Alejandro Hernandez (MEX) 6–4 7–6(7–5), Yevgeney Kafelnikov & Marat Safin (RUS) bt Barry Cowan & Kyle Spencer (GBR) 7–6(7–2) 6–4, Mark Knowles & Mark Merklein (BAH) bt Nuno Marques & Bernardo Mota (POR) 6–7 (7–9) 6–4 7–5

Second Round:

Todd Woodbridge & Mark Woodforde (AUS)(1) bt Bhupathi & Paes 6–3 7–6(7–1), Hrbaty & Kucera bt Bertolin & Brandi(8) 6–4 6–7(5–7) 6–3, Corretja & Costa bt Jiri Novak & David Rikl (CZE)(3) 6–7(6–8) 7–5 6–4, Mirnyi & Voltchkov bt Clement & Escude 6–4 7–6(7–4), Haas & Prinosil bt Lee & Yoon 6–4 7–5, Lareau & Nestor (4) bt Szymanski & De Armas 6–3 6–4, Adams & De Jager(5) bt Kafelnikov & Safin 6–3 3–6 9–7, Knowles & Merklein bt Alex O'Brien & Jared Palmer (USA)(2) 6–2 6–4

Quarter-final:

Woodbridge & Woodforde(1) bt Hrbaty & Kucera 7–6(7–5) 6–4, Corretja & Costa bt Mirnyi & Voltchkov 6–7(4–7) 6–3 7–5, Lareau & Nestor(4) bt Haas & Prinosil 6–0 6–4, Adams & De Jager(5) bt Knowles & Merklein 4–6 6–2 14–12

Semi-final:

Woodbridge & Woodforde(1) bt Corretja & Costa 6–3 7–6(7–5), Lareau & Nestor(4) bt Adams & De Jager(5) 6–1 6–2

Final:

Lareau & Nestor(4) (Gold) bt Woodbridge & Woodforde(1) (Silver) 5–7 6–3 6–4 7–6(7–2)

Third Place Play-off:

Corretja & Costa (Bronze) bt Adams & De Jager(5) 2–6 6–4 6–3

Ladies' Doubles – First Round:

Elena Tatarkova & Anna Zaporozhanova (UKR) bt Janet Lee & Tzu-Ting Weng (TPE) (WC) 6–3 7–6(7–4), Serena Williams & Venus Williams (USA) bt Sonya Jeyaseelan & Vanessa Webb (CAN) 6–3 6–1, Elena Likhovtseva & Anastasia Myskina (RUS) bt Tina Krizan & Katarina Srebotnik (SLO)(7)(WC) 7–6(7–4) 6–3, Laura Montalvo & Paola Suarez (ARG)(3) bt Silvia Farina-Elia & Rita Grande (ITA) 6–0 6–0, Milagros Sequera & Maria Alejandra Vento (VEN)(WC) bt Emmanuelle Gagliardi & Miroslava Vavrinec (SUI) 6–2 7–5, Karina Habsudova & Janette Husarova (SVK) bt Yoon-Jeong Cho & Sung-Hee Park (KOR)(WC) 7–5 6–7(2–7) 6–4, Els Callens & Dominique Van Roost (BEL)(5) bt Iva Majoli & Silvija Talaja (CRO)(WC) 6–2 5–7 6–2, Jelena Dokic & Rennae Stubbs (AUS)(6) bt Manisha Malhotra & Nirupama Vaidyanathan (IND) 6–0 6–0, Kristie Boogert & Miriam Oremans (NED) bt Julie Pullin & Lorna Woodroffe (GBR) 6–2 6–1, Benjamas Sangaram & Tamarine Tanasugarn (THA) bt Mariana Mesa & Fabiola Zuluaga (COL)(WC) 7–6(7–4) 5–7 6–4, Nana Miyagi & Ai Sugiyama (JPN) (4) bt Yayuk Basuki & Wynne Prakusya (INA)(WC) 6–2 5–7 6–4, Petra Mandula & Katalin Marosi-Aracama (HUN) bt Amanda Coetzer & Leizel Horn (RSA)(8) 6–4 6–3, Joana Cortez & Vanessa Menga (BRA) bt Na Li & Ting Li (CHN) 6–4 6–2, Olga Barabanschikova & Natasha Zvereva (BLR) bt Barbara Schett & Patricia Wartusch (AUT) 6–2 6–2, Conchita Martinez & Arantxa Sanchez-Vicario (ESP)(2) bt Daniela Bedanova & Kveta Hrdlickova (CZE)(WC) 6–4 6–3

Second Round:

Julie Halard-Decugis & Amelie Mauresmo (FRA)(1) bt Elena Tatarkova & Anna Zaporozhanova 6–2 6–4, Serena Williams & Venus Williams bt Elena Likhovtseva & Anastasia Myskina 4–6 6–2 6–3, Milagros Sequera & Maria Alejandra Vento bt Laura Montalvo & Paola Suarez(3) 6–4 6–1, Els Callens & Dominique Van Roost(5) bt Karina Habsudova & Janette Husarova 6–3 6–2, Kristie Boogert & Miriam Oremans bt Jelena Dokic & Rennae Stubbs(6) 2–6 7–6 (7–4) 6–4, Benjamas Sangaram & Tamarine Tanasugarn bt Nana Miyagi & Ai Sugiyama(4) 2–6 7–5 6–2, Petra Mandula & Katalin Marosi-Aracama bt Joana Cortez & Vanessa Menga 6–2 6–3, Olga Barabanschikova & Natasha Zvereva bt Conchita Martinez & Arantxa Sanchez-Vicario(2) 6–4 7–5

Quarter-final:

Serena Williams & Venus Williams bt Julie Halard-Decugis & Amelie Mauresmo(1) 6–3 6–2, Els Callens & Dominique Van Roost(5) bt Milagros Sequera & Maria Alejandra Vento 4–6 7–5 6–4, Kristie Boogert & Miriam Oremans bt Benjamas Sangaram & Tamarine Tanasugarn 6–4 3–6 7–5, Olga Barabanschikova & Natasha Zvereva bt Petra Mandula & Katalin Marosi-Aracama 6–3 7–5

Semi-final:

Serena Williams & Venus Williams bt Els Callens & Dominique Van Roost(5) 6–4 6–1, Kristie Boogert & Miriam Oremans bt Olga Barabanschikova & Natasha Zvereva 6–3 6–2

Final:

Serena Williams & Venus Williams (Gold) bt Kristie Boogert & Miriam Oremans (Silver) 6–1 6–1

Third Place Play-off:

Els Callens & Dominique Van Roost(5) (Bronze) bt Olga Barabanschikova & Natasha Zvereva 4–6 6–4 6–1

(Referee Stefan Fransson, SWE)

2004 – Athens

Olympic Tennis Centre, 15–22 August

Men's Singles – First Round:

Roger Federer (SUI)(1) bt Nikolay Davydenko (RUS) 6–3 5–7 6–1, Tomas Berdych (CZE) bt Florian Mayer (GER) 6–3 7–5, Fabrice Santoro (FRA) bt Filippo Volandri (ITA) 6–2 6–1, Tommy Robredo (ESP)(15) bt Lamina Quahab (ALG)(WC) 6–3 6–4, Joachim Johanssson (SWE) bt Paradorn Srichaphan (THA)(12) 6–2 6–3, Ivan Ljubicic (CRO) bt Sargis Sargsian (ARM) 6–3 6–4, Dominik Hrbaty (SVK) bt Younes El Aynaoui (MAR) 6–3 6–4, Taylor Dent (USA) bt Frederic Nemeyer (CAN) 6–2 3–6 6–4, Carlos Moya (ESP)(3) bt Thomas Enqvist (SWE) 7–6(9–7) 6–7(8–10) 9–7, Oliver Rochus (BEL) bt Mark Philippoussis (AUS) 3–6 6–0 6–1, Arnaud Clement (FRA) bt Nicolas Lapentti (ECU)(WC) 7–6(7–5) 6–2, Ivo Karlovic (CRO) bt Andrei Pavel (ROM)(13) 6–4 6–7(10–12) 6–2, Nicolas Massu (CHI) (10) bt Gustavo Kuerten (BRA) 6–3 5–7 6–4, Vince Spadea (USA) bt Jurgen Melzer (AUT) 6–0 6–1, Agustin Calleri (ARG) bt Karol Beck (SVK) 2–6 6–3 8–6, Igor Andreev bt Rainer Schuettler (GER)(7) 6–7(5–7) 7–6(7–2) 6–2, Juan Carlos Ferrero (ESP)(5) bt Hicham Arazi (MAR) 6–3 6–1, Mardy Fish (USA) bt Jonas Bjorkman (SWE) 7–6(9–7) 1–0 retd, Jarkko Nieminen (FIN) bt Yen-Hsun Lu (TPE)(WC) 6–3 6–3, Max Mirnyi (BLR) bt Juan Ignacio Chela (ARG)(11) 3–6 7–6(7–0) 6–4, Nicolas Kiefer (GER)(14) bt Vladimir Voltchkov (BLR) 6–2 6–4, Marcos Baghdatis (CYP)(WC) bt Gregory Carraz (FRA) 5–7 7–6(7–5) 7–5, Mikhail Youzhny (RUS) bt Xavier Malisse (BEL) 6–2 6–2,

Jiri Novak (CZE) bt Tim Henman (GBR)(4) 6–3 6–3, Sebastien Grosjean (FRA) bt Luis Horna (PER)6–2 7–5, Wayne Arthurs (AUS)(WC) bt Victor Hanescu (ROM)(WC) 6–4 7–6(7–4), Feliciano Lopez (ESP) bt Robin Soderling (SWE) 6–3 3–6 6–4, Marat Safin (RUS)(9) bt Karol Kucera (SVK)(WC) 6–0 6–4, Fernando Gonzalez (CHI)(16) bt Konstantinos Economidis (GRE)(WC) 7–6(8–6) 6–2, Hyung-Taik Lee (KOR)(WC) bt Mariano Zabaleta (ARG) 4–6 6–3 6–2, Tommy Haas (GER) bt Mario Ancic (CRO) 6–1 7–5, Andy Roddick (USA)(2) bt Flavio Saretta (BRA) 6–3 7–6(7–4)

Second Round:
Berdych bt Federer(1) 4–6 7–5 7–5, Robredo(15) bt Santoro 1–6 6–3 6–4, Ljubicic bt Johansson 7–6(7–3) 6–4, Dent bt Hrbaty 7–6(7–4) 6–3, Moya(3) bt Rochus 6–0 7–6(7–3), Karlovic bt Clement 7–6(7–4) 4–6 6–4, Massu(10) bt Spadea 7–6(7–3) 6–2, Andreev bt Calleri w.o., Fish bt Ferrero(5) 4–6 7–6(7–5) 6–4, Mirnyi bt Nieminen 6–3 6–4, Kiefer(14) bt Baghdatis 6–2 3–6 6–3, Youzhny bt Novak 6–4 6–3, Grosjean(8) bt Arthurs 7–6(7–2) 6–3, Lopez bt Safin(9) 7–6(7–4) 6–3, Gonzalez(16) bt Lee 7–5 6–2, Roddick(2) bt Haas 4–6 6–3 9–7

Third Round:
Berdych bt Robredo(15) 7–6(7–2) 4–6 8–6, Dent bt Ljubicic 6–4 6–4, Moya(3) bt Karlovic 4–6 7–6(7–3) 6–4, Massu(10) bt Andreev 6–3 6–7(4–7) 6–4, Fish bt Mirnyi 6–3 4–6 6–1, Youzhny bt Kiefer(14) 6–2 3–6 6–2, Grosjean(8) bt Lopez 6–7(4–7) 6–4 6–0, Gonzales(16) bt Roddick(2) 6–4 6–4

Quarter-final:
Dent bt Berdych 6–4 6–1, Massu(10) bt Moya(3) 6–2 7–5, Fish bt Youzhny 6–3 6–4, Gonzalez(16) bt Grosjean(8) 6–2 2–6 6–4

Semi-final:
Massu(10) bt Dent 7–6(7–5) 6–1, Fish bt Gonzalez(16) 3–6 6–3 6–4

Final:
Massu(10) (Gold) bt Fish (Silver) 6–3 3–6 2–6 6–3 6–4

Third Place Play-off:
Gonzales (Bronze) bt Dent 6–4 2–6 16–14

Ladies' Singles – First Round:
Justine Henin-Hardenne (BEL)(1) bt Barbara Strycova (CZE) 6–3 6–4, Maria Vento-Kabchi (VEN) bt Anne Kremer (LUX) 6–3 6–4, Nicole Pratt (AUS) bt Myriam Casanova (SUI) 6–3 7–5, Tathiana Garbin (ITA) bt Anna Smashnova-Pistolesi (ISR)(13) 6–2 6–1, Nadia Petrova (RUS)(9) bt Martina Sucha (SVK) 6–3 6–3, Mary Pierce (FRA) bt

Anabel Medina Garrigues (ESP) 6–3 7–5, Maja Matevzic (SLO) bt Saori Obata (JPN) 7–6(7–3) 7–5, Venus Williams (USA)(6) bt Melinda Czink (HUN)(WC) 6–1 6–2, Anastasia Myskina (RUS)(3) bt Magui Serna (ESP) 6–0 6–1, Kristina Brandi (PUR) bt Jelena Kostanic (CRO) 7–5 6–1, Eleni Daniilidou (GRE) bt Catalina Costano (COL) 6–2 6–1, Magdalena Maleeva (BUL)(15) bt Klara Koukalova (CZE) 6–1 6–4, Francesca Schiavone (ITA)(11) bt Shinobu Asagoe (JPN) 6–3 7–6(7–4), Yoon Jeong Cho (KOR) bt Kaia Kanepi (EST)(WC) 7–6(7–1) 6–1, Fabiola Zuluaga (COL) bt Jelena Jankovic (SCG) 6–4 6–1, Paola Suarez (ARG)(7) bt Nathalie Dechy (FRA) 6–7(1–7) 7–6(7–5) 9–7, Ai Sugiyama (JPN)(8) bt Jie Zheng (CHN) Tatiana Perebiynis (UKR)(WC) bt Dally Randriantefy (MAD)(WC) 6–3 6–4, Angelique Widjaja (INA)(WC) bt Tamarine Tanasugarn (THA) 1–6 6–2 6–1, Karolina Sprem (CRO)(12) bt Gisela Dulko (ARG) 7–6(8–6) 7–5, Silvia Farina-Elia (ITA)(14) bt Sandrine Testud (FRA) 6–2 6–0, Lisa Raymond (USA) bt Lubomira Kurhajcova (SVK) 6–4 4–6 6–3, Katarina Srebotnik (SLO) bt Maria Sanchez-Lorenzo (ESP) 6–3 0–6 6–4, Alicia Molik (AUS) bt Elena Dementieva (RUS) (4) 4–6 6–0 6–3, Svetlana Kuznetsova (RUS)(5) bt Mariana Diaz-Oliva (ARG) (WC) 6–3 6–3, Akiko Morigami (JPN) bt Iveta Benesova (CZE) 6–1 6–4, Daniela Hantuchova (SVK) bt Claudine Schaul (LUX) 6–1 6–1, Patty Schnyder (SUI)(10) bt Petra Mandula (HUN) 6–3 6–4, Chanda Rubin (USA)(16) bt Samantha Stosur (AUS) 6–2 6–7(8–10) 6–0, Cara Black (ZIM)(WC) bt Tina Pisnik (SLO) 6–3 5–7 6–4, Maria Elena Camerin (ITA) bt Mervana Jugic-Salkic (BIH)(WC) 6–4 6–3, Amelie Mauresmo (FRA)(2) bt Conchita Martinez (ESP) 6–1 6–4

Second Round:

Justine Henin-Hardenne(1) bt Maria Vento-Kabchi 6–2 6–1, Nicole Pratt bt Tathiana Garbin 1–6 7–6(7–5) 6–2, Mary Pierce bt Nadia Petrova(9) 6–2 6–1, Venus Williams(6) bt Maja Matevzic 6–0 6–0, Anastasia Myskina(3) bt Kristina Brandi 6–2 3–6 6–4, Eleni Daniilidou bt Magdalena Maleeva(15) 2–6 6–4 6–4, Francesca Schiavone bt Yoon Jeong Cho 2–6 7–6(7–0) 6–4, Fabiola Zuluaga bt Paola Suarez (7) 4–6 7–6(7–1) 6–1, Ai Sugiyama(8) bt Tatiana Perebiynis 7–5 6–4, Karolina Sprem(12) bt Angelique Widjaja 6–3 6–1, Lisa Raymond bt Silvia Farina Elia(14) 6–1 6–2, Alicia Molik bt Katarina Srebotnik 7–5 6–4, Svetlana Kuznetsova(5) bt Akiko Morigami 7–6(7–5) 6–2, Patty Schnyder(10) bt Daniela Hantuchova 3–6 6–1 6–4, Chanda Rubin(16) bt Cara Black 6–4 3–6 6–3, Amelie Mauresmo(2) bt Maria Elena Camerin 6–0 6–1

Third Round:

Justine Henin-Hardenne(1) bt Nicole Pratt 6–1 6–0, Mary Pierce bt Venus Williams(6) 6–4 6–4, Anastasia Myskina(3) bt Eleni Daniilidou 7–5 6–4, Frances Schiavone(11) bt Fabiola Zuluaga 6–7(5–7) 6–1 6–3, Ai Sugiyama(8) bt Karolina Sprem(12) 7–6(8–6) 6–1, Alicia Molik bt Lisa Raymond 6–4 6–4, Svetlana Kuznetsova(5) bt Patty Schnyder(10) 6–3 6–3, Amelie Mauresmo(2) bt Chanda Rubin(16) 6–3 6–1

Quarter-final:

Justine Henin-Hardenne(1) bt Mary Pierce 6–4 6–4, Anastasia Myskina(3) bt Francesca Schiavone(11) 6–1 6–2, Alicia Molik bt Ai Sugiyama(8) 6–3 6–4, Amelie Mauresmo(2) bt Svetlana Kuznetsova(5) 7–6(7–5) 4–6 6–2

Semi-final:

Justine Henin-Hardenne(1) bt Anastasia Myskina(3) 7–5 5–7 8–6, Amelie Mauresmo(2) bt Alicia Molik 7–6(10–8) 6–3

Final:

Justine Henin-Hardenne(1) (Gold) bt Amelie Mauresmo(2) (Silver) 6–3 6–3

Third Place Play-off:

Alicia Molik (Bronze) bt Anastasia Myskina(3) 6–3 6–4

Men's Doubles – First Round:

Bob Bryan & Mike Bryan (USA)(1) bt Marat Safin & Mikhail Youzhny (RUS) 6–1 6–2, Max Mirnyi & Vladimir Voltchkov (BLR) bt Hicham Azazi & Younes El Aynaoui (MAR) w.o., Fernando Gonzales & Nicolas Massu (CHI) bt Mark Knowles & Mark Merklein (BAH) 7–5 6–4, Gaston Etlis & Martin Rodriguez (ARG)(6) bt Feliciano Lopez & Tommy Robredo (ESP) 6–3 6–4, Michael Llodra & Fabrice Santoro (FRA)(3) bt Xavier Malisse & Oliver Rochus (BEL) 6–3 6–2, Daniel Nestor & Frederic Niemeyer (CAN) bt Karol Beck & Dominik Hrbaty (SVK) 6–2 7–5, Mario Ancic & Ivan Ljubicic (CRO) bt Jonas Bjorkman & Joachim Johansson (SWE) w.o.,Martin Damm & Cyril Suk (CZE) (7) bt Konstantinos Economidis & Vasilis Mazarakis (GRE) 6–1 6–3, Mahesh Bhupathi & Leander Paes (IND)(5) bt Mardy Fish & Andy Roddick (USA) 7–6(7–5) 6–3, Yves Allegro & Roger Federer (SUI) bt Mariusz Fyrstenberg & Marcin Matkowski (POL) 6–3 6–2, Andre Sa & Flavio Saretta (BRA) bt Carlos Moya & Rafael Nadal (ESP) 7–6(8–6) 6–1, Wayne Black & Kevin Ullyett (ZIM)(4) bt Arnaud Clement & Sebastien Grosjean (FRA) 5–7 6–4 9–7, Jonathan Erlich & Andy Ram (ISR)(8) bt Thomas Enqvist & Robin Soderling (SWE) 7–5 6–3, Igor Andreev & Nikolay Davydenko (RUS) bt Juan Ignacio Chela & Mariano Zabaleta (ARG) 3–6 6–3 6–4, Nicolas Kiefer & Rainer Schuettler (GER) bt Victor Hanescu & Andrei Pavel (ROM) 7–5 7–6(7–3), Wayne Arthurs & Todd Woodbridge (AUS)(2) bt Tomas Berdych & Jiri Novak (CZE) 6–4 6–3

Second Round:

Bryan & Bryan(1) bt Mirnyi & Voltchkov 6–3 6–3, Gonzalez & Massu bt Etlis & Rodriguez(6) 6–3 7–6(7–2), Llodra & Santoro(3) bt Nestor & Niemeyer 6–3 6–7 5–7 6–3, Ancic & Ljubicic bt Damm & Suk(7) 7–6(8–6) 6–7(2–7) 7–5, Bhupathi &

Paes(5) bt Allegro & Federer 6–2 7–6(9–7), Black & Ullyett(4) bt Sa & Saretta 6–3 6–4, Erlich & Ram(8) bt Andreev & Davydenko 6–4 6–1, Kiefer & Schuettler bt Arthurs & Woodbridge(2) 7–6(8–6) 6–3

Quarter-final:
Gonzalez & Massu bt Bryan & Bryan 7–5 6–4, Ancic & Ljubicic bt Llodra & Santoro 4–6 6–3 9–7, Bhupathi & Paes(5) bt Black & Ullyett(4) 6–4 6–4, Kiefer & Schuettler bt Erlich & Ram(8) 2–6 6–2 6–2

Semi-final:
Gonzales & Massu bt Ancic & Ljubicic 7–5 4–6 6–4, Kiefer & Schuettler bt Bhupathi & Paes(5) 6–2 6–3

Final:
Gonzales & Massu (Gold) bt Kiefer & Schuettler (Silver) 6–2 4–6 3–6 7–6(9–7) 6–4

Third Place Play-off:
Ancic & Ljubicic (Bronze) bt Bhupathi & Paes(5) 7–6(7–5) 4–6 16–14

Ladies' Doubles – First Round:
Svetlana Kuznetsova & Elena Likhovtseva (RUS)(1) bt Libuse Prusova & Barbora Strycova (CZE) 6–2 3–6 6–1, Nathalie Dechy & Sandrine Testud (FRA) bt Tina Krizan & Katarina Srebotnik (SLO) 7–5 6–3, Akiko Morigami & Saori Obata (JPN) bt Melinda Czink & Aniko Kapros (HUN) 3–6 7–5 6–3, Paola Suarez & Patricia Tarabini (ESP)(7) bt Anabel Medina Garrigues & Arantxa Sanchez-Vicario (ESP) 6–7(8–10) 7–5 6–2, Alicia Molik & Rennae Stubbs (AUS)(4) bt Maret Ani & Kaia Kanepi (EST) 6–4 6–1, Catalina Castano & Fabiola Zuluaga (COL) bt Anne Kremer & Claudine Schaul (LUX) 7–6(9–7) 2–6 9–7, Silvia Farina Elia & Francesca Schiavone (ITA) bt Lubomira Kurhajcova & Martina Sucha (SVK) 6–2 6–4, Ting Li & Tian Tian Sun (CHN)(8) bt Chanda Rubin & Venus Williams (USA) 7–5 1–6 6–3, Shinobu Asagoe & Ai Sugiyama (JPN)(5) bt Elena Dementieva & Anastasia Myskina (RUS) 5–7 7–5 6–3, Jelena Kostanic & Karolina Sprem (CRO) bt Wynne Prakusya & Angelique Widjaja (INA) 6–3 6–2, Amelie Mauresmo & Mary Pierce (FRA) bt Eleni Daniilidou & Christina Zachariadou (GRE) 7–5 6–1, Martina Navratilova & Lisa Raymond (USA) bt Yulia Beygelzimer & Tatiana Perebiynis (UKR) 6–0 6–2, Myriam Casanova & Patty Schnyder (SUI)(6) bt Daniela Hantuchova & Janette Husarova (SVK) 6–3 6–4, Zi Yan & Jie Zheng (CHN) bt Maja Matevzic & Tina Pisnik (SLO) 6–2 6–1, Tathiana Garbin & Roberta Vinci (ITA) bt Nicole Pratt & Samantha Stosur (AUS) 6–0 6–1, Conchita Martinez & Virginia Ruano Pascual (ESP) bt Petra Mandula & Kyro Nagy (HUN) 6–4 6–0

Second Round:

Nathalie Dechy & Sandrine Testud bt Svetlana Kuznetsova & Elena Likhovtseva 2–6 7–6(7–5) 6–3, Paola Suarez & Patricia Tarabini(7) bt Akiko Morigami & Saori Obata 6–4 6–2, Alicia Molik & Rennae Stubbs(4) bt Catalina Castano & Fabiola Zuluaga 6–4 6–2, Ting Li & Tian Tian Sun bt Silvia Farina Elia and Francesca Schiavone 6–1 7–6(7–1), Shinobu Asagoe & Ai Sugiyama(5) bt Jelena Kostanic & Karolina Sprem 6–3 7–5, Martina Navratilova & Lisa Raymond(3) bt Amelie Mauresmo & Mary Pierce w.o., Zi Yan & Jie Zheng bt Myriam Casanova & Patty Schnyder(6) 6–3 6–3, Conchita Martinez & Virginia Ruano Pascual bt Tathiana Garbin & Roberta Vinci 6–3 6–3

Quarter-final:

Paola Suarez & Patricia Tarabini(7) bt Nathalie Dechy & Sandrine Testud 6–4 1–6 6–4, Ting Li & Tian Tian Sun bt Alicia Molik & Rennae Stubbs(4), Shinobu Asagoe & Ai Sugiyama(5) bt Martina Navratilova & Lisa Raymond (3) 6–4 4–6 6–4, Conchita Martinez & Virginia Ruano Pascual(2) bt Zi Yan & Jie Zheng 6–1 6–1

Semi-final:

Ting Li & Tian Tian Sun(8) bt Paola Suarez & Patricia Tarabini(7) 6–2 2–6 9–7, Conchita Martinez & Virginia Ruano Pascual(2) bt Shinobu Asagoe & Ai Sugiyama(5) 6–3 6–0

Final:

Ting Li & Tian Tian Sun(8) (Gold) bt Conchita Martinez & Virginia Ruano Pascual(2) (Silver) 6–3 6–3

Third Place Play-off:

Paola Suarez & Patricia Tarabini(7) (Bronze) bt Shinobu Asagoe & Ai Sugiyama(5)

(Referee: Stefan Fransson, SWE)

2008 – Beijing

Olympic Tennis Centre, 10–17 August

Men's Singles – First Round:
Roger Federer (SUI)(1) bt Dmitry Tursunov (RUS)
6–4 6–2, Rafael Arevalo (ELS)(WC) bt Hyung-Taik Lee
(KOR) 4–6 6–3 6–4, Andreas Seppi (ITA) bt Tommy
Robredo (ESP) 6–4 4–6 8–6, Tomas Berdych (CZE)(17) bt
Xin Yuan Yu (CHN) 6–1 6–2, Gilles Simon (FRA)(10) bt
Robin Soderling (SWE) 6–4 6–4, Guillermo Canas (ARG)
bt Frederic Niemeyer (CAN) 3–6 4–2 retd, Dominik Hrbaty
(SVK) bt Thomaz Bellucci (BRA) 2–6 6–4 6–2, James Blake
(USA)(8) bt Chris Guccione (AUS) 6–3 7–6(7–3), Nikolay Davydenko (RUS)(4) bt Ernests
Gulbis (LAT) 6–4 6–2, Paul-Henri Mathieu (FRA) bt Nicolas Lapentti (ECU) 7–6(7–4)
6–2, Kevin Anderson (RSA)(WC) bt Komlavi Loglo (TOG)(WC) 6–3 6–2, Nicolas Kiefer
(GER)(15) bt Max Mirnyi (BLR)(WC) 6–3 6–1, Fernando Gonzales (CHI)(12) bt Peg Sun
(CHN)(WC) 6–4 6–4, Marin Cilic (CRO) bt Juan Monaco (ARG) 6–4 6–7(5–7) 6–3,
Oliver Rochus (BEL) bt Ivo Minar (CZE) 6–3 3–6 6–3, Janko Tipsarevic (SRB) bt David
Ferrer (ESP)(5) 7–6(10–8) 6–2, David Nalbandian (ARG)(7) bt Shao-Xuan Zeng (CHN)
6–2 6–1, Nicolas Massu (CHI)(WC) bt Steve Darcis (BEL) 6–4 7–5, Victor Hanescu
(ROM) bt Simone Bolelli (ITA) 7–5 3–6 6–4, Gael Monfils (FRA) bt Nicolas Almagro
(ESP)(11) 6–4 3–6 6–3, Mikhail Youzhny (RUS)(13) bt Jiri Vanek (CZE) 6–4 6–1, Thomas
Johansson (SWE) bt Jarkko Nieminen (FIN) 4–6 6–4 6–4, Rainer Schuettler (GER) bt Kei
Nishikori (JPN)(WC) 6–4 6–7(5–7) 6–3, Novak Djokovic (SRB)(3) bt Robby Ginepri
(USA) 6–4 6–4, Yen-Hsun Lu (TPE) bt Andy Murray (GBR) (6) 7–6(7–5) 6–4, Agustin
Calleri (ARG) bt Devin Mullings (BAH) 6–1 6–1, Jurgen Melzer (AUT) bt Marcos Daniel
(BRA) 6–7(7–9) 6–1 8–6, Stanislas Wawrinka (SUI) bt Frank Dancevic (CAN) 4–6 6–3
6–2, Michael Llodra (FRA) bt Radek Stepanek (CZE)(16) 4–6 7–6(7–5) 11–9, Igor
Andreev (RUS) bt Sam Querrey (USA) 6–4 6–4, Lleyton Hewitt (AUS) bt Jonas Bjorkman
(SWE)(WC) 7–5 7–6(7–5) Rafael Nadal (ESP)(2) bt Potito Starace (ITA) 6–2 3–6 6–2

Second Round:
Federer(1) bt Arevalo 6–2 6–4, Berdych(17) bt Seppi 6–3 7–6(7–4), Simon(10) bt Canas
7–5 6–1, Blake(8) bt Hrbaty 7–6(7–3) 4–6 6–3, Mathieu bt Davydenko(4) 7–5 6–3,
Kiefer(15) bt Anderson 6–4 6–7(4–7) 6–4, Gonzales(12) bt Cilic 6–4 6–2, Rochus bt
Tipsarevic 7–6(7–5) 2–3 retd, Nalbandian(7) bt Massu 7–6(7–0) 6–1, Monfils bt Hanescu
6–4 7–6(7–5), Youzhny(13) bt Johansson 7–5 6–2, Djokovic(3) bt Schuettler 6–4 6–2,
Lu bt Calleri 6–4 6–4, Melzer bt Wawrinka(8) 6–4 6–0, Andreev bt Llodra 6–4 3–6 6–1,
Nadal(2) bt Hewitt 6–1 6–2

Third Round:

Federer(1) bt Berdych(17) 6–3 7–6(7–4), Blake(8) bt Simon(10) 6–4 6–2, Mathieu bt Kiefer(15) 6–3 7–5, Gonzales(12) bt Rochus 6–0 6–3, Monfils bt Nalbandian(7) 6–4 6–4, Djokovic(3) bt Youzhny(13) 7–6(7–3) 6–3, Melzer bt Lu 6–2 6–4, Nadal(2) bt Andreev 6–4 6–2

Quarter-final:

Blake(8) bt Federer(1) 6–4 7–6(7–2), Gonzales(12) bt Mathieu 6–4 6–4, Djokovic(3) bt Monfils 4–6 6–1 6–4, Nadal(2) bt Melzer 6–0 6–4

Semi-final:

Gonzales(12) bt Blake(8) 4–6 7–5 11–9, Nadal(2) bt Djokovic(3) 6–4 1–6 6–4

Final:

Nadal(2) (Gold) bt Gonzales(12) (Silver) 6–3 7–6(7–2) 6–3

Third Place Play-off:

Djokovic(3) (Bronze) bt Blake(8) 6–3 7–6(7–4)

Ladies' Singles – First Round:

Mariya Koryttseva (UKR) bt Tzipora Obziler (ISR) 5–7 7–5 6–4, Lucie Safarova (CZE) bt Maret Ani (EST) 6–4 6–2, Sybille Bammer (AUT) bt Anabel Medina Garrigues (ESP) 6–4 4–6 6–4, Patty Schnyder (SUI)(13) bt Jill Craybas (USA) 6–3 6–2, Vera Zvonareva (RUS)(8) bt Zi Yan (CHN) 6–2 6–0, Shahar Peer (ISR) bt Sorana Cirstea (ROM) 6–3 5–7 6–0, Francesca Schiavone (ITA) bt Akul Amanmuradova (UZB) 6–4 6–2, Agnieszka Radwanska POL(8) bt Yung-Jan Chan (TPE)(WC) 6–1 7–6(8–6), Serena Williams (USA) (4) bt Olga Govorstsova (BLR) 6–3 6–1, Samantha Stosur (AUS) bt Sara Errani (ITA) 6–3 6–2, Shaui Peng (CHN) bt Carla Suarez Navarro (ESP) 7–5 7–6(7–2), Alize Cornet (FRA)(15) bt Nicole Vaidisova (CZE) 4–6 6–1 6–4, Daniela Hantuchova (SVK)(10) bt Ai Sugiyama (JPN) 6–2 7–5, Caroline Wozniacki (DEN) bt Selima Sfar (TUN)(WC) 6–4 6–1, Sofia Arvidsson (SWE) bt Tamarine Tanasugarn (THA)(WC) 6–2 6–1, Elena Dementieva (RUS)(5) bt Kateryna Bondarenko (UKR) 6–1 6–4, Venus Williams (USA) (7) bt Timea Bacsinzky (SUI) 6–3 6–2, Iveta Benesova (CZE) bt Sania Mirza (IND) 6–2 2–1 retd, Casey Dellacqua (AUS) bt Gisela Dulko (ARG) 6–3 6–4, Victoria Azarenka (BLR)(12) bt Tatiana Perebiynis (UKR) 6–4 5–7 6–4, Kaia Kanepi (EST) bt Flavia Pennetta (ITA)(14) 6–2 7–6(8–6), Virginie Razzano (FRA) bt Eleni Daniilidou (GRE) 6–3 6–3, Ayumi Morita (JPN)(WC) bt Marina Erakovic (NZL) 5–7 7–6(9–7) 6–4, Na Li (CHN) bt Svetlana Kuznetsova (RUS)(3) 7–6(7–5) 6–4, Dinara Safina (RUS)(6) bt Mara Santangelo (ITA) 6–3 7–6(7–1), Maria Martinez Sanchez (ESP) bt Alicia Molik (AUS) (WC) 6–1 6–1, Nuria Llagostera Vives (ESP)(WC) bt Klara Zakopalova (CZE) 2–6 6–3

7–5, Jie Zheng (CHN) bt Agnes Szavay (HUN)(11) 4–6 6–3 7–5, Dominika Cibulkova (SVR)(16) bt Pauline Parmentier (FRA) 6–1 7–5, Tsvetana Pironkova (BUL) bt Marta Domachowska (POL) 6–3 6–4, Alona Bondarenko (UKR) bt Milagros Sequerra (VEN) 3–6 0–1 retd, Jelena Jankovic (SRB)(2) bt Cara Black (ZIM)(WC) 6–3 6–3

Second Round:
Lucie Safarova bt Mariya Koryllseva 2–6 6–1 7–5, Sybille Bammer bt Patty Schnyder(13) 6–4 6–4, Vera Zvonareva(9) bt Shahar Peer 6–3 7–6(7–4), Francesca Schiavone bt Agnieszka Radwanska(8) 6–3 7–6(8–6), Serena Williams(4) bt Samantha Stosur 6–2 6–0, Alize Cornet(15) bt Shaui Peng 6–2 6–2, Caroline Wozniacki bt Daniela Hantuchova(10) 6–1 6–3, Elena Dementieva(5) bt Sofia Arvidsson 6–3 6–4, Venus Williams bt Iveta Benesova 6–1 6–4, Victoria Azarenka(12) bt Casey Dellacqua 6–2 6–2, Kaia Kanepi bt Virginie Razzano 6–4 7–5, Na Li bt Ayumi Morita (JPN) 6–2 7–5, Dinara Safina(6) bt Maria Martinez Sanchez 7–6(7–3) 6–1, Jie Zheng bt Nuria Llagostera Vives 6–7(7–9) 6–1 6–4, Dominika Cibulkova(16) bt Tsvetana Pironkova 6–2 6–2, Jelena Jankovic(2) bt Alona Bondarenko 7–5 6–1

Third Round:
Sybille Bammer bt Lucie Safarova 7–5 6–4, Vera Zvonareva(9) bt Francesca Schiavone 7–6(7–4) 6–4, Serena Williams(4) bt Alize Cornet(15) 3–6 6–3 6–4, Elena Dementieva(5) bt Caroline Wozniacki 7–6(7–3) 6–2, Venus Williams(7) bt Victoria Azarenka(12) 6–3 6–2, Na Li bt Kaia Kanepi 4–6 6–2 6–0, Dinara Safina(6) bt Jie Zheng 6–4 6–3, Jelena Jankovic(2) bt Dominika Cibulkova(16) 7–5 6–1

Quarter-final:
Vera Zvonareva(9) bt Sybille Bammer 6–3 3–6 6–3, Elena Dementieva(5) bt Serena Williams(4) 3–6 6–4 6–3, Na Li bt Venus Williams(7) 7–5 7–5, Dinara Safina(6) bt Jelena Jankovic(2) 6–2 5–7 6–3

Semi-final:
Elena Dementieva(5) bt Vera Zvonareva(9) 6–3 7–6(7–3), Dinara Safina(6) bt Na Li 7–6(7–3) 7–5

Final:
Elena Dementieva(5) (Gold) bt Dinara Safina(6) Silver 3–6 7–5 6–3

Third Place Play-off:
Vera Zvonareva(9) (Bronze) bt Na Li 6–0 7–5

Men's Doubles – First Round:

Bob Bryan & Mike Bryan (USA)(1) bt Mark Knowles & Devin Mullins (BAH) 6–2 6–1, Julian Knowle & Jurgen Melzer (AUT) bt Nicolas Kiefer & Rainer Schuettler (GER)(WC) 6–7(3–7) 6–3 6–1, Chris Guccione & Lleyton Hewitt (AUS)(WC) bt Agustin Calleri & Juan Monaco (ARG)(WC) 4–6 7–6(7–4) 18–16, Rafael Nadal & Tommy Robredo (ESP)(6) bt Jonas Bjorkman & Robin Soderling (SWE)(4) 6–3 6–3, Roger Federer & Stanislas Wawrinka (SUI)(4) bt Simone Bolelli & Andreas Seppi (ITA) 7–5 6–1, Dmitry Tursunov & Mikhail Youzhny (RUS) bt Fernando Gonzales & Nicolas Massu (CHI)(WC) 7–6(7–5) 6–4, Marcelo Melo & Andre Sa (BRA) bt Tomas Berdych & Radek Stepanek (CZE) 5–7 6–2 8–6, Mahesh Bhupathi & Leander Paes (IND)(7) bt Gael Monfils & Gilles Simon (FRA) 6–3 6–3, Igor Andreev & Nikolay Davydenko (RUS)(8) bt James Blake & Sam Querry (USA) 6–3 6–4, Steve Darcis & Oliver Rochus (BEL) bt Guillermo Canas & David Nalbandian (ARG) 6–7(6–8) 7–6(7–5) 6–3, Andy Murray & Jamie Murray (GBR) bt Daniel Nestor & Frederic Niemeyer (CAN) 4–6 6–3 6–4, Arnaud Clement & Michael Llodra (FRA) bt Jonathan Erlich & Andy Ram (ISR)(3) 6–4 6–4, Nicolas Almagro & David Ferrer (ESP)(5) bt Kevin Anderson & Jeff Coetzee (RSA) 3–6 6–3 6–4, Simon Aspelin & Thomas Johansson (SWE) bt Paul Hanley & Jordan Kerr (AUS) 7–6(9–7) 6–3, Mariusz Fyrstenberg & Marcin Matikowski (POL) bt Xin Yuan Yu & Shao-Xuan Zeng (CHN)(WC) 6–3 6–4, Martin Damm & Pavel Vizner (CZE) bt Novak Djokovic & Nenad Zimonjic (SRB)(2) 3–6 6–0 6–2

Second Round:

Bryan & Bryan bt Knowle & Melzer 7–6(7–2) 6–4, Guccione & Hewitt bt Nadal & Robredo(6) 6–2 7–6(7–5), Federer & Wawrinka(4) bt Tursunov & Youzhny 6–4 6–3, Bhupathi & Paes(7) bt Melo & Sa 6–4 6–2, Andreev & Davydenko(8) bt Darcis & Rochus 7–6(8–6) 6–2, Clement & Llodra bt Murray & Murray 6–1 6–3, Aspelin & Johansson bt Almagro & Ferrer(5) 7–6(8–6) 6–4 Fyrstenberg & Matkowski bt Damm & Vizner 1–6 7–6(7–3) 7–5

Quarter-final:

Bryan & Bryan(1) bt Guccione & Hewitt 6–4 6–3, Federer & Wawrinka(4) bt Bhupathi & Paes(7), 6–2 6–4, Clement & Llodra bt Andreev & Davydenko 6–2 6–7(4–7) 6–4, Aspelin & Johansson bt Fyrstenberg & Matkowski 7–6(7–5) 6–4

Semi-final:

Federer & Wawrinka(4) bt Bryan & Bryan(1) 7–6(8–6) 6–4, Aspelin & Johansson bt Clement & Llodra 7–6(8–6) 4–6 19–17

Final:

Federer & Wawrinka(4) (Gold) bt Aspelin & Johansson (Silver) 6–3 6–4 6–7(4–7) 6–3

Third Place Play-off:

Bryan & Bryan(1) (Bronze) bt Clement & Llodra 3–6 6–3 6–4

Ladies' Doubles – First Round:

Svetlana Kuznetsova & Dinara Safina (RUS)(1) bt Mara Santangelo & Roberta Vinci (ITA) 6–1 3–6 7–5, Sania Mizra & Sunitha Rao (IND)(WC) bt Tatiana Golovin & Pauline Parmentier (FRA) w.o., Emmanuelle Gagliardi & Patty Schnyder (SUI)(WC) bt Eleni Daniilidou & Anna Gerasimou (GRE)(WC) 6–0 6–4, Zi Yan & Jie Zheng (CHN)(8) bt Daniela Hantuchova & Janette Husarova (SVK) 6–1 7–6(11–9), Anabel Medina Garrigues & Virginia Ruano Pascual (ESP)(4) bt Mariya Koryttseva & Tatiana Perebiynis (UKR) 6–3 6–4, Samantha Stosur & Rennae Stubbs (AUS) bt Petra Kvitova & Lucie Safarova (CZE) 6–1 6–0, Victoria Azarenka & Tatiana Poutchek (BLR) bt Maret Ani & Kaia Kanepi (EST)(WC) 6–2 6–2, Lindsay Davenport & Leizel Huber (USA) (5) bt Klalidia Jans & Alicia Rosolska (POL) 6–2 6–1, Alona Bondarenko & Kateryna Bondarenko (UKR)(6) bt Marta Domachowska & Agnieszka Radwanska (POL) 6–3 6–2, Olga Govortsova & Darya Kustova (BLR) bt Shuai Peng & Tian Tian Sun (CHN) 7–6 (7–1) 7–6(7–3), Flavia Pennetta & Francesca Schiavone (ITA) bt Casey Dellacqua & Alicia Molik (AUS) 6–4 6–4, Yung-Jan Chan & Chia-Jung Chang (TPE)(3) bt Alize Cornet & Virginie Razzano (FRA) 7–6(7–2) 6–7(3–7) 7–5, Elena Vesnina & Vera Zvonareva (RUS)(7) bt Nuria Llagostera Vives & Maria Martinez Sanchez (ESP) 2–6 6–1 6–3, Gisela Dulko & Betina Jozami (ARG)(WC) bt Tzipora Obziler & Shahar Peer (ISR)(WC) 6–3 6–2, Ayumi Morita & Ai Sugiyama (JPN) bt Greta Arn & Agnes Szavay (HUN)(WC) 6–3 6–3, Serena Williams & Venus Williams (USA)(2) bt Iveta Benesova & Nicole Vaidisova (CZE) 4–6 7–5 6–1

Second Round:

Svetlana Kuznetsova & Dinara Safina(1) bt Sania Mizra & Sunitha Rao 6–4 6–4, Zi Yan & Jie Zheng(8) bt Emmanuelle Gagliardi & Patty Schnyder 6–3 7–6(7–2), Anabel Medina Garrigues & Virginia Ruano Pascual(4) bt Samantha Stosur & Rennae Stubbs 4–6 6–4 6–4, Lindsay Davenport & Leizel Huber(5) bt Victoria Azarenka & Tatiana Poutchek 6–4 4–6 6–3, Alona Bondarenko & Kateryna Bondarenko(6) bt Olga Govortsova & Darya Kustova 6–1 6–3, Flavia Pennetta & Francesca Schiavone bt Yung-Jan Chan & Chia-Jung Chuang(3) 7–6(7–1) 1–6 8–6, Elena Vesnina & Vera Zvonareva(7) bt Gisela Dulko & Betina Jozami 6–2 6–3, Serena Williams & Venus Williams(2) bt Ayumi Morita & Ai Sugiyama 7–5 6–2

Quarter-final:

Zi Yan & Jie Zheng(8) bt Svetlana Kuznetsova & Dinara Safina(1) 6–3 5–7 10–8, Anabel Medina Garrigues & Virginia Ruano Pascual(4) bt Lindsay Davenport & Leizel Huber(5) 5–7 7–6(8–6) 8–6, Alona Bondarenko & Kateryna Bondarenko(6) bt Flavia Pennetta &

Francesca Schiavone 6–1 3–6 7–5, Serena Williams & Venus Williams(2) bt Elena Vesnina & Vera Zvonareva(7) 6–4 6–0

Semi-final:
Anabel Medina Garrigues & Virginia Ruano Pascual(4) bt Zi Yan & Jie Zheng(8) 6–4 7–6(7–5), Serena Williams & Venus Williams(2) bt Alona Bondarenko & Kateryna Bondarenko(6) 4–6 6–4 6–1

Final:
Serena Williams & Venus Williams(2) (Gold) bt Anabel Medina Garrigues & Virginia Ruano Pascual(4) (Silver) 6–2 6–0

Third Place Play-off:
Zi Yan & Jie Zheng(8) (Bronze) bt Alona Bondarenko & Kateryna Bondarenko (6) 6–2 6–2

(Referee: Stefan Fransson, SWE)

Demonstration Event

1968 – Guadalajara, Mexico, 14–20 October

Men's Singles – First Round:

Manuel Santana (ESP)(1) bt Humberto Camarotti (CUB) 6–1 6–1 6–2, Inge Buding (FRG) bt Jun Kamiwazumi (JPN) 6–4 2–6 4–6 2–2 retd, Jurgen Ulrich (DEN) bt James Osborne (USA)(8) 6–3 7–5 6–3, Juan Gisbert (ESP)(4) bt Yashin Shretta (KEN) 6–3 6–1 6–0, James McManus (USA) bt Anatoly Volkov (URS) 6–2 2–6 3–6 6–4 7–5, Rafael Osuna (MEX)(5) bt Stanley Pasarell (USA) 6–3 6–2 6–2, Miguel Olvera (MEX) bt Tony Ortiz (PUR) 6–1 6–0 6–0, Manuel Orantes (ESP) bt Toshiro Sakai (JPN) 6–310–8 6–0, Nicola Pietrangeli (ITA)(6) bt Meghji Abdul-Aziz (KEN) 6–1 6–3 6–2, Teimuraz Kukulia (URS) bt Jurgen Fassbender (FRG) 5–7 6–4 6–4 6–2, Joaquim Loyo-Mayo (MEX)(3) bt Juan-Manuel Brito (CUB) 6–0 6–0 6–1, Torben Ulrich (DEN) bt Francisco Guzman (ECU) 6–8 7–5 5–2 retd, Pierre Darmon (FRA)(7) bt Alberto Carrero (PUR) 6–1 10–8 6–1, Eugenio Castigliano (ITA) bt Vladimir Korotkov (URS) 6–4 6–2 6–2, Herbert Fitzgibbon (USA)(2) bt Hans Nerell (SWE) 3–6 6–4 6–3 7–5

Second Round:

Santana(1) bt Buding 6–3 7–5 6–4, Zarazua bt J. Ulrich 6–4 6–1 6–1, Gisbert(4) bt McManus 6–2 8–6 6–2, Osuna(5) bt Olvera 6–4 6–3 6–4, Orantes bt Pietrangeli(6) 3–6 6–1 6–3 7–5, Loyo-Mayo(3) bt Kakulia 5–7 6–1 6–3 5–7 6–3, T. Ulrich bt Darmon(7) 6–2 2–6 6–3 1–6 7–5,Fitzgibbon(2) bt Castigliano 7–5 6–2 6–3

Quarter-final:

Santana(1) bt Zarazua 6–1 6–0 6–2, Osuna(5) bt Gisbert(4) 6–4 4–6 1–6 8–6 6–1, Orantes bt Loyo-Mayo(3) 2–6 6–2 6–4 6–1, Fitzgibbon(2) bt T. Ulrich 6–3 6–2 6–1

Semi-final:

Santana(1) bt Osuna(5) 6–3 6–4 6–3, Orantes bt Fitzgibbon(2) 6–4 6–4 6–3

Final:

Santana(1) bt Orantes 2–6 6–3 3–6 6–3 6–4

Third Place Play-off:

Fitzgibbon(2) bt Osuna(5) 6–4 6–3 7–5

Ladies' Singles – First Round:

Edda Buding (FRG) bt Patricia Montano (MEX) 7–5 2–6 6–4, Lourdes Gongora (MEX) bt Valerie Ziegenfuss (USA) 6–1 6–2, Maria-Eugenia Guzman (ECU) bt Zaiga Yansone

(URS) 6–2 6–2, Julie Heldman (USA) bt Suzana Petersen (BRA) 6–1 6–2, Rosie Darmon (FRA) bt Ana-Maria Yeaza (ECU) 6–1 6–1

Quarter-final:

Jane Bartkowicz (USA)(1) bt Edda Buding 4–6 6–4 7–5, Lourdes Gongora bt Maria-Eugenia Guzman 6–2 6–2, Julie Heldman bt Rosie Darmon 6–3 6–3, Helga Niessen (FRG)(2) bt Cecilia Rosado (MEX) 6–1 6–1

Semi-final:

Jane Bartkowicz(1) bt Lourdes Gongora 6–2 6–2, Helga Niessen(2) bt Julie Heldman 6–3 1–6 6–3

Final:

Helga Niessen(2) bt Jane Bartkowicz(1) 6–4 6–3

Third Place Play-off:

Julie Heldman bt Lourdes Gongora 6–4 6–3

Men's Doubles – First Round:

Vladimir Korotkov & Anatoly Volkov (URS) bt Inge Buding & Jurgen Fassbender (FRG) 6–4 11–9 7–5, Pierre Darmon (FRA) & Joaquim Loyo-Mayo (MEX)(4) bt Jorgen Ulrich & Torbin Ulrich (DEN) 4–6 6–1 7–5 6–3, Alberto Carrero (POR) & Stanley Pasarell (USA) bt Juan-Manuel Brito & Humberto Camarotti (CUB) 3–6 2–6 8–6 6–3 6–4, Francisco Guzman & Miguel Olvera (ECU) bt Eugenio Castigliano & Massimo Di Domenico (ITA) 7–5 4–6 6–2 3–6 8–6, James McManus & James Osborne (USA)(3) bt Meghji Abdul-Aziz & Yashvin Shretta (KEN) 6–3 6–2 6–3, Manuel Orantes (ESP) & Nicola Pietrangeli (ITA) bt Jun Kamiwazumi & Toshiro Sakai (JPN) 6–1 6–2 6–3, Rafael Osuna & Vicente Zarazua (MEX)(2) bt Telmuraz Kakulia (URS) & Hans Nerell (SWE) 5–7 6–4 6–3 5–7 6–4

Quarter-final:

Juan Gisbert & Manuel Santana (ESP)(1) bt Korotkov & Volkov 3–6 6–4 6–3 6–4, Darmon & Loyo-Mayo(4) bt Carrero & Pasarell 6–3 6–1 6–2, Guzman & Olvera bt McManus & Osborne(3) 6–2 3–6 6–1 1–6 6–4, Osuna & Zarazua(2) bt Orantes & Pietrangeli 6–2 6–4 8–6

Semi-final:

Gisbert & Santana(1) bt Darmon & Loyo-Mayo(4) 6–3 6–4 6–4, Osuna & Zarazua(2) bt Guzman & Olvera 10–8 6–4 7–5

Final:

Osuna & Zarazua(2) bt Gisbert & Santana(1) 6–4 6–3 6–3

Third Place Play-off:

Darmon & Loyo-Mayo(4) bt Guzman & Olvera 6–4 1–6 6–1 6–3

Ladies' Doubles – First Round:

Rosie Darmon (FRA) & Julie Heldman (USA) bt Suzane Petersen (BRA) & Cecilia Rosado (MEX) 7–5 6–0, Lourdes Gongora & Patricia Montano (MEX) bt Maria-Eugenia Guzman & Ana Maria Ycaza (ECU) 7–5 3–6 6–3

Semi-final:

Rosie Darmon & Julie Heldman bt Jane Bartkowicz & Valerie Ziegenfuss (USA)(1) 2–6 6–4 6–3, Edda Buding & Helga Niessen (FRG)(2) bt Lourdes Gongora & Patricia Montano 6–4 6–1

Final:

Edda Buding & Helga Niessen(2) bt Rosie Darmon & Julie Heldman 6–3 6–4

Third Place Play-off:

Jane Bartkowicz & Valerie Ziegenfuss(1) bt Lourdes Gongora & Patricia Montano 6–2 6–1

Demonstration event

1984 – Los Angeles, USA, 6–11 August

Men's Singles – First Round:

Jimmy Arias (USA)(1) bt Jaime Yzago (PER) 6–1 6–4, Kelly Jones (USA) bt Suharyadi Scharyadi (INA) 2–6 6–2 6–3, Eric Amend (USA) bt Manuel Tolentino (PHI) 6–3 3–6 6–3, Michael Westphal (FRG)(6) bt Gap-Taik Roh (KOR) 6–3 7–5, Stefan Edberg (SWE) (3) bt Ronald Agenor (HAI) 6–4 6–2, Carlos Di Laura (PER) bt Amos Mansdorf (ISR) 6–2 7–6 (7–1), Thomas Muster (AUT) bt Olli Rahnasto (FIN) 6–4 6–4, Guy Forget (FRA)(8) bt Orlando Lourenco (ZIM) 6–3 6–1, Jakob Hlasek (SUI)(5) bt Loic Courteau (FRA) 6–0 4–6 6–4, Jorge Bardou (ESP) bt Anastasios Bavelas (GRE) 6–1 6–4, Francisco Maciel (MEX) bt Derrek Rostagno (USA) 6–4 7–6, Emilio Sanchez (ESP)(4) bt Michele Fioroni (ITA) 6–4 6–1, Simon Youl (AUS)(7) bt Yakuba Suleiman (NGR) 6–0 4–6 6–2, Stuart Bale (GBR) bt Gopinath Nair (IND) 6–2 6–1, Arafat Chekrouni (MAR) bt De-Peng Li (CHN) 6–2 3–6 6–3, Paolo Cane (ITA) bt Pat Cash (AUS)(2) 6–3 7–6

Second Round:

Arias (1) bt Jones 6–2 6–4, Westphal (6) bt Amend 7–5 6–2, Edberg(3) bt Di Laura 7–6(7–2) 7–6(7–1), Forget(8) bt Muster 4–6 6–3 6–2, Hlasek(5) bt Bardou 6–2 6–2, Maciel bt Sanchez(4) 6–4 6–4, Youl(7) bt Bale 4–6 6–4 7–5, Cane bt Chekrouni 6–2 6–4

Quarter-final:

Arias(1) bt Westphal(6) 7–5 6–4, Edberg(3) bt Forget(8) 6–4 7–5, Maciel bt Hlasek(5) 3–6 6–2 7–5, Cane bt Youl(7) 0–2 retd

Semi-final:

Edberg(3) bt Arias(1) 6–2 6–1, Maciel bt Cane 6–2 6–0

Final:

Edberg(3) bt Maciel 6–1 7–6(8–6)

Ladies' Singles – First Round:

Katheen Horvath (USA)(1) bt Petra Huber (AUT) 6–3 6–3, Myriam Schropp (FRG) bt Gigi Fernandez (PUR) 6–3 7–5, Patricia Hy (HKG) bt Marianne Groal (CAN) 6–0 6–3, Sabrina Goles (YUG)(7) bt Suzanne Lee (KOR) 6–0 6–2, Catherine Tanvier (FRA)(4) bt Gretchen Rush (USA) 6–7(8–10) 7–5 6–1, Jill Hetherington (CAN) bt Carin Anderholm (SWE) 6–3 6–1, Angeliki Kanellopoulou (GRE) bt Mei-Chu Hsu (TPE) 6–0 6–2, Andrea Leand (USA)(5) bt Simone Schilder (NED) 6–4 6–2, Raffaella Reggi (ITA)(6) bt Rina Einy (GBR) 6–0 6–0, Amanda Brown (GBR) bt Mercedes Paz (ARG) 6–2 6–3, Lilian Drescher (SUI) bt Elizabeth Minter (AUS) 7–5 6–2, Renata Sasak (YUG) bt Laura Arraya (PER)(3) 1–6 6–1 6–1, Steffi Graf (FRG)(8) bt Etsuko Inoue (JAP) 6–3 7–5, Anna-Maria Cecchini (ITA) bt Akiko Kijmuta (JPN) 6–3 6–2, Pascale Paradis (FRA) bt Silvana Campos (BRA) 6–3 7–5, Andrea Jaeger (USA)(2) bt Tine Scheuer-Larsen (DEN) 2–6 6–2 6–3

Second Round:

Kathleen Horvath(1) bt Myriam Schropp 6–2 6–2, Sabrina Goles(7) bt Patricia Hy 6–4 4–6 9–7, Catherine Tanvier(4) bt Jill Hetherington 2–6 6–2 6–4, Angeliki Kanellopoulou bt Andrea Leand(5) 6–3 6–3, Raffaella Reggi(6) bt Amanda Brown 6–2 0–6 6–3, Lilian Dreshcer bt Renata Sasak 6–1 6–3, Steffi Graf(8) bt Anna-Maria Cecchini 0–6 6–3 6–4, Pascale Paradis bt Andrea Jaeger(2) w.o.

Quarter-final:

Sabrina Goles(7) bt Kathleen Horvath(1) 6–2 7–6(7–2), Catherine Tanvier(4) bt Angeliki Kanellopoulou 6–2 6–1, Raffaella Reggi(6) bt Lilian Drescher 6–1 6–2, Steffi Graf(8) bt Pascale Paradis 6–0 6–1

Semi-final:

Sabrina Goles(7) bt Catherine Tanvier(4) 6–2 6–2, Steffi Graf(8) bt Raffaella Reggi(6) 7–6(7–1) 6–4

Final:

Steffi Graf(8) bt Sabrina Goles(7) 1–6 6–3 6–4

Exhibition Event

1968 – Mexico City, Mexico, 24–26 October

Mens' Singles – First Round:

Inge Buding (FRG) bt Joaquin Loyo-Mayo (MEX) 6–4 6–3, Francisco Guzman (ECU) bt Juan-Manuel Brito (CUB)

Second Round:

Vladimir Korotkov (URS) bt Herbert Fitzgibbon (USA)(1) 6–4 6–1, Pierre Darmon (FRA) bt Humberto Camarotti (CUB) 6–0 6–0, Jun Kamiwazumi (JPN) bt James McManus (USA) 6–3 6–3, Buding bt Teimuraz Kakulia (URS) 6–4 6–2, Nicola Pietrangeli (ITA) bt Guzman 6–4 6–4, Vincente Zarazua (MEX) bt Toshiro Sakai (JPN) 6–3 8–6, Anatoly Volkov (URS) bt Yashvin Shretta (KEN) w.o., Rafael Osuna (MEX)(2) bt Meghji Abdul-Aziz (KEN) w.o.

Quarter-final:

Korotkov bt Darmon 6–4 6–4, Buding bt Kamiwazumi 6–0 6–2, Pietrangeli bt Zarazua 6–4 6–0, Osuna(2) bt Volkov 6–2 7–5

Semi-final:

Buding bt Korotkov 6–4 4–6 6–2, Osuna(2) bt Pietrangeli 6–4 6–2

Final:

Osuna(2) bt Buding 6–2 3–6 6–3

Ladies' Singles – First Round:

Rosie Darmon (FRA) bt Valerie Ziegenfuss (USA) 6–1 6–2, Suzana Petersen (BRA) bt Patricia Montano (MEX) 3–6 6–1 6–4, Julie Heldman (USA) bt Cecilia Rosado (MEX) 6–1 6–0

Quarter-final:

Jane Bartkowicz(1) bt Zaigo Yansone (URS) 6–3 7–5, Suzana Petersen bt Rosie Darmon 7–5 5–7 6–4, Julie Heldman bt Lourdes Gongora (MEX) 6–2 6–4, Eugenia Guzman (ECU) bt Helga Niessen (FRG)(2) w.o.

Semi-final:

Jane Bartkowicz (USA)(1) bt Suzana Petersen 6–4 6–2, Julie Heldman bt Eugenia Guzman 6–1 6–2

Final:

Jane Bartkowicz(1) bt Julie Heldman 6–3 6–2

Men's Doubles – First Round:

Rafael Osuna & Vicente Zarazua (MEX)(1) bt Inge Buding & Jurgen Fassbender (FGR) w.o., Francisco Guzman (ECU) & Teimuraz Kakulia (URS) bt Juan-Manuel Brito & Humberto Camarotti (CUB) 6–4 6–3, Vladimir Korotkov & Anatoly Volkov (URS) bt Jun Kamiwazumi & Toshiro Sakai (JPN) 3–6 6–4 6–0, Pierre Darmon (FRA) & Joaquin Loyo-Mayo (MEX)(2) bt Herbert Fitzgibbon & James McManus (USA) 7–5 6–3

Semi-final:

Osuna & Zarazua(1) bt Guzman & Kakulia 4–6 8–6 6–0, Darmon & Loyo-Mayo(2) bt Korotkov & Volkov 7–5 1–6 6–2

Final:

Osuna & Zarazua(1) bt Darmon & Loyo Mayo(2) 6–4 3–6 14–12

Ladies' Doubles – First Round:

Maria-Eugenia Guzman (ECU) & Suzana Petersen (BRA) bt Lourdes Gongora & Patricia Montano (MEX) 6–4 4–6 6–1

Semi-final:

Jane Bartkowicz & Valerie Ziegenfuss (USA)(1) bt Maria-Eugenia Guzman & Suzana Petersen 6–2 6–2, Rosie Darmon (FRA) & Julie Heldman (USA)(2) bt Cecilia Rosado (MEX) & Zaiga Yansone (URS) 6–2 4–6 6–1

Final:

Rosie Darmon & Julie Heldman(2) bt Jane Bartkowicz & Valerie Ziegenfuss(1) 6–0 10–8

Mixed Doubles – First Round:

Vladimir Korotkov & Zaiga Yansone (URS) bt Vicente Zarazua & Lourdes Gongora (MEX) w.o., Pierre Darmon & Rosie Darmon (FRA) bt James McManus & Valerie Ziegenfuss (USA) 6–1 6–2

Quarter-final:

Teimuraz Kakulia (URS) & Suzana Petersen (BRA) bt Herbert Fitzgibbon & Julie Heldman (USA)(1) w.o., Korotkov & Zaiga Yansone bt Francisco Guzman & Maria-Eugenia Guzman w.o., Darmon & Rosie Darmon bt Joaquin Loyo-Mayo (MEX) & Patricia Montana (MEX) 7–5 1–6 6–2, Inge Buding (FRG) & Jane Bartkowicz (USA) bt Jurgen Fassbender & Helga Niessen (FRG)(2) w.o.

Semi-final:

Korotkov & Zaiga Yansone bt Kakulia & Suzana Petersen 6–1 6–3, Buding & Jane Bartkowicz bt Darmon & Rosie Darmon 3–6 6–2 6–1

Final:

Korotkov & Zaiga Yansone bt Buding & Jane Bartkowicz 7–5 6–4

All England Lawn Tennis Club Chief Executive, Ian Ritchie, at Wimbledon with the Olympic Handover Flag. On 24th August, 2008 at 2.30pm, this flag was raised at the Club in common with over 500 others worldwide. This marked the moment when Beijing handed over to London as the Olympic City for 2012.

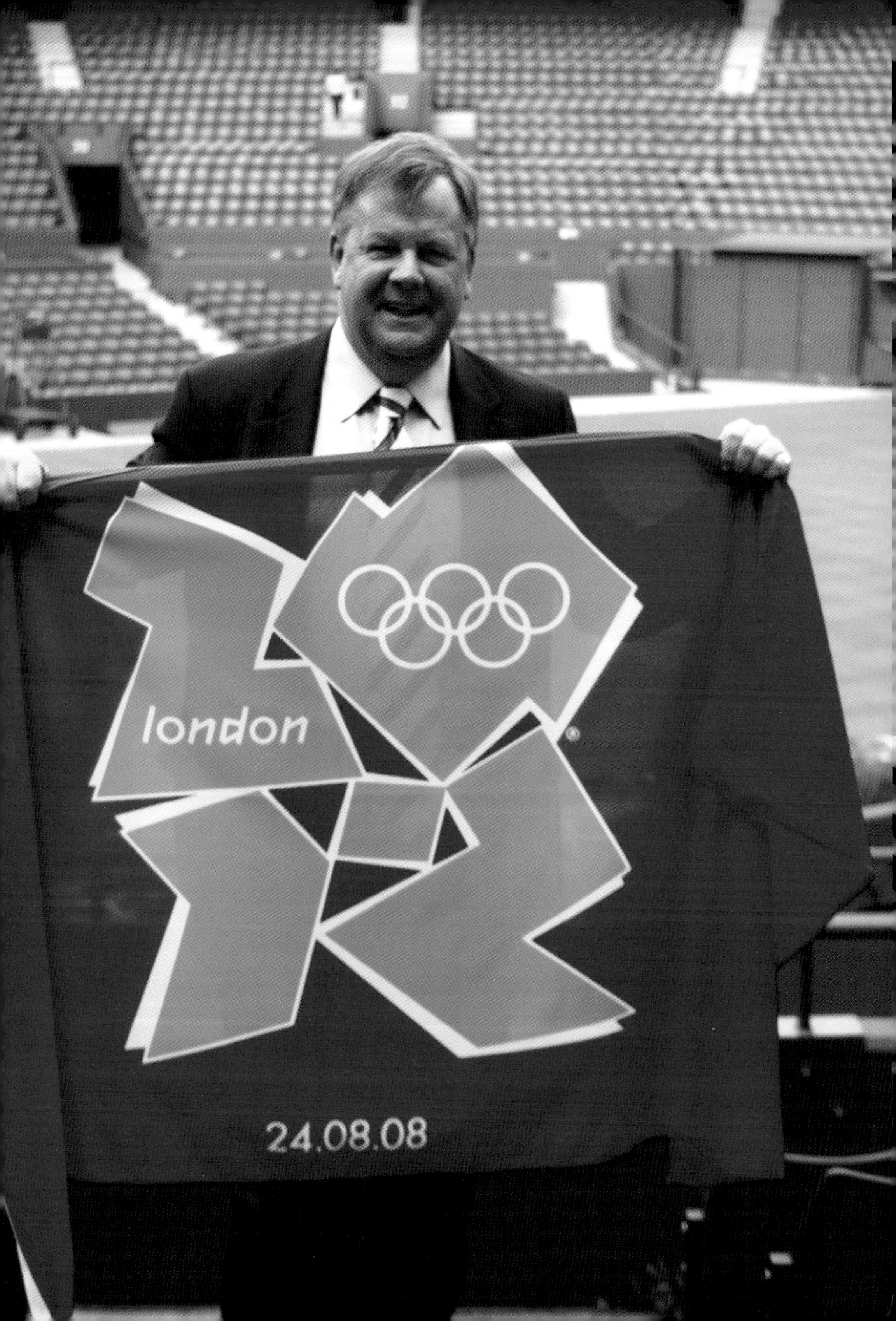
london
24.08.08

Summary of Olympic Games

Olympiad	Year	Venue	Dates	Participants	Men
1	1896	Athens	6–15/4	211	211
2	1900	Paris	14/5–28/10	1,225	1206
3	1904	St. Louis	1/7–23/11	687	681
★	1906	Athens	22/4–2/5	826	820
4	1908	London	24/4–31/10	2035	1999
5	1912	Stockholm	5/5–22/7	2547	2490
7	1920	Antwerp	20/4–12/9	2668	2591
8	1924	Paris	4/5–27/7	3092	2956
9	1928	Amsterdam	17/5–12/8	3014	2724
10	1932	Los Angeles	30/7–14/8	1408	1281
11	1936	Berlin	1/8–16/8	4066	3738
14	1948	London	27/7–14/8	4099	3714
15	1952	Helsinki	19/7–3/8	4925	4407
16	1956	Melbourne	27/10–8/12	3184	2813
17	1960	Rome	25/8–11/9	5346	4736
18	1964	Tokyo	10/10–24/10	5140	4457
19	1968	Mexico City	12/10–27/10	5530	4749
20	1972	Munich	26/8–11/9	7123	6065
21	1976	Montreal	17/7–1/8	6028	4781
22	1980	Moscow	19/7–3/8	5217	4043
23	1984	Los Angeles	28/7–12/8	6797	5230
24	1988	Seoul	17/9–2/10	8465	6279
25	1992	Barcelona	25/7–8/8	9364	6657
26	1996	Atlanta	19/7–4/8	10310	6797
27	2000	Sydney	15/9–1/10	10651	6582
28	2004	Athens	13/8–29/8	10625	6296
29	2008	Beijing	8/8–24/8	11028	6286
30	2012	London			

Ladies	Nations	Sports	Events
0	14	9	43
19	26	24	178
6	13	16	104
6	20	9	74
36	22	21	110
57	28	13	102
77	29	21	154
136	44	17	126
290	46	14	109
127	37	14	117
328	49	19	129
385	39	17	136
518	69	17	149
371	67	17	151
610	83	17	150
683	93	19	163
781	112	18	172
1058	121	21	195
1247	92	21	198
1124	80	21	204
1567	140	21	221
2186	159	23	237
2707	169	24	257
3513	197	26	271
4069	199	31	300
4329	201	28	301
4742	204	28	302

NOTES

★Games of 1906 designated Intercalated Olympics

Games of 6th Olympiad cancelled because of World War I

Games of the 12th and 13th Olympiad cancelled because of World War II

Abbreviations

ALG	Algeria	DOM	Dominican Republic	PAR	Paraguay
ARG	Argentina	ECU	Ecuador	PER	Peru
ARM	Armenia	ELS	El Salvador	POL	Poland
AUL	Australasia	ESP	Spain	POR	Portugal
AUS	Australia	EST	Estonia	PUR	Puerto Rico
AUT	Austria	FIN	Finland	ROM	Romania
BAH	Bahamas	FRA	France	RSA	South Africa
BEL	Belgium	FRG	Federal Republic	RUS	Russia
BEN	Benin		of Germany	SAN	San Marino
BER	Bermuda	GER	Germany	SCG	Serbia &
BIH	Bosnia &	GRE	Greece		Montenegro
	Herzegovina	GBR	Great Britain	SLO	Slovenia
BLR	Belarus	HAI	Haiti	SRB	Serbia
BOH	Bohemia	HOL	Holland	SUI	Switzerland
BOL	Bolivia	HUN	Hungary	SVK	Slovak Republic
BRA	Brazil	INA	Indonesia	SWE	Sweden
BRI	British Isles	IND	India	TCH	Czechoslovakia
BUL	Bulgaria	IRE	Ireland	THA	Thailand
CAN	Canada	ISR	Israel	TPE	Chinese Taipei
CHI	Chile	ITA	Italy	TUN	Tunisia
CHN	China	JAP	Japan	UKR	Ukraine
CIS	Commonwealth of	KOR	Korea	URS	Union of Soviet
	Independent States	LAT	Latvia		Socialist Republics
CIV	Ivory Coast	LUX	Luxembourg	URU	Uruguay
COL	Colombia	MAD	Madagascar	USA	United States
CRC	Costa Rica	MOR	Morocco	UZB	Uzbekistan
CRO	Croatia	MEX	Mexico	VEN	Venezuela
CYP	Cyprus	NGR	Nigeria	YUG	Yugoslavia
CZE	Czech Republic	NOR	Norway	ZIM	Zimbabwe
DEN	Denmark	NZL	New Zealand		